Displacing the State

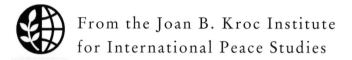

From the Joan B. Kroc Institute
for International Peace Studies

*Kroc Institute Series on Religion, Conflict,
and Peacebuilding*

Displacing the State

Religion and Conflict in Neoliberal Africa

Edited by

James Howard Smith *and* Rosalind I. J. Hackett

Foreword by R. Scott Appleby

University of Notre Dame Press
Notre Dame, Indiana

Manufactured in the United States of America

Library of Congress Cataloging-in-Publication Data

Displacing the state : religion and conflict in neoliberal Africa / edited by James Howard Smith and Rosalind I. J. Hackett ; foreword by R. Scott Appleby.
    p.   cm. — (Kroc Institute Series on religion, conflict, and peacebuilding)
"The volume has its remote origins in an international conference held in Jinja, Uganda, from March 31 to April 3, 2004, and sponsored by the Kroc Institute for International Peace Studies, University of Notre Dame"—Foreword.
Includes bibliographical references and index.
ISBN-13: 978-0-268-03095-7 (pbk. : alk. paper)
ISBN-10: 0-268-03095-2 (pbk. : alk. paper)
1. Social conflict—Africa—Religious aspects. 2. Religion and state—Africa. 3. Africa—Religious life and customs. 4. Peace-building—Africa—Religious aspects. I. Smith, James Howard. II. Hackett, Rosalind I. J. III. Series: Kroc Institute series on religion, conflict, and peace building.
BL2400.D57   2011
201.72096—dc23

                                                                    2011040049

Contents

Foreword

R. Scott Appleby

A friend and colleague in the study of Catholic modernism once remarked that the modernists, who wanted the Catholic Church to rediscover a forgotten or suppressed awareness of God's *immanence*, or indwelling presence in the individual soul, were convinced that "the world is so completely suffused with the divine presence that it was no longer meaningful for them to speak of the *supernatural*." Although accused of polytheism and paganism, as well as a dreadful heresy the pope termed *immanentism*, the Catholic modernists insisted that the indwelling presence of the divine was a *transcendent* presence, as paradoxical as that might appear at first blush. The presence of the living God, as God, they believed, was the power animating human creativity, industry, hope, and vulnerability, among other modes of the religious imagination.

Significantly, the modernists were students of comparative religion. They would find Africa today an intriguing confirmation of their theories about religion's ubiquitous presence—religion in the way they defined it, at least, as a diverse array of historically contingent expressions of the divine presence in human action.

Whether or not one is a believer in a God or gods, transcendent or immanent or immanent-in-transcendence, it is impossible to deny that Africa is a "furiously religious" place, to borrow Peter Berger's term for the "de-secularized world" in which we all live. Indeed, it is also impossible to understand cultures, politics, societies, and economies in Africa without struggling to comprehend the continent's long history of colonization (cultural, religious, military, political, and economic) and its dizzying diversity of indigenous, imported, imposed, transplanted, and transformed religious and spiritual practices, institutions, networks, and media.

Yet surprising numbers of scholars have attempted to do just that—to ignore or treat superficially an interpretive problem that will not go away. For religion, defined to include ancestor worship as well as the sacrifice of the Eucharist, the umma as well as the clan, is implicated in almost every aspect of social life in Africa. Conflict is a constant of social life in Africa, as elsewhere, and so we should not be surprised that religions and religious actors are embroiled in ethnic clashes, resource wars, political violence, and other human rights abuses from the Maghreb to the Horn, from Cairo to Cape Town. Again, let us think of religion in this context as a complex, hybrid, fluid, lived reality rather than a neat ideal type found in a textbook or sacred scripture.

Even less examined in the scholarly literature, with some laudable exceptions noted by the editors of this volume, is the phenomenon of religious peace-building. Religion is implicated in urban, regional, and international violence in numerous ways—among others, as a direct instigator, a passive aggressor, and a breeder of intolerance that can erupt into hatred at the slightest manipulation. But religious communities and actors also help to prevent or limit violence, heal the psychic and spiritual wounds of victims, demand justice for the oppressed, mediate between warring parties, provide good offices for negotiations, and promote forgiveness and reconciliation, among other acts of "conflict transformation."

The growing literature on peace-building views the process as continual and comprehensive of all phases of a conflict. Thus peace-builders work at one or more of the following tasks: *preventing violence* through programs of social and economic development to address inequalities, and through education and dialogue across lines of social division; *managing conflict* when it erupts into violence, through mediation, negotiation, and trust-building exercises; and *transforming conflicts* through resolution of "presenting issues" but also via longer-term structural reforms and social reconstruction after periods of violence and human rights abuses. In each of these overlapping phases of peace-building, recent research has shown, religious actors have contributed in significant ways, owing to a longstanding record of religious service to the community and a style of presence and agency that draws upon rituals, memory, and symbols that resonate with the deepest values of a community.

This volume illustrates the diversity of religious influences on the character and dynamics of conflict in Africa by examining vivid cases, settings, and situations chosen to underscore the range of acts, ideas, social movements, and political decisions affected by what Africans believe and practice in and through their churches, mosques, media, and other religious spaces. There is no attempt to be comprehensive of any one region, much less the continent. Nor do all religious and spiritual practices and practitioners of religiously sanctioned violence or religiously empowered peace-building make an appearance in these pages. Whatever case is being discussed, however, the authors never stray far from an awareness of how religion in Africa is shaped by the legacy of European colonialism and the slave trade, the continuing effects of cultural, economic, and religious imperialism in an age of globalization, and the depressing record of corrupt and incompetent governance in many of the new African nations.

The volume has its remote origins in an international conference held in Jinja, Uganda, from March 31 to April 3, 2004, and sponsored by the Kroc Institute for International Peace Studies, University of Notre Dame (United States). I say "remote" because, although many of the authors participated in the conference, others joined the project subsequent to the event, and every chapter has been recast around a common set of questions that provided specific content to the broad theme of the conference: "Religion in African Conflicts and Peace-building Initiatives: Problems and Prospects for a Globalizing Africa." Although several papers presented at the conference were not included in the volume, they shaped its themes and arguments, often by raising theoretical as well as empirical questions that gestated for months after conferees departed Jinja to their homes in Gulu, Dar es Salaam, Nairobi, Dakar, Lagos, Khartoum, Cape Town, The Hague, Bayreuth, Chicago, New York, Lexington, South Bend, and Knoxville.

A "furiously religious" world need not be incomprehensible, or flattened in its rich complexities to familiar and reductive social scientific categories. The signal contribution of this volume is that it begins to plumb the more engrossing, and perplexing, depths of the human imagination that have inspired women and men of Africa to describe, enact, politicize, and justify their deepest aspirations and strivings within a world they experience as suffused with a presence they deem "sacred."

Acknowledgments

While there are many people who were involved in the making of this book, and who deserve our thanks, we would like to especially acknowledge a few individuals without whom this book would not have been finished: E. Scott Appleby, director of the Kroc Institute for International Peace Studies, University of Notre Dame, and his wonderful staff, notably Barbara Lockwood, who welcomed and supported us as Visiting Rockefeller Fellows in 2003–4; Rashied Omar, then director of the Program on Religion, Conflict and Peacebuilding for invaluable discussions; Patrick Mason, his successor, for superb editorial assistance; Sakah Mahmud, our Rockefeller colleague, who helped lay the foundations for this book; and Jean Comaroff and Charles Villa-Vicencio for their thoughtful commentaries on the essays at an earlier stage. In sum, we are indebted to the Kroc Institute for providing a space for us to think and write about issues pertaining to religion, conflict, and peace.

Religious Dimensions of Conflict and Peace in Neoliberal Africa

An Introduction

James Howard Smith

It is difficult to imagine a place where religion's ambivalent power (Appleby 2000) has been more profoundly experienced than in Africa. In colonial Africa, for example, Christianity often bolstered, sustained, and legitimated the violent process of governance. But more recently, movements that draw their authority from "otherworldly" rather than "this-worldly" sources have mobilized African publics against corrupt and abusive temporal regimes and facilitated innovative new forms of reconciliation and cooperation.[1] This essay, and the volume it introduces, illustrates the power of religion in making and unmaking social and political orders in Africa. The authors represent diverse disciplines and backgrounds, but certain themes unite them, and in turn hold the volume together. The first is a shared emphasis on the socially and politically transformative power of religion, and its capacity to foster conflict and peace simultaneously. The second is that, in making sense of the relationship between religion and conflict, each essay dwells on the actual and ideal status of religion vis-à-vis the state and other secular institutions in Africa. And so, taken together, the essays question, in different ways, the relevance of the separation of the sacred from the secular, as well as the very categories themselves, in specific African contexts. This approach is prescient because the separation of religion from politics is often held to be a prerequisite for modern democratic societies, but this very separation conceals the fact that secular values are as predicated on belief as religious ones (Asad 2003). The distinction of the secular from the sacred also undergirds temporal authority by implying that state violence is more reasonable and legitimate than its religious counterpart, an always dubious position that African history has rendered absurd. Finally, the essays in this volume respond—some directly and some implicitly—to the fact that the relationship between religious and secular categories and institutions is undergoing a profound shift in a neoliberal Africa gutted by structural adjustment programs (SAPs), as states become increasingly incapable of governing their territories and as religious groups take on many of the functions formerly reserved for states.

For post-Enlightenment secularists, the relationship between religion and politics has always been fairly straightforward: religion, because it is based on particularistic faith, is inherently non-rational and parochial, and its intrusion into politics is thus suspect at best; however, it is widely held that, because religion is grounded in morality, it is also uniquely capable of "speaking truth to temporal power" (Comaroff 2003), and so serves as a moral foundation for civil society (see Asad 2003 for an overview). For most secularists, then, religion is an essentially ambivalent force that must be controlled by more legitimate secular power, to which religious actors must ultimately submit in the interest of democracy. This position is often defended through a particular reading of European history. Religious sentiment has, according to this view, contributed to senseless and irrational death and violence, especially in the dreadful medieval and early modern past, and so the modern, democratic secular state evolved to protect people from the violent excesses of other people's faith. Religion, in this widely held view, is vestigial—a stubbornly resilient, potentially dangerous trace of an earlier time whose social function in modern times is held to be the satisfaction of basic human needs that modern, secular societies neglect or repress, such as the need for meaning or social connection.

All of this has little to do with African understandings of or historical experiences with religion and politics. For one, most African religious thought and practice is not focused on the transcendent, but is explicitly concerned with the reinvigoration and expansion of social relationships in the present (Ellis and Ter Haar 2004). For example, the idea that ancestors influence events in the present is widespread in much of Africa, even among professed Christians, and can clearly be interpreted as a religious belief; however, the whole point about the ancestors is that they live among and impact the lives of the living, and that they want to be shown affection by being included in everyday human activities, like eating, drinking, and participating directly in political life. Moreover, modernist assumptions about how religion and politics should relate to one another, if at all—including the idea that religion may be inimical to modern political life—have little relevance to African experiences of state politics or religion, as certain religions (especially Christianity) have long been seen, by Europeans in Africa and Africans alike, as synonymous with modernity and progress.

In addition, the pairing of the categories "religion" and "conflict" implies a normative social order, or peace, that is secular and presumably state-centered. Conflict, cast as a pathology, acquires meaning in relationship to peace, a supposedly normative condition, but to what actual social-political condition does the term *peace* refer? Recent social theory has made the violent conceptual and operational foundations of states, and of secular law, abundantly clear (see, for example, Agamben 1998). The inherent violence of law and the state makes normative understandings of the concept of "peace," which are usually synonymous with nation-state sovereignty and legal convention, seem naïve and misguided. Contemporary events have borne out the fact that peace is itself a fraught concept that often conceals the violence upon which apparent peace depends. It is interesting, in this regard, that, since the suicide bombings of 9/11 and the subsequent (2003) U.S. invasion and occupation of Iraq, the terms *empire* and *imperialism* have reemerged in popular and academic discourse after a long hiatus, fueling the popularity of books such as Michael Hardt and Antonio Negri's *Empire,* and feeding discussion about the true reasons for and consequences of Iraq's so-called liberation. In this context, it has become common for scholars to connect peace with domination and to point out, as Partha Chatterjee has put it, that "the first and most important function of empire is to maintain the peace" (Chatterjee 2004, 98). Thus, in the context of real-world imperial politics, the imposition of peace exacerbates discontent and violence which, as everyone watching the news is all too aware, is often articulated in a religious idiom (see, for example, Juergensmeyer 2008; Lincoln 2003).

Africans have been very much aware of the relationship between empire and putative peace since the beginning of colonialism. Colonial rule, one of the most violent and transformative episodes of Africa's shared history, was rhetorically framed, by its proponents, as a peace-building project: an effort to forge a universalizing hegemony over what was imagined to be the chaotically pluralistic violence of African life. One of the primary stated reasons for missionization and administrative colonialism was the protection of Africans from themselves: from their own inherent violence, from their absence of reason, and from their childlike inability to distinguish truth from falsehood (see, for example, Mamdani 1996). This underpinned the religious and secular dimensions of the colonial project, including the artificial imposition of the colonial boundaries that would later become the material and imaginative pretexts for postcolonial national sovereignty and peace.

Thus Africans experienced colonial and postcolonial nation-states as violent and coercive intrusions into preexisting, dynamic social and political orders, and not as reasonable institutions that promised the alleviation of pain and the promulgation of peace through the attenuation of religious unreason. Therefore, we should be wary of projecting onto Africa the liberal Western notion that the state is a reasonable artifice designed to replace irrational conflict and war with peace and happiness. Moreover, in many parts of the continent, Christianity fostered and legitimated class formation in Africa; conversion came to be synonymous with the acquisition of modernity and its fruits (such as schooling and formal employment), while non-Christian beliefs and practices came to be associated, for many, with backwardness and poverty. African cultural and ritual practices were at first stigmatized by missionaries, and later were coupled by real political, geographic, and economic marginalization, which shaped the way these vernacular activities, and the people who practiced them, were perceived. Schooling, which was usually predicated on conversion to Christianity, promised an avenue of escape from the restrictions created by colonial policies of indirect governance, customary law, and apartheid rules regulating labor migration to urban centers, and so cemented the equation of certain religions, such as Christianity, with modernity and progress.

Given the relationships among religion, governance, and the making of African elites in colonial Africa, it is not surprising that most popular anti-colonial movements channeled the power of religion, often in ways that transgressed upon established secular and religious powers simultaneously. Typically, these new, popular religious movements attempted to either (1) appropriate potent aspects of colonial orders while making them more amenable to African conditions (for example, syncretic "break-away" schools and churches) or (2) completely transform political arenas by creating new, religiously inspired realities that never existed before, but which drew on earlier cultural and historical symbolic resources—such as millenarian movements, neo-traditionalist movements, Islamic brotherhoods, and, in a somewhat different vein, certain "born-again" forms of Christianity seeking a break with the past. For example, in Kenya, defense of female genital-cutting, banned by the Christian missions and government in 1929, was the issue that initially popularized and empowered the first anti-colonial political association, the Kikuyu Central Association, which launched the career of Jomo Kenyatta, Kenya's first president, who went on to write a full-scale ethnography defending the practice. The new African independent schools and churches that formed, at first in response to the ban, were able, over time, to collapse and transcend the powerful oppositions that had been central to colonial rule—most important, the divide separating African things from European things.

Other anti-colonial movements focused specifically on mobilizing the power of the past in opposition to abusive authorities. In Zimbabwe during the 1960s and 1970s, traditional spirit mediums, in constant dialogue with ancestors, led the Shona guerilla war against the colonial regime, and greatly enlarged the scale of the anti-colonial resistance (Lan 1985). And throughout the continent, new religious movements have challenged colonial and postcolonial regimes, deploying ritual and magic to unite large groups of people, while simultaneously offering an alternative, often millennialist, vision that runs counter to the state (Hackett 2010; Comaroff 2001). Examples of socially marginalized groups mobilizing cultural resources to resist and reinvent oppressive social orders are too numerous to detail, but include the Tanzanian Maji Maji rebellion of the 1910s, the eastern Congolese Simba secessionist rebellion of the mid-1960s, and Alice Lakwena's Acholi insurrection against Ugandan President Yoweri Museveni's government in the 1980s. Throughout colonial and post-colonial Africa, armed insurgencies drew on culturally and histori-cally entrenched idioms, framing them in an innovative way in an ef-fort to generate new, inclusive social and political orders.

Postcolonial African regimes seeking to consolidate their control over territories that were nation-states in name only sought, like their colonial predecessors, to manage religion and religious differences as part of the political project of nation-building. In many new nations, educated Christian elites, many of whom had acquired prestige and position as colonial functionaries within colonial systems, monopo-lized the avenues to and symbols of success in the postcolonial period. Supported by mainline church leaders, in many postcolonies politi-cians and educated civilian leaders used the entrenched belief that Af-rican life and culture was synonymous with "witchcraft and savagery" to cajole populations to leave "traditional" cultural and religious prac-tices behind in the interest of national development. But this was cer-tainly not the only variation on the theme of religious politics, as oth-ers sought to ground the state in more authentically African cultural repertoires: for example, in 1960s Zaire, Mobutu Sese Seko banned Christian baptism and names, while Africanizing dress and crimi-nalizing the tie as part of his attempt to forge an outwardly egalitarian national culture with himself at its center. In 1970s Mozambique, FRELIMO (Frente de Libertação de Moçambique), the anti-colonial guerilla insurgency–turned Marxist-Leninist government, tried to make its influence felt in regions where it was unknown and its moti-vations suspect by taking dramatic measures against Christian church leaders and "traditional" ritual and religious authorities alike (Lubke-mann 2008). In response to the demonization of African culture by colonial and postcolonial authorities, and in an effort to create a truly decolonized African sensibility, many African intellectuals and cul-tural leaders have long tried to resurrect African religious concepts and practices by making them look more like their direct competitors, especially Christianity. For example, they have resorted to the politics of capital letters and acronyms in order to make African religions resemble something like a church, while sanitizing and homogenizing what were, in actuality, incredibly diverse cultural practices (and so these diverse beliefs and practices are now called, in African academic circles, "African Traditional Religion" or the even more official and organized sounding acronymic "ATR").

In short, throughout the continent, arguments about what counts as religious and irreligious continue to be linked to now thoroughly Africanized ideas about modernity, progress, and the ideal foundations of political community. These debates erupt in emerging public spheres, and largely define public debate about a range of issues. For example, I once watched an African Pentecostal preacher in Nairobi try to demonstrate, through elaborate interpretations involving numerology, that condoms were part of a satanic conspiracy spearheaded by whites, in consort with African elites, to kill off the poor and appropriate the land of the deceased. An irate and well-dressed African businessman responded to him, and the growing crowd, with the provocative question, "But how can the whites be devils, since they are the ones who brought light to a dark continent?!" And, for a conference on religion, conflict, and peace-building in Africa held in Uganda, I was part of a panel on African neo-traditionalist political movements, including the Congolese Mai Mai and the Kenyan Mungiki. After the presentations concluded, a sizable group of African religious leaders stood up and vocally complained, "That is not religion!" These social movements, they argued, were the violent work of the devil, who seeks to turn society backward by playing on the immature passions of the poor.

In the post–Cold War era, the imposition of neoliberal economic policies has further blurred, and at times inverted, whatever boundary can be said to have existed between religion and formal politics in Africa. During the 1980s and 1990s, the International Monetary Fund (IMF)– and World Bank–mandated deregulation of African economies led to currency devaluation, slashed public services, the erosion of political patronage, and, ironically, increased corruption. As a result, governance has become progressively more fragmentary and multiple, and in many places no single political entity exercises the right to kill, while religiously inspired movements excise taxes and impose levies; as Achille Mbembe has put it,

> Many African states can no longer claim a monopoly on violence and on the means of coercion within their territory. Nor can they claim a monopoly on territorial boundaries. Coercion itself has become a market commodity. Military manpower is bought and sold on a market in which the identity of suppliers and purchasers means almost nothing. Urban militias, private armies, armies of regional lords, private security firms, and state armies all claim the right to exercise violence or to kill. Neighboring states or rebel movements lease armies to poor states. . . . Increasingly, the vast majority of armies are composed of citizen soldiers, child soldiers, and privateers. (Mbembe 2003, 32)

In this structurally maladjusted Africa, religious organizations have taken on many state functions, from holding court to controlling media to, in some instances, delivering the mail. At the same time, state regimes have drawn on religious sources to bolster their authority, calling on citizens to reclaim sacred land and establishing official commissions to investigate alleged cases of devil worship among itinerant, underemployed youth. And so states have become more like religious organizations at the same time as religions have come to look more like states. And all of the diverse political players competing for legitimacy and power have drawn on—and will no doubt continue to draw on—religious narratives, symbols, and concepts to establish and extend their authority. In this context of waning state power and legitimacy, repressed political and religious identities have erupted again, in novel guises, giving birth to a torrent of cultural revivalist movements and new religious movements that dwell on memories of violent pasts that postcolonial regimes have tried, unsuccessfully, to banish to the dustbins of history.

While the influence of religion may be growing, the expansion and privatization of media has deterritorialized religion, and reduced complex problems to potent religious signs and symbols (see, for example, Hackett, this volume). This is a crucial, relatively recent phenomenon that has not yet been subject to the critical attention it deserves. Media have contributed directly to the popularity and scale of religious movements, and have shaped the way publics understand them—the urban Mungiki movement in Kenya (see Wamue, this volume) and the state's violent reaction to it, for example, has been a media-promoted national spectacle, which would never have reached its present scale had it not been nurtured and sensationalized by Kenyan newspapers and television. Internationally, too, the media have drawn attention to the outwardly religious dimensions of African conflicts, while obscuring the more subtle historical factors that precipitated specific conflicts. For example, the conflict in Darfur has been widely portrayed, in the international media, as a religiously inspired Arab Muslim genocide against Africans, but this position ignores the fact that there are Muslims on both sides of the conflict, and that the events in the western Sudan have a complex array of historical and contemporary causes, including the impact of global warming on the ecology of the region and the related competition among pastoralists for dwindling water resources. Another example is the Lord's Resistance Army (LRA) in northern Uganda, which has been portrayed as an irrational religious genocide against the Acholi people. However, Acholi are just as likely to blame the secular Ugandan government for their situation as they are the LRA, and many commentators have argued that the international community's complicity in the secular, anti-LRA narrative has helped extend the Ugandan government's control over the region, causing much anxiety and resentment among Acholi (Ayesha Nibbe and Adrian Yen, personal communications).

We can derive a few closing points from this admittedly broad and somewhat generalizing history, before moving on to our contribution, and our contributors. First, religion in Africa was never relegated, even superficially, to a space outside politics and current events, or to benign places of private worship. Rather, because of the history of religion and religious transformation in Africa, religion has always been perceived, by Africans, as having the power to radically change social life and history, and religious practitioners have employed religious symbolism and enthusiasm in their efforts to totally reinvent social orders in opposition to that which came before. So it comes as no real surprise that, today in Africa, religion emerges everywhere, in places that Westerners are perhaps not accustomed to finding it (although, these days, they should be). And this should not be taken as evidence of either African backwardness or failure to separate naturally given categories (such as the public and the private or the sacred and the secular) which are, in fact, historically and culturally particular. Moreover, because of this transformative capacity, religion has always been both conflict-making and peace-making. Also, because of the historical struggles discussed above, African religious thought and practice has always had to confront the consequences of conflict-ridden histories, and is always struggling to transform the present by engaging in some way with the past—either by drawing on its power and channeling it into efficacious directions or by ritually destroying the past's power over the present. Religious values and practices thus express, but can also not be reduced to, larger social issues—pertaining to class, generation, gender, ethnicity, and the like—and so become a prism for accessing and overcoming historical and structural conflict and violence. Finally, because other African power brokers, such as militias and state institutions, are often illegitimate in the eyes of the public, the normative Western idea that religious actors should obey secular laws and institutions, or that there is a fundamental difference between these spheres of thought and action, is not immediately obvious, especially to Africans themselves.

As a result of these issues we, as thinkers interested in Africa's history and future, have to be prepared to pose difficult questions that have rarely, if ever, been seriously posed before (see also Mbembe 2001). For example, is it possible that an "extremist" religion that is manifestly uncivil, to the point of disregarding national law, breaking away from the nation-state, or condemning nonmembers as being beyond the pale of moral order, may actually influence people's habits, expectations, and dispositions in positive ways that cannot yet be foreseen? Might it be that the violence of religious groups or organizations is directly proportional to the scale and severity of the historically given structures they are trying to transform? And might religiously inspired conflict be part of the longer historical process through which Africans create political communities with which they actually identify, and confront unequal and authoritarian political structures that are equally embedded in religious histories? This volume does not resolve these questions, but productively works through them, bearing and retaining the trace of the conflicts and struggles that have shaped Africa's histories.

In selecting chapters for this volume, we chose pieces that take counterintuitive and original approaches to the complex imbrications of religion, conflict, and peace in neoliberal Africa. Most of the chapters are historical and ethnographic in method and scale, and focus on the everyday activities, processes, and structures that engender conflict and peace: liturgical verse, movies and street pamphlets, church services, secret societies, legal debates surrounding domestic arrangements, and so on. In this way, these chapters pull focus away from dramatic and highly mediated violent conflicts by examining the role of religious practices in the making and umaking of social orders from the bottom up, in stark contrast to conventional top-down approaches.

The first section of three, "Historical Sources of Religious Conflict and Peace," examines how aspects of African history have laid the foundation for very divergent models of peace: one stressing reconciliation and cooperation between formerly opposed parties, and another relying on the ongoing perpetuation of conflict and the persistent demonization of others, especially the poor or marginal. In "Forgiveness with Consequences: Scriptures, *Qenē,* and Traditions of Restorative Justice in Nineteenth-Century Ethiopia," historian Charles Schaefer delineates a tradition of restorative justice in Ethiopia that extends back to the medieval period, elements of which can be found in Ethiopian political thought and practice in the twenty-first century. Schaefer argues that Ethiopian restorative justice has allowed for the forgiveness of vanquished parties, but that forgiveness has always come with consequences; this "conditional clemency" has implied that the "one seeking forgiveness [was] obligated to show contrition and to be accountable for future actions; in other words, to correct their criminal . . . ways." Schaefer argues that this understanding of justice has enabled post-conflict peace and reconciliation at various moments in Ethiopian history. Moreover, and crucially, this tradition of justice drew its legitimacy, and was arguably derived from, the religious thought of Coptic Christianity and the Ethiopian Orthodox Church, epitomized by the sophisticated *qenē* tradition of liturgical poetry. But, more recently, Western-derived notions of retributive justice have been both adopted by and foisted onto the Ethiopian and Eritrean regimes with often devastating consequences. Schaefer argues eloquently for the need for both foreign diplomats and national political leaders to take seriously the lessons of Ethiopian restorative justice, a religious and cultural tradition that remains a central part of Ethiopian life and thought.

Schaefer's chapter dwells at length on the peaceful potential of religion and religious discourse, and argues that these aspects of religious belief and practice should be developed so that religion can contribute effectively to peace-building. In contrast, in his chapter, entitled "Making Peace with the Devil: The Political Life of Devil Worship Rumors in Kenya," James Howard Smith focuses on the productive dimensions of the concept of evil, epitomized by the idea of the devil; he argues that specific, culturally nuanced ideas about the devil and devil worshipers have been central to governance in Kenya from the colonial period, and that diverse Kenyan groups have tried to use these concepts to "make peace" by destroying that which threatens their vision of social order. Smith shows how, in Kenya, the idea that the devil exists on the existential limits of rational governance, and that those frustrated and marginalized by the colonial project are tempted to serve him, came to inform colonial and postcolonial state governance, as well as popular resistance. During the 1950s Mau Mau insurgency, state officials, abetted by anthropologists and psychologists, elaborated and acted upon an idea of devil worship that portrayed an underground satanic society divided into cells, predicated upon ghastly oathing rituals, and led by a diabolical and "detribalized" native leader. This theory shaped the way the colonial state handled Mau Mau (through the use of witchdoctors and the mass detention of the Kikuyu population, for example) and later contributed to postcolonial state policies on allegedly subversive groups and populations.

Smith traces how, over time, this discourse about devil worship was deployed by different groups in Kenyan society (those critical of the Moi regime, the Moi regime itself, the Mungiki neo-traditionalist movement, etc.) that sought to shore up threatened moral and political boundaries and forge viable national communities predicated on shared moral values. The essay makes it abundantly clear that contemporary conflicts rooted in current conditions are understood and acted upon through the prism of traumatic historical memories and historically entrenched structural conflicts. Moreover, the discourse of devil worship has established a tense peace through the radical, violent Othering of those whose existence has been held to threaten the peace. Thus, Smith's chapter dwells on the unseemly aspects of peace—the fact that real-world peace often involves scapegoating and the perpetuation of tension (in this case, framed in a religious idiom; see also Ring 2006).

The following three chapters comprise a section entitled "New Religious Movements, Enduring Social Tensions"; these chapters foreground the present, but emphasize how contested historical memories shape the way Africans experience and respond to the structural transformations associated with neoliberalism. In these memories, which have indeed flashed up in a moment of intense danger (paraphrasing Benjamin 1968, 267), an invented history is alternately sacralized and demonized by differentially positioned social groups, becoming fodder for a religious imagination that deploys invented traditions to admonish the present. Grace Nyatugah Wamue-Ngare, in "The Mungiki Movement: A Source of Religio-Political Conflict in Kenya," examines a Gikuyu neo-traditionalist religious and political movement whose members and leadership have struggled to retain their original utopian religious foundations at the same time as the organization has morphed into a powerful shadow state and mafia. Mungiki's membership consists mainly of poor young men who have, in the past, sought to impose a strict gendered and generational orthodoxy upon the Kikuyu public, blaming the spread of HIV/AIDS on the waning of cliterodectomy, and even going so far as to attack "indecently" dressed women on Nairobi's streets. Urban Mungiki activists are known by what are, in the predominantly Christian region of central Kenya, highly transgressive and symbolically loaded stylistic acts: donning dreadlocks in the style of 1950s Mau Mau insurgents, praying to the Gikuyu God Ngai while facing Mount Kenya, and snorting snuff tobacco, a historically stigmatized practice associated with senior males in rural areas. In doing so, Mungiki embody and act on their belief that Kenyan society and the state have lost their grounding in what Mungiki gloss as traditional African values.

Although Kenyans often criticize Mungiki for being anachronistically obsessed with the past, Mungiki leaders have spoken publicly, to the media, on issues of current national concern, including the need for land tenure reform and the destructive consequences of IMF-mandated SAPs. Because of their public, exaggerated performance of a violent and repressed history (mainly, the legacy of the Mau Mau insurgency), the group struck a profound chord in Kenyan society, provoking a great deal of discussion and, ultimately, violent repression from the Moi and Kibaki regimes. But over time, with the help of the media's quest for spectacle, Mungiki has become a sign unleashed from the original intentions that gave birth to it, as idle young men are arrested by police under suspicion of being Mungiki and as others commit crimes of their own only to later blame them on an increasingly spectral Mungiki (see also Smith, this volume). While she recognizes that Mungiki is no longer a singular entity, and that there are now indeed many "Mungikis" at work in Kenyan society, Wamue chooses to focus on an aspect of the Mungiki phenomenon that has been systematically ignored by the Kenyan media, and by most Kenyans: mainly, the positive moral vision that has sustained and motivated many Mungiki despite the fact that these utopian hopes have been consistently corrupted by politicians and unscrupulous entrepreneurs seeking to perpetuate violent conflict. These utopian imaginings entail a model of peace that has always included the potential for violence against those who threaten Mungiki's pristine and impossible vision of the past.

Wamue emphasizes the religious dimensions of Mungiki in reaction to those who have portrayed the movement as a mafia organization with no redeeming moral virtues. In contrast, Koen Vlassenroot, in his chapter on Mai Mai militias in the eastern Congo ("Magic as Identity Maker: Conflict and Militia Formation in Eastern Congo"), minimizes the occult dimensions of a similar, equally heterogeneous, youth-based movement in the eastern Congo in an effort to draw out their often unrecognized political and sociological motivations and historical underpinnings. Media representations of Mai Mai militias have made them internationally famous for their transgressive deployment of traditional religious ritual, their occasional acts of cannibalism, and the youth of their leadership. But Vlassenroot maintains that, in the wake of a collapsed and defunct Zairean state, religious ritual has enabled militias to forge alternative sovereign orders, in the process blurring the distinction between peace-building and conflict-making. He convincingly argues that Mai Mai militias have struggled to violently overhaul local life from the bottom up, and that this total transformation of society has been oriented toward the remaking of historically entrenched local authority structures—this in contrast to analyses of Mai Mai that have portrayed the movement as solely an autochthonous reaction to foreign, Rwandan occupation. In their efforts to determine whether these neo-traditionalist movements are predominantly religious or predominantly political, Wamue and Vlassenroot draw attention to an even more fundamental issue: mainly, that the new religious movements at work in Africa challenge entrenched Western understandings of religion as belief in a transcendental truth above and beyond political realities. Rather, these religious/political movements are firmly grounded in real-world struggles and transformations, and are the principal mechanism through which people try to bend overarching structures to their wills.

Isabel Mukonyora confronts this issue directly in her chapter, "Religion, Politics, and Gender in Zimbabwe: The Masowe Apostles and Chimurenga Religion." She examines a religious movement that has taken on many social functions (including those formerly reserved for states), while in some ways echoing Zimbabwean state ideology about the sacral power of stolen lands. Mukonyora begins by showing how, in the context of a declining patronage state and the attendant devaluation of men's labor and social position, political leaders like President Robert Mugabe have drawn on the concept of the sacred power of ancestors and ancestral land to bolster their diminished position. They have thus based their political legitimacy on a vanquished model of masculine authority that real life has made all too chimerical. But Mukonyora's analysis of the Masowe Apostolic Church makes it abundantly clear that local debates about the value of men's and women's work and natures are played out in the public sphere constituted by the church, with members of each sex performing a particular, divergent model of moral authority. While the author clearly sympathizes with women's inchoate vision of a society united by horizontal networks over and against men's aggressive posturing, what emerges in the analysis is that the church has become a space for ritually negotiating and resolving endemic, historically enduring social conflicts that originate in the home itself. The political-economic withdrawal and declining legitimacy of the state has enabled domestic politics to become public politics at the same time as the state increasingly draws on the embattled ideal of the patriarchal household to extend its authority. Moreover, Mukonyora's analysis demonstrates a profound ambivalence about tradition among Masowe Apostles: while they incorporate many elements of Shona culture into their rituals, and emphasize the symbolic significance of land, Masowe religious ritual is ultimately aimed at curtailing the power of ancestors, and hence the past, over living populations in the present (and thus shares much in common with other popular religious movements, such as Pentecostalism). Like the Mai Mai and Mungiki youth—though in a way fundamentally less violent than either of them—the Masowe Apostles strive to effect a total transformation of the world from the bottom up by changing and disciplining people's attitudes and behavior. All of this work is made more profound by the fact that it takes place in a social and political context defined by the violent caprice of abusive masculine authorities in the larger Zimbabwean political arena.

While our second section emphasized how religion engenders new forms of social and political identification in the wake of state transformation and, in many instances, decline and collapse, the chapters in the third section ("New Religious Public Spheres and the Crisis of Regulation") highlight the conflict between state structures and the new ideologies and institutions associated with neoliberal globalization (international religious nongovernmental organizations [NGOs], new forms of media, and discourses of human rights, for example). In this vein, Rosalind I. J. Hackett, in "'Devil Bustin' Satellites': How Media Liberalization in Africa Generates Intolerance and Conflict," argues that, contrary to all expectations that a liberalized print and electronic media would engender peaceful, open public discussion and dialogue among religions, the recent proliferation of new media images (pamphlets, radio broadcasts, television, and the Internet) is in fact "replicating, if not intensifying, old, as well as generating new, forms of religious conflict." Drawing on a wealth of primary and secondary sources, Hackett homes in on a single aspect of neoliberal rupture, explaining the consequences of the fact that large media organizations, once owned and controlled by states, are now "owned by private entrepreneurs, religious organizations, political parties, existing media houses, development organizations, and local communities." In an overarching context of social and political fragmentation, media have become a mechanism for producing new forms of social belonging, often through the demonization of others. Rather than suggest that religious media determine behavior or lead to violence, Hackett draws attention to the fallacies of the post-Enlightenment assumption that unfettered communication necessarily generates the social good in a peaceful manner. Rather, she argues, media are integral, even essential, to the production of the new religiously inspired political communities that are emerging throughout the continent. This deterritorialization of religion has changed the nature of religious belief and belonging, as meaningful religious images and sentiments commonly transcend historically enduring boundaries of religious cleavage, providing new opportunities for conflict *and* understanding.

In his chapter, "Mediating Armageddon: Popular Christian Video Films as a Source of Conflict in Nigeria," Asonzeh F.-K. Ukah examines the popular and legal controversy surrounding the release of the Nigerian Pentecostal film *Rapture*. His chapter expands upon the themes that Hackett introduced by examining a single example of antagonistic religious imagery made possible by a newly liberalized media. Ukah argues that, in the bankrupt, criminalized, and structurally maladjusted Nigerian postcolony, video film and new religious movements (especially Pentecostalism, the fastest growing religious movement in Africa) have erupted, phoenix-like, from the ashes, each fueling the other. Together they comprise a new moral and commercial economy that challenges the state, as well as established dynamics of religious growth and identification. Ukah holds that this dynamic growth, when combined with general economic and state collapse, has the potential to exacerbate violent conflict and national fragmentation. The analysis centers on a provocative and symbolically rich film in which Pentecostals are raptured into heaven, while a thinly veiled Catholic Church spearheads the apocalypse and the subsequent, terrorizing reign of the Beast over all misguided humanity. The film generated a great deal of controversy, though no violence, in Nigeria, and Ukah focuses at length on the legal issues surrounding the film's release. Interestingly, the on-the-ground debate assumed a form that would be very familiar to a Western, and especially U.S. American, audience (highlighting the conflict between freedom of religious expression and respect for the beliefs of others) and demonstrated a certain legal meticulousness among a wide swath of the Nigerian public. But ultimately these legal debates, and the public censure of *Rapture*'s producer, turned out to be of little consequence because the state could not effectively regulate video films. And so, ironically, the state's banning of the film seems to have actually fueled its popularity and exacerbated its influence—no doubt confirming, for many, the truth of its message.

Ukah writes as an interested and involved student of Nigeria, clearly concerned about the rise of unyielding religious activism in a nation historically known for a religious tolerance born of manifest diversity. He is also committed to a particular vision of social order, in which the state is the legitimate legal authority and religious groups monitor their statements and images with a view to maintaining national peace. But his analysis draws attention to the existence of an alternative model of peace whose epistemological foundations are neither provable nor disprovable, and whose power over the public's imagination is incontestable: mainly, the widely held evangelical and, by extension, Pentecostal notion that genuine peace can only emerge if all citizens transform the state of their souls by establishing a direct relationship with Christ/God (becoming "saved," or "born again"). In this view, pluralism and relativism, rather than being synonymous with peace, are productive of social decay and violence, and the problem of national security (a more limited and secular version of peace) is of secondary importance to those who are trying to forge a new world and a whole new dispensation, or way of being human. Moreover, all manifestations of tradition are reinterpreted as demonic by this religious perspective that seeks nothing less than what Birgit Meyer, in a somewhat more positive discussion of Pentecostalism, has referred to as a complete "break with the past" (Meyer 1998). While it may be that this religion is driven, in large part, by the desire for profits and, as Ukah puts it, "market share," its leaders can only succeed commercially to the extent that they speak to the public's desire to shore up moral boundaries in the wake of widespread social and economic crisis, which is in turn interpreted in moral terms.

Ukah's chapter reveals an attitude toward the state that is as widespread among African citizens as it is among Westerners: mainly, the belief that, regardless of what the representatives of any specific state *actually* do, the ideal-typical state is *supposed* to function according to impartial and universalizing legal codes that are removed from private interests and personal emotions. This legal-bureaucratic state system, it is widely held, should be grounded in universal reason, and therefore be above the fray of religions and religious conflicts, which are held to be manifestations of particular beliefs. But the Ugandan literary scholar Abasi Kiyimba's chapter on the fraught history of the Ugandan Domestic Relations Bill ("'The Domestic Relations Bill' and Inter-Religious Conflict in Uganda: A Muslim Reading of Personal Law and Religious Pluralism in a Postcolonial Society") suggests a more complex relationship between the state and religion in contemporary Africa. Kiyimba shows how a proposed bill designed to legislate domestic arrangements (most controversially, by criminalizing polygamy) has been promulgated by Ugandan legislators and other educated elites. These self-professed modernists, supported by a wide cross-section of the non-Muslim population, view polygamy as backward and perceive its current protection under the law as a byproduct of the limiting, divisive colonial policy of indirect rule (by which so-called "natives" were governed by "traditional authorities" and "customary law"). In contrast, Uganda's rather large Muslim population, both male and female, claims the right to organize domestic relationships as they see fit, and in turn argue that Qur'anic authority is greater than secular authority.

While this seems to be a classic case of a modern, universalizing secular state in opposition to heterogeneous religious traditions, Kiyimba's analysis makes it clear that both positions in the Domestic

Relations Bill debate are equally contemporary. Each position emerges from opposed sides of the paradox that was the colonial state, whose bifurcated political system envisioned Africans as both citizen and subject (Mamdani 1996); the colonial regime codified Islamic self-governance in customary law, which was separated from general law. In addition, this state, far from being a paragon of secular authority, is actually shaped by religious histories, a fact that Ugandan Muslims are quick to grasp. These critics of the bill argue that putatively secular authority is actually Christian authority in a secular guise, as the bill that pretends to encode universal values actually upholds prejudices that are decidedly particular and no more modern than polygamy (again, because both legal systems trace their origins to colonial governance and law). The Muslim perspective makes all the more sense, in the context of Ugandan history, because Christianity, schooling, and career success have been indissoluble in colonial and postcolonial Uganda, as Uganda's governing and civil service elites have long been mission-educated Christians. Thus, while many Ugandans rhetorically frame the state and religion as separate, religion is deeply cemented in state governance. And so the state's regulation of religious heterogeneity suddenly takes on a completely different pallor: the state is always already a religious actor, just as religion has been imbricated in state governance from the inception of the colonial state apparatus. Conflict emerges from the structural contradictions of the postcolonial state, whose sovereignty would seem to be a precondition for peace.

And so a number of more specific issues, or themes, emerge from these pieces. The first is that the declining moral and political authority of states in neoliberal Africa has precipitated an eruption of repressed conflicts, memories, and alternative models of social-political order. These repressed imaginaries have come to appear sacred to many, in part because of the violence and energy that have been invested in their repression. This is evident in neo-traditional revivalist movements in Kenya, the Democratic Republic of the Congo, and Zimbabwe; in Ethiopian debates about repressed traditions of restorative justice; in the progressive politicization of Islam in Uganda; and in widespread reactions to patriarchal and gerontocratic authority from youth and women at all levels of the social hierarchy—from households to state houses. This revalorization of repressed traditions and values is related to the second theme, which is the growing chasm separating the rich from the poor in neoliberal Africa. This widening divide is often understood and articulated in religious terms, as evidenced by the Mungiki in Kenya, the Masowe Apostles in Zimbabwe, and the Mai Mai militias in eastern Congo who have mobilized, in part, against the expropriation of Congolese resources by outsiders and people they imagine to be outsiders. This religious conflict reflects the fact that inequality and poverty are widely understood, by Africans, to be serious moral problems that must be redressed through religious and spiritual means (Ferguson 2006). This connects to a third theme, which is the religiously inspired reaction, in Africa, to "market fundamentalism," or the foreign-imposed belief—no less mystical because it is secular—that the market unfettered will magically generate the social good. This is evidenced, for example, in Kenyan rumors concerning an international conspiracy of devil worshipers at the IMF, and finds its way into public debates about the potentially violent consequences of religious profiteering in neoliberal Nigeria. Writing in the midst of a global economic meltdown, African religious insights into the violence and injustice of neoliberal reforms seem all the more prescient.

A fourth theme is the fact that the transformations taking place in Africa are understood and acted upon from within historically enduring idioms of gender and generation; this is exemplified by the Masowe Apostles' reaction to patriarchal politics; the youthful Mai Mai's and Mungiki's embrace of masculine values in opposition to the perceived empowerment of women; and the debate over the Domestic Relations Bill in Uganda. The downsizing of historically male-controlled formal economies and the growth of youth militias are widely understood in terms of gender and generation, and thus represent the culmination, in larger social arenas, of conflicts rooted in the household and in kinship. Religious arenas in turn become spaces for articulating and negotiating the changing statuses of men and women, and of youth and seniors, with respect to one another, especially given the absence of viable spaces for political dialogue in many parts of the continent. This politicization of kinship is related to a fifth, disconcerting trend, which is the tendency of these religiously inspired attempts to transform social and political orders to be meted out on the bodies of women, who are widely identified with a morally vulnerable nation in contrast to a state marked as male; we see this particularly in the case of eastern Congolese militias and Mungiki youth gangs, and in the pornographic imagery deployed by Pentecostal filmmakers in Nigeria to shore up moral boundaries, while developing a consumer base in a competitive commercial environment. And finally, there is a sixth theme, which is the growing significance of electronic media and mass-mediated images and texts in African political and religious life; this has significantly altered the scope and reach of religious movements, allowing them to constitute new publics and to challenge the hegemony of secular values and institutions, as evidenced by the public debate, in Nigeria, over the Pentecostal film *Rapture,* and in the rapid proliferation and privatization of media organizations throughout the continent outlined by Hackett.

In conclusion, it is our hope that readers of this volume will emerge from it with a new appreciation of the specificity of African social and political contexts, which resist conventional Western typologies and conceptualizations, notably with respect to the sacred and the secular, conflict and peace, and religion and politics. Notwithstanding the particularities of these contexts, the insights to be found here concerning the perduring power of religion have comparative value for those interested in the imbrications of religion, conflict, and peace in diverse regions of the world.

NOTE

1. I have in mind here the multiparty democracy movements that swept Africa in the early 1990s and religiously inspired interventions such as the post-apartheid South Africa Truth and Reconciliation Commission.

REFERENCES

Agamben, Giorgio. 1998. *Homo Sacer: Sovereign Power and Bare Life.* Stanford, CA: Stanford University Press.

Appleby, R. Scott. 2000. *The Ambivalence of the Sacred: Religion, Violence, and Reconciliation*. New York and Oxford: Rowman and Littlefield Publishers.

Asad, Talal. 2003. *Formations of the Secular*. Stanford, CA: Stanford University Press.

Benjamin, Walter. 1968. *Illuminations: Essays and Reflections*. New York: Schocken Books.

Chatterjee, Partha. 2004. *The Politics of the Governed: Reflections on Popular Politics in Most of the World*. New York: Columbia University Press.

Comaroff, Jean. 2003. "Critical Reflections on Religion in Conflict and Peacebuilding in Africa." Unpublished paper presented in Jinja, Uganda.

Comaroff, Jean, and John Comaroff, eds. 2001. *Millennial Capitalism and the Culture of Neoliberalism*. Chicago: University of Chicago Press.

Ellis, Stephen, and Gerrie ter Haar. 2004. *Worlds of Power: Religious Thought and Political Practice in Africa*. New York: Oxford University Press.

Ferguson, James. 2006. *Global Shadows: African in the Neoliberal World Order*. Durham, NC: Duke University Press.

Hackett, Rosalind. 2010. "Millennial and Apocalyptic Movements in Africa: From Neotraditionals to Neo-Pentecostals." In *Oxford Handbook of Millennialism*, edited by Catherine Wessinger. New York: Oxford University Press.

Hardt, Michael, and Antonio Negri. 1999. *Empire*. Cambridge: Harvard University Press.

Juergensmeyer, Mark. 2008. *Global Rebellion: Religious Challenges to the Secular State, from Christian Militias to al Qaeda*. Comparative Studies in Religion and Society. Berkeley: University of California Press.

Lan, David. 1985. *Guns and Rain: Guerillas and Spirit Mediums in Zimbabwe*. Berkeley: University of California Press.

Lincoln, Bruce. 2003. *Holy Terrors: Thinking about Religion after September 11*. Chicago: University of Chicago Press.

Lubkemann, Stephen. 2008. *Culture in Chaos: An Anthropology of the Social Condition in War*. Chicago: University of Chicago Press.

Mamdani, Mahmood. 1996. *Citizen and Subject: Contemporary Africa and the Legacy of Late Colonialism*. Princeton, NJ: Princeton University Press.

Mbembe, Achille, Necropolitics Public Culture 15(1): 11–40.

Meyer, Birgit. 1998. "'Make a Complete Break with the Past': Memory and Post-Colonial Modernity in Ghanaian Pentecostalist Discourse." *Journal of Religion in Africa* 27(3):316–49.

Ring, Laura. 2006. *Zenana: Everyday Peace in a Kerachi Apartment Building*. Bloomington: Indiana University Press.

PART I

HISTORICAL SOURCES OF RELIGIOUS CONFLICT AND PEACE

CHAPTER I

Forgiveness with Consequences
Scriptures, *Qenē,* and Traditions of Restorative Justice in Nineteenth-Century Ethiopia

Charles Schaefer

Secession, War, and a Fitful Peace

Portrayed as comrades-in-arms, victorious rebels, bush-educated politicians, simple-living, and incorruptible, Ethiopian Prime Minister Meles Zenawi and Eritrean President Isaias Afewerki were heralded as the poster boys of Africa's new leadership. Until 1996, both men proclaimed brotherly love, mutual admiration, a desire for economic federation, and a genuine belief that the secession of Eritrea from Ethiopia was right and just. Zenawi and Afewerki celebrated what they believed to be a common political culture and independence, cultivated during their protracted resistance struggle against the Marxist dictatorship of Mengistu Haile Mariam, known as the Derg. Their common experience left them with a sense of optimism about the pursuit of a shared, bright future. These were the same men who criticized other African leaders as greedy, uncaring, and vengeful.

And then things changed, rather dramatically. First, there was a currency war of sorts. Following the printing of the nafka (Eritrean currency), Ethiopia demonetized its own currency and reprinted a different-colored birr in order to prevent Eritrea from cashing in on Ethiopia's foreign reserves. There followed a full-scale para-statal conflict over markets and, finally, the costly Eritrean-Ethiopian war, which area specialist Patrick Gilkes likened to two bald men fighting over a comb, yet which resulted in the loss of seventy thousand lives.[1]

Gone was any semblance of trust or vision of a common good, and suddenly the disparaging monikers with which Zenawi and Afewerki had been assailing other African leaders were leveled at them.

After the end of the war and the signing of a peace treaty in December 2000, rancor and hostility between the two nations prevailed. In March 2003, the United Nations Eritrean-Ethiopia Border Commission published its findings, which demarcated the border between the two countries and gave the town of Badme to Eritrea. Simmering tensions heated to a boil. After January 2004, the United Nations, the European Union (EU), Great Britain, and the United States all sent special envoys to squelch the fire. Former German Prime Minister Helmet Schroeder and U.S. Secretary of State Condoleezza Rice, among other dignitaries, stopped in Addis Ababa to try their hands at bringing about a rapprochement between the two leaders, to no avail. Pronouncements about the inevitability of renewed war continued to come from both Asmara and Addis Ababa with no abatement in sight. In a remarkably candid interview, Zenawi described the deteriorating relations with Eritrea, stating, "I think it would be fair to say that they are quite bad." He went on to elaborate: "We have no intention of going to war with Eritrea again, we would not want to do so. . . . Nevertheless that doesn't mean there's going to be peace, it could mean that the current status of stalemate and tension could persist for months and perhaps years."[2] The peace treaty and border demarcation proved colossal failures, in part owing to the Horn of Africa's buying into Western ideas about justice to bring about peace. An assumption of retributive justice is that there is a winner and a loser. Yet neither the Ethiopian government nor the Eritrean government wants to be seen as a loser in the eyes of its people or the international community. Essentially, they seek an alternative to resolve the impasse and save face.

Likewise, the 1991 decision of the Ethiopian People's Revolutionary Democratic Front (EPRDF) to use a tribunal to try high-ranking Derg officials, who had committed genocidal acts against students and educated elites during the Red Terror (1976–78), led Zenawi to ponder whether the trial was an appropriate expression of retributive justice. Basically, the Ethiopian leadership painted itself into a corner. Although the verdict was passed in January 2007, twelve years after the prosecution began presenting its case, the Ethiopian population had come to consider the trial irrelevant. Worse, Ethiopians viewed the standards by which Derg officials were being tried as hypocritical, a betrayal of the values of the EPRDF. It is no surprise, then, that the trial failed to reconcile the past and bring national healing to address the future.[3] Zenawi claimed that "we didn't think of a truth and reconciliation commission. In any case there was no such experience at that time [circa 1991]."[4] It is true that South Africa's Truth and Reconciliation Commission did not exist at the time, and perhaps Zenawi's lack of awareness concerning the low-profile truth commissions in Latin America was understandable. Less excusable was his and the EPRDF's ignorance of and failure to consider Ethiopia's own traditions of restorative justice.

What appears to be lacking in the political culture of Ethiopia and Eritrea is the ability to forgive. Perhaps memories are too keen and people assume that to forgive means to forget. (The vast literature critiquing concepts of restorative justice certainly dwells on this connection.) But long memories were never considered an impediment to forgiveness in traditional Ethiopian society; to the contrary, forgiveness was given conditionally and the conditions were not forgotten. When those conditions were abused, the original terms were recalled and consequences for deceitfulness and malfeasance were prescribed according to the seriousness of the individual case. In short, traditional Ethiopia subscribed to the idea of "forgiveness with consequences" and took Christian scriptures as the generative text modeling their conception of restorative justice.

Would a retrieval of Ethiopian traditional concepts and practices of justice prove more effective than Western trials and notions of retribution? That is the question addressed by this chapter, which traces the link between the teachings of the Ethiopian Orthodox Church and the political culture of nineteenth-century Ethiopia in order to assess the rationale for opting for forms of restorative justice and the conditions under which it was deployed. Three issues are examined: first, the connection between the church establishment and the political hierarchy; second, why restorative justice was considered the best option for feudal Ethiopia; and third, the manner in which conditional clemency was granted. If the terms of clemency were violated, payment or punishment was exacted; this retribution provided the bite in Ethiopia's conception of restorative justice.

In what follows I focus on the application of forms of justice to instances of mass or collective violence against the citizenry or the state of Ethiopia prior to the twentieth century. This study is confined to the Christian highlands of Ethiopia and concentrates almost exclusively on the connection between the Ethiopian Orthodox Church and the polity—this is not to ignore other religious groups (that is, Muslims and those who practice what is sometimes referred to, problematically, as African Traditional Religion) and their values, but simply to represent the prevailing culture and religious traditions in eighteenth- and nineteenth-century Ethiopia.

Ethiopia has a complex judicial system. A comprehensive analysis would have to start with the roots of customary law, the Jewish Pentateuch and the Syrian and Roman codes, all of which were synthesized into the *Fetha Nagast*—Ethiopia's common law. Indeed, in Zenawi's own words, "Ethiopians have had courts for many years, for thousands of years," and the only court that may have a longer lifespan is "the court in the sky."[5] Historically the *Fetha Nagast* did not adjudicate matters of state; that was left for the *chelot,* the imperial court, to resolve. It was made up of the emperor and the *tachawoch,* which included trusted members of the *makwanent* (the high ruling class consisting of nobles, provincial governors, and high-ranking military and ecclesiastical officials) and the *afa negus* (the "Mouth of the Emperor," equivalent to a chief justice). The manner in which the *chelot* resolved treasonous acts, gross human rights abuses, or political crimes is the focus of the present discussion of Ethiopia's traditions of restorative justice.

FUSING OF RELIGIOUS AND POLITICAL DISCOURSE

Monophysite Christianity was introduced to Ethiopia in the early fourth century by two brothers from Tyre, Frumentius and Aedesius, the former of whom was later consecrated bishop of Axum by the Coptic patriarch in Alexandria. Frumentius's lasting achievement was to convert Emperor Ezana and his family to Christianity. Thus began the union between creed and court that dominated Ethiopia into the twentieth century. As it took hundreds of years for the vast majority of Ethiopians to profess Christianity, a unique indigenized form of the faith took shape, synthesizing the doctrine of Antioch, the theocracy of Alexandria, and a storehouse of cultural and social elements borrowed from African religious thought, pre-rabbinic Judaism, and other archaic Semitic religions.[6] This syncretized Ethiopian Orthodoxy nevertheless became the foundation of individual identity and national character.

In highland Ethiopia the parish determined or designated virtually everything: locality, taxes, administrative region, judicial zone, schools, social safety nets, and even land tenure. Geographically, the highlands were speckled with conical-shaped churches consisting of three concentric circles, with the innermost room containing the *tabot*—the holy ark or wooden tablet representing the saint to whom the church was dedicated. Churches were typically the largest structures in the parish. Administration was largely conducted out of the house of the *chiqa shum,* a peasant elder appointed yearly by the feudal *gult*-holder (lord). Land arbitration, dispute resolution, and divorce courts tended to be open-air affairs or were conducted on the terrace of the church.[7] Schools, if they existed, were mostly staffed by either priests or deacons, also on the terraces of the church. The church as the local meeting place was central to the lives of peasants. Beyond baptisms, marriages, and burials, services, saints' days, festivals, and self-help meetings were all conducted in the church or on church property. Sociologist Donald Levine estimates that if a person were to have observed every church holiday in Manz, his fieldwork site, a peasant would go to Mass and either fast or refrain from hard labor every other day—fully 50 percent of the time.[8]

As stated above, Emperor Ezana was the first political leader to convert, and virtually an unbroken line of Christian kings succeeded him until 1974. So fused was Ethiopian religious and political ideology that in its final redaction in the early fourteenth century the *Kebre Nagast,* or national epic, defined the institution of the emperor and counseled him on how to govern.[9] The *Kebre Nagast* legitimated the emperor by claiming his descent from Menilek I, the son of King Solomon and the queen of Sheba, who as an adult traveled to Israel to visit his father and acquire statecraft and wisdom. Much of what defined good governance, therefore, was lifted straight from the Old Testament, specifically the books of Judges and 1 and 2 Kings. The ultimate legitimation was the abduction of the ark of the covenant to Axum and God's proclamation that Ethiopia was the new Zion. That the historicity of the national epic is shaky seems not to trouble Orthodox Ethiopians, for their beliefs are situated more comfortably in the Old Testament than the New.[10]

Zar'a Ya'cob, a model feudal emperor, stipulated that the whole Bible was to be read in its entirety during church services in the course of the year and that special emphasis be placed on the Law and the Prophets. Language, idiomatic expression, metaphor, and in fact the ideation of the world and society were all shaped by scriptures. In the royal chronicles the hagiography of emperors is referred to in biblical terms. In reading the chronicles of Zar'a Ya'cob, 'Amda Seyon, Takla Giyorgis, Galawdewos, Yohannis, Menilek, or even despised emperors like Tewodros, one wonders if one is indeed reading Ethiopian history or simply a rearranged history of Israel, for the personalities, wisdom imparted, victories, and defeats are all compared to those of Elijah, Elisha, Saul, David, Solomon, and the like.[11] The names and titles of Ethiopian emperors emphasized this connection; for example, Ras Tafari took the coronation name Haile Selassie, which means "Might of the Trinity," and his full title was His Imperial Majesty, Haile Selassie, King of Kings and Lion of Judah. The British explorer Henry Salt noted while traveling through the country in 1809, "The reader conversant in Scripture, cannot fail . . . to remark [on] . . . the general resemblance existing throughout between the manners of [Ethiopians] and those of Jews previously to the reign of Solomon."[12] The ideation of scriptural norms was pervasive throughout Ethiopian society among both elites and commoners. Indeed, the pervasiveness of religious instruction lent a certain fluidity to the Ethiopian feudal system, as social classes shared much of the same Christian worldview.

CONCEPTS OF RESTORATIVE JUSTICE IN ETHIOPIAN POLITICAL DISCOURSE

Certainly the Old Testament, held in such regard within Ethiopian Orthodoxy, invokes both retribution and magnanimity. Similarly, it would be naïve to disregard vengeance and war as major features of Ethiopian political history. Admittedly, standard interpretations of fifteenth- through nineteenth-century Ethiopian history characterize it as a period of recurrent warfare. The *zamana mesafint* ("Era of the Princes"), a period of constant feudal rivalries during the eighteenth and nineteenth centuries, provided numerous European travelers ample opportunity to witness and write about the ravages of war. Cruelty elicited much commentary by foreign observers, as it complemented their racialized view of the world by positing that Ethiopians, like all Africans, were uncivilized. For example, the nineteenth-century British traveler Cornwallis Harris claimed, "Monstrous and appalling crimes are dictated by the desire to obtain the insignia of valor,"[13] while Henry Salt observed, "The Ras finding that he could make only a trifling impression on the enemy he had to encounter, burnt the town of Mokiddo, and left the country."[14] The first generation of Western historians dealing with nineteenth-century Ethiopian history relied on these depictions when they attempted to gauge the trajectory of history and trace its evolution from disunity to unity.

Ignored by European travel narratives and scholarly treatises was an assessment of what took place in Ethiopia between battles that allowed social and political hierarchies to reconstitute themselves so effectively that in short order new skirmishes could be waged. To a certain extent, the persistence of war in feudal Ethiopia was a result of the effective application of indigenous conflict resolution techniques.[15] As the historian Shiferaw Bekele states, "Ethiopia's rulers spent probably as much time making peace as warfare. . . . Indeed the history of the country over the last three centuries suggests that peace making was an integral part of the political and institutional architecture of the Ethiopian polity. The chronicles and other sources shed light on numerous peace building efforts."[16]

Particularly noteworthy is what happened after most battles.[17] Arnauld d'Abbadie, a French explorer and entrepreneur who lived in Ethiopia from 1838 to 1848 and took part in a number of battles during the *zamana mesafint*, was unable to comprehend what he saw at the conclusion of hostilities. In his memoir he described a celebrative reunion of cousins fighting on opposite sides and, from d'Abbadie's European perspective, the lack of fear on the part of the vanquished soldiers. D'Abbadie recorded, "Ethiopian soldiers are so secure in the solemnity of warfare that these beliefs contribute to their ability to give clemency to the vanquished. One observes the victorious and the defeated recognizing each other, embracing, inquiring with concern about the wellbeing of recent adversaries, or interposing in order to improve the fortunes of friends."[18] Others noted similar occurrences. Henry Dufton, who was in a position to witness the transformation of Emperor Tewodros into a despot by the mid-nineteenth century, noted that in his early reign Tewodros acted with magnanimity: "Whether from policy, or in obedience to the better impulses of his nature, he did not allow his conquests to be marked by even the ordinary cruelties of Abyssinian warfare. . . . He exercised the utmost clemency towards the vanquished, treating them rather as his friends than his enemies."[19] These actions were not uncommon, for it was considered good form for victors to grant clemency to the defeated as part of the ruling elites' understanding of restorative justice.

The rationale for these and other acts of forgiveness, as part of the package of restorative justice, was woven into the economic and social fabric of Ethiopia and expressed in religious idioms. Historian Tsegaye Tegenu describes how Ethiopian aristocrats, knowing that agrarian, feudal societies are dependent on their cultivators, mobilized peasant-soldiers according to the seasonal demands of crop cultivation and made efforts to start or stop campaigns accordingly.[20] Since revenge against rank-and-file peasant-soldiers would only hurt the economy and citizenry of the conquered areas, Ethiopian rulers seldom, if ever, sought retribution against commoners. Some have argued that the practice of leaving farmers alone provided a kind of insurance that roving armies would always have someone to plunder as they moved around the countryside from one battle to the next, but that view does not resonate with the respect accorded peasants in either the Royal

Chronicles or *qenē*. *Qenē* was an extremely sophisticated form of liturgical poetry that carried double meanings in which social memory and wisdom were passed down to all who heard it. It was not reserved only for elites—to the contrary, it also served as a vehicle for articulate commoners to warn and admonish those in power. The same benevolence was extended to rival aristocrats. Typically a victor would require an act of submission from the vanquished, often involving an oath taken on a cross or the Bible. In addition, acts of submission were often cemented by arranging single or double intermarriages.[21] An example is seen in the magnanimity shown by Emperor Menilek toward his rival Tigrian kings, who had sided with the Italians prior to the Battle of Adwa in 1896. By finding common cause, honoring provincial suzerainty, and insisting only on rather perfunctory acts of submission to the Showan throne, Menilek managed to regain the allegiance of a number of other nobles and could then count on their support and that of their armies at the Battle of Adwa.[22] In general, then, outright punishment by the victors was considered bad form; the idealized role of the emperor was to restore the body politic, not exact punishment. Indeed, legal scholar Heinrich Scholler states that reconciliation was the mantra of court life and that, after listening to all sides, the emperor was expected to stay neutral in order to formulate a restorative justice position.[23]

How was this tradition of restorative justice imparted? As stated above, Christian scriptures were the wellspring iterated in Mass, court and civic ceremonies, and the *Kebre Nagast*. The concepts of benevolence and forgiveness were universally understood and can be traced in the veneration of the saints, religious education, and the double meanings embedded in *qenē*.

While religious iconography did not necessarily inculcate the semi- and non-literate Ethiopian populace with a complex ethical code, the pervasive religious imagery and lessons taught on various saints' days did extend the parameters of ethical reasoning and options available therein to the people. Orthodox hagiographic literature is replete with examples of the miracles of Jesus, various angels, saints, and, especially, the Virgin Mary. Numerous versions of the *Miracles of Mary* exist, producing what art historian Marilyn Heldman terms the rise of the "cult of Mary" in the fifteenth century.[24]

The veneration of saints is a prominent feature of Ethiopian Ortho-doxy; religious feast days dedicated to St. Mikael occur on the twelfth day of each month (Ethiopian calendar), while thirty-three days are given to honoring the Virgin Mary per year. Around the veneration of saints has developed an iconic tradition whereby a person prays to a saint while holding the icon of that saint, for the icon is believed to function as an intermediary and even possess some of the saint's power. Saints represent many human characteristics from powerful warriors, like St. George and St. Mikael, who were favorites of emper-ors bound for war, to St. Tekla Haymanot and St. Mary, "Mother of Peace," who are viewed as intercessors bringing peace and under-standing. Even the *tabot,* the representative ark found in the inner sanctuary of each church, is personified by the saint to whom the church is dedicated; thus, "arks of Mikael are vengeful while arks of Mary are compassionate."[25] Often the images of the saints communi-cate their place on the spectrum between wrath and forgiveness: thus, if the saint is viewed as bringing peace and understanding to the world, he is depicted with doves surrounding his head; if the saint is quelling the forces of anarchy and disharmony (sometimes signified by a leop-ard or hyena), he or the angels are made to carry spears.

Traditions of restorative justice were also disseminated through religious education—the only form of formal education operating in Ethiopia before the twentieth century. As far back as the fifteenth century, religious instruction was mandated as part of the religious service. More formal education was available to all who could afford it. At the lowest level, the village priest taught the Ethiopic syllabary, arithmetic, and the Psalter. Beyond this basic instruction, education followed two tracks: the first taught priests and monks scriptures, lit-urgy, doctrine, and the *Fetha Nagast,* while the second went beyond this into the creative realm of composition, including *qenē.* Students of this second track were mostly studying to be *dabtarās* (cantors); *dabtarās* were respected for their learning and their ability to use bib-lical teachings as commentary on everyday occurrences in the form of *qenē.*

Qenē is an exceptionally sophisticated liturgical "doubletalk" that in poetic form carries a "wax" (surface) level of meaning and a "gold" (deep, ambiguous) level that may be arguing just the opposite. To become an accomplished *qenē* composer takes years of study, as each verse is supposed to be unique, with strict rules of meter and rhyme. Never is the author of *qenē* supposed to repeat it, for once composed and spoken, it enters the public domain to be committed to memory by all listeners (primarily the Christian population, although particularly inspired phrases were used among non-Christians as well), repeated hundreds of times in houses and public spaces throughout the country, and ruminated upon as part of a robust oral tradition. *Qenē* was memorized by peasants and aristocrats alike. As recently as the Derg period (1974–91) peasants, taxi drivers, and even professors at Addis Ababa University often expressed their grievances about the autocratic regime by repeating *qenē* they had heard directly from a *dabtarā* or by repeating a particularly pithy poem that had entered into public discourse. *Dabtarās* most adept at capturing deep meanings and/or subtle criticism of prevailing socio-political conditions in the country became celebrities. *Qenē* can be pro-vengeance or pro-forgiveness, as both forms of justice were portrayed in the Old Testament.

Qenē epitomizes the Ethiopian personality that Donald Levine coined in the title to his landmark book, *Wax and Gold,* in which seeing both sides of the proverbial coin is central to intergroup understanding and the long-term success of governance. Thus, warfare may lead a Ras to victory, but *qenē* highlights the long-term or unintended consequences of conquest. Likewise, retribution may be the preferred way to deal with an enemy, but *qenē* argues that forgiveness may be more salutary. Historically, the lessons of *qenē* touched the highest aristocrat and the lowest peasant. Notably, Ethiopian elites were given religious instruction as part of their education, but the emphasis was on issues of justice. The principal goal was to cultivate the ability to perceive ambiguity; here noted *dabtarās* were sought to help the scions of the *makwanent* appreciate the complexities of human nature. They were taught that true justice is not codified, but rather is circumstantial and tries to achieve reconciliation between disputants.[26] These lessons proved invaluable to the emperor and the *chelot* (imperial court) when called upon to render justice in matters of state or to resolve national conflict.

The above discussion begs the following question: was forgiveness, as a central component of Ethiopia's understanding of restorative justice, a political ideology and strategy grounded in religion, or was it a general cultural ethos? The short answer is that it was both. Christianity was practiced by the dominant political clique and, as argued above, was the basis of their education, ideology, and identity; moreover, scriptures provided examples and strategies upon which to model justice for the imperial state and agrarian society. But forgiveness was also a part of the cultural ethos. Language, idiomatic expression, metaphor, and in fact the entire ideation of the world and society were shaped by scriptures for all major ethnic groups and religions in Ethiopia.[27] Tadesse Tamrat observes that it was sometimes difficult for Ethiopians to differentiate between political and religious offices because the terms used to describe them were often synonymous.[28] This chapter argues exclusively from the perspective of the Christian highlands, yet understanding, tolerance, and forgiveness were also hallmarks of other religious and political communities within the larger Ethiopian polity, including Islam and African cosmologies in southern and western Ethiopia.[29]

Forgiveness with a Bite

In the twenty-first century, the Ethiopian public may be recalling the wisdom of their tradition of restorative justice that encourages forgiveness but does not necessarily forgo punishment. In an open letter written by former Derg officials being tried for crimes against humanity to Prime Minister Meles Zenawi and given to the Ethiopian Human Rights Council (EHRCO) to broadcast widely, the defendants asked for forgiveness for the crimes they had committed thirty years before. They appeared to be harkening back to Ethiopia's well-developed tradition of asking for forgiveness while acknowledging that forgiveness is conditional: "We plead to you [Zenawi], with due humility and respect, to accept our genuine request and to grant us a forum whereon we, on behalf of all those who stood on our side, and on our own behalf, can ask for forgiveness for our wronged compatriots."[30] Mesfin Wolde-Mariam, the president of EHRCO, added,

"These people are prepared to ask for forgiveness—not mercy or [for] the trials to be stopped, they just want to release what is in their conscience—to cleanse themselves."[31]

That forgiveness is not free but rather comes with requirements and consequences is a concept rooted in Ethiopia's particular theological tradition. For example, in the Ethiopian Orthodox Church, the sacrament of Holy Communion is extremely important and a sine qua non for engaging in the important events of life; participation in the sacrament requires the confession of sins and true repentance. Those who have broken a fast, worked on a religious feast day, committed adultery, stolen money, or murdered someone are expected to confess their sin, perform acts of penance commensurate with the gravity of the sin, and purify themselves of the sinful behavior. Forgiveness is thus freely given to those who acknowledge their sinful ways and seek to change them.[32] If the process of repentance and purification was not performed satisfactorily, then absolution is withdrawn, the offender is damned in theological terms, and communion can be withheld.

This religious understanding of the conditional nature of repentance and forgiveness was appropriated into political and judicial realms. Acts of magnanimity assume that the beneficiary will demonstrate remorse and a willingness to change, but in cases in which the person granted forgiveness does not live according to the agreed upon conditions, consequences such as payments or punishments were applied. Two examples from Ethiopian history illustrate forgiveness with consequences: the Battle of Adwa and the Battle of Sagale. These are particularly powerful examples because they constitute the bedrock of Ethiopians' popular invention of a halcyon past.[33] For the masses they conjure up the glory days when Ethiopia defeated a European power, or when the virtuous forces subdued the malevolent threat to the throne. To elites, the battles represent a time when the political hierarchy ruled to maintain the suzerainty of the nation as well as the wellbeing of the citizenry. Both elites and the masses call for a return to the principled politics of this heroic past as an alternative to the conflict and corruption of the modern period.

At the Battle of Adwa on March 1, 1896, Menilek's army routed an Italian army that had set out the night before to mount a surprise attack. Conservative estimates claim four thousand Italian and two thousand *askari* (Ethiopian/Eritrean soldiers under Italian command) casualties, while close to another two thousand Italians were captured.[34] News of the Battle of Adwa immediately became headline news around the world. The majority of Western newspaper editors cast it as Italy's shameful defeat, but for black and colonial native presses it was celebrated as Africa's victory over colonial aggression. That the victory was a signature event was beyond doubt, but equally noteworthy were Emperor Menilek's charitable acts toward the defeated Italians afterward. While historians debate precisely why the emperor granted amnesty to the Italian soldiers taken captive at the battle, the magnanimity shown toward them is remarkable.[35] Of the 49 Italian officers and 1656 soldiers taken captive, less than 100 died from their wounds in Ethiopia. The rest were transported to hospitals in Addis Ababa or Harar, sheltered in the houses of the Ethiopian *makwanent,* or settled in Italian neighborhoods and were employed as skilled laborers on building projects throughout Ethiopia. After some time the soldiers and officers were allowed to return home, but to the chagrin of Italian politicians who publicly condemned the treatment of their countrymen by the savage Abyssinians; many of the POWs, who had married Ethiopian women, chose to stay in Ethiopia for the rest of their lives.

On the one hand Adwa and its aftermath simply illustrate the rules of war that Arnauld d'Abbadie observed regarding Ethiopian techniques of conflict resolution fifty years earlier. But Ethiopian benevolence was not universal in the aftermath of Adwa, with harsh punishment leveled at the native Ethiopian *askari* who had fought on the Italian side. Augustus Wylde, one of the few people to travel into the interior of Ethiopia shortly after the Battle of Adwa, reported:

> The Italian native prisoners, soldiers in the Italian service who had fought against the Abyssinians, were tried by a council of war consisting of all the chief Abyssinian leaders, and the horrible sentence of mutilation was passed; which Menelek sanctioned, after, it is said, great pressure had been brought to bear upon him, he being greatly against any harsh measures being used. The sentence of mutilation—that is, the cutting off the right hand and the

left foot—is customary punishment for the offences of theft, sac-
rilege and treason, of which many of these men were judged to be
clearly guilty.[36]

The mutilation of the *askari* seems harsh, especially in contrast with
the magnanimity shown toward the Italian captives. Such punishment, however, makes more sense in the broader context of conditional clemency. In the Ethiopian model, which was drawn from
biblical sources,[37] forgiveness assumes obligation, for while the power
to be merciful lies with the forgiver, the one seeking forgiveness is obligated to show contrition and to be accountable for future actions, in
other words, to turn away from criminal—or in this case treasonous—
ways. In the case of recalcitrance on the part of the forgiven, punishment became the bite, or condition, implied in this understanding of
forgiveness. For approximately ten years, Menilek's forces had warned
the *askari* that if they continued to fight on the side of the Italians
they would be viewed as traitors. Wylde observed, "Those soldiers
who had served at the defense of Macalle [Meqele] had been warned
of what punishment they would receive if they were again found in
arms against Abyssinia."[38] Menilek found the *askari* unworthy of forgiveness, for they had willfully fought against their Ethiopian brothers and did not show remorse for their treasonous actions. Severing
the right hand (the sword hand) and the left foot (used to mount a
horse), while seemingly harsh, was a traditional punishment for treason that in fact showed restraint and the possibility of social reintegration into society; certainly it was more munificent than execution.

The Battle of Sagale in 1916 illustrated the range of options available to Ethiopian political leaders to reconcile adversaries in a struggle
over dynastic succession. Lij Iyasu had succeeded his grandfather
Emperor Menilek in 1913. Many consider Lij Iyasu a progressive and
a visionary for he saw Ethiopia as a kaleidoscope of ethnicities and religions and sought to develop a policy of inclusion. Unfortunately,
this went against the entrenched interests of the Ethiopian Orthodox
highlanders. Lij Iyasu was accused of converting to Islam, resulting in
Abuna (Archbishop) Mattewos charging him with apostasy and thus
releasing the *makwanent* from the oath of allegiance to him.[39] The
aristocracy split in two and battled over the crown at Sagale in 1916,

with Lij Iyasu's forces being defeated. Following the Battle of Sagale the *makwanent* followed the traditional Ethiopian rule by granting the defeated soldiers amnesty to return to their homes in Wollo Province, for as Ras Tafari reputedly said, "We are all Ethiopians."[40] The *makwanent,* and later Ras Tafari/Emperor Haile Selassie, also determined appropriate punishments for Lij Iyasu. Originally he was imprisoned and put in gold chains (as befitting an emperor); then he was put into nominal house arrest and priests, consorts, and friends were allowed to visit him freely. When he escaped and was caught a second time plotting to reassert his claim to the throne, he was imprisoned again in less comfortable circumstances.[41]

CONCLUSION

Not all conflicts over dynastic succession or issues surrounding the survival of the state were resolved in a benevolent, affirming manner. Ethiopian history is full of contradictions, yet while there are numerous examples of revenge and other atrocities, there are an equal number of circumstances where the political establishment forgave the offenders in hopes of bringing about reconciliation and national healing.

Restorative justice has elicited significant attention in recent years, and is frequently condemned for having no bite. Truth commissions, blanket amnesties, and various forms of clemency, critics argue, simply promote the idea of "forgive and forget" and thus condemn a country and its people to repeated misuse of power and gross human rights abuses.[42] Yet evaluating the rationale and practices for granting conditional clemency to the vast majority of Italians and Eritreans, while punishing some *askari* after the Battle of Adwa, provides a powerful example of restorative justice with bite, or forgiving without forgetting.[43] Memory of warnings given and recollection of continued disregard for the precepts of Ethiopian feudal society resulted in the Ethiopian emperor punishing the *askari* for not being accountable to the obligations implied in the understanding of forgiveness.

The understanding of forgiveness in Ethiopia, strongly informed by scriptures, was reiterated time and again in *qenē* as perhaps the most subtle, sagacious commentary on politics and society that emperors and the *makwanent* heard and studied. Forgiveness was both a cultural ethos as well as a political stratagem grounded in the Ethiopian Orthodox appropriation of Christianity, which dominated the polity at the time. In instances where retribution was applied, justice was swift and often bloody; however, equal if not greater attention was given to applying a conditional form of restorative justice in order to establish the basis for future peace and restore balance and sociopolitical harmony. This form of justice, though borrowing heavily from a distinct religious ideology, was primarily a fluid stratagem concerned with the temporal affairs of state. Forgiveness was granted conditionally and, when conditions were not met, grades and levels of punishment could change, as illustrated by Lij Iyasu's varying compliance with the terms of his amnesty after the Battle of Sagale. Fundamentally, however, the purpose of justice was to restore society to health. Ethiopia's restorative justice tradition is, therefore, one resource that can be retrieved from the past in order to more effectively address contemporary crises. Although it did not always define actual behavior, and other reconciliation processes existed among the Islamic and Oromo populations, the Christian, imperial tradition represents an indigenous aspect of Ethiopian religion and history that could be lifted up in current discussions of how to deal with conflict and perceived injustice in the region.

Perhaps the Derg defendants realized they and Ethiopia needed to put closure on seventeen years of senseless brutality and to bring Africa's ineffective, Western-style human rights trial to an appropriate end after fourteen years. Returning to a more fluid, nuanced, conditional sense of justice would facilitate resolving a number of political disputes, not simply limited to the border demarcation between Ethiopia and Eritrea. Moreover, within the emerging field of transitional justice there is a new emphasis on finding bridges between restorative or retributive justice to implement a system endogenously prescribed to the time, place, and particulars of each case.[44] Ethiopia's historical record, exemplified by countless examples of conditional clemency, points to a general cultural ethos supported by a dominant religious-political ideology that championed reconciliation, harmony, and peacemaking, including the integration of rivals and competing political and religious institutions. Precautions were taken, in that amnesty was granted with conditions and recourse, and circumstances of the original conflicts were not forgotten. Such an ethos of understanding and forgiveness with limits would help Ethiopia as it negotiates implementing democracy, incorporating opposition parties into a representative parliament, tolerating a free press, and supporting ethnic, civic, and religious freedoms.

Eritrea too would do well to be more tolerant and forgiving, as encouraged by the so-called Group of Fifteen (G-15). In May 2001, fifteen senior military and civilian leaders within the Eritrean People's Liberation Front (EPLF) leadership wrote an Open Letter criticizing President Isaias Afewerki and the direction of their own government in terms of its governance, judiciary, and human rights record. The G-15 criticized Afewerki's dictatorial methods and "kangaroo courts," saying that the Eritrean people should be enjoying their constitutional rights; for their outspokenness, eleven were imprisoned. Opposition parties have been outlawed and the Eritrean government appears to be on a manhunt to eliminate members of the EPLF and its scions. Freedom of the press does not exist; university students have been arrested and tortured, and parents of those students have likewise been arrested simply for going to the authorities to inquire about the wellbeing of their children. Current travails seem far removed from the bygone era when cousins and friends fought each other on the battlefield and afterward the victors sought out the vanquished and did all that was in their power to assist the defeated and improve their fortunes, but perhaps there is a lesson in this not-so-distant past for today.

NOTES

1. Tekeste Negash and Kjetil Tronvoll, *Brothers at War: Making Sense of the Eritrean-Ethiopian War* (Athens: Ohio University Press, 2000), 30–45. The Gilkes comment came in a personal conversation.

2. Andrew Simmons, Al Jazeera, http://english.aljazeera.net/NR/exeres/80AA000E-7081-4D35-B0F4-25902CC79D04.htm, accessed March 19, 2007.

3. For a more in-depth assessment of the rationale behind the EPRDF's choice of a tribunal as opposed to a truth commission, see Charles Schaefer, "The Derg Trial versus Traditions of Restorative Justice in Ethiopia," in *The Ethiopian Red Terror Trials: Transitional Justice and Human Rights Denied,* ed. Kjetil Tronvoll, Charles Schaefer, and Girmachew A. Aneme (Oxford: James Currey, 2009).

4. Quoted from Kjetil Tronvoll's interview with Meles Zenawi, Addis Ababa, January 16, 2002.

5. Ibid.

6. Edward Ullendorff, *Ethiopia and the Bible* (London: Oxford University Press, 1968), 15.

7. Heinrich Scholler, "Open Air Courts in Popular Paintings," *Afrika und Übersee* (1985).

8. Donald Levine, *Wax and Gold: Tradition and Innovation in Ethiopian Culture* (Chicago: University of Chicago Press, 1965), 60. Although the number of days varies by region, if strictly counted there are more than 260 religious days to be observed in Debra Damot.

9. Marilyn E. Heldman, "The Kebran Gospels: Ethiopia and Byzantium," in *Proceedings of the Fifth International Conference on Ethiopian Studies, Session B* (Chicago, 1978), 363.

10. Perhaps the most thorough examination of the Old Testament roots in Ethiopian Orthodoxy was undertaken by Ullendorff in *Ethiopia and the Bible,* which details the depth and breadth of the Hebraic influence.

11. Two English translations that communicate this point are G. W. B. Huntingford, *The Glorious Victories of 'Amda Seyon, King of Ethiopia* (Oxford: Clarendon Press, 1965); and H. Weld Blundell, *The Royal Chronicle of Abyssinia 1769–1840* (repr., Osnabruck: Otto Zeller Verlag, 1989).

12. Henry Salt, *A Voyage to Abyssinia and Travels into the Interior of that Country* (repr., London: Frank Cass, 1967), 306.

13. Cornwallis Harris, *Adventure in Africa* (Philadelphia: T. B. Peterson, 1843), 183.

14. Salt, *A Voyage to Abyssinia,* 305–6.

15. Charles Schaefer, "Reexamining the Ethiopian Historical Record on the Continuum between Vengeance and Forgiveness," in *Proceedings of the 15th International Conference on Ethiopian Studies,* ed. Siegbert Uhlig (Wiesbaden: Harrassowitz, 2006), 348–55.

16. Shiferaw Bekele, "The Peace Making Process in the History of Ethiopia," unpublished paper, July 2001. The first phase of this long-term project is being undertaken in Ethiopia and Italy and will result in a work tentatively titled "Reconstructing the First Reign of Tekle Giyorgis I (1779–1784)."

17. Again, in an attempt not to be misleading, there are passages in the travel literature and Ethiopian Royal Chronicles that discuss barbarous acts

after battles. See Harris, *Adventures in Africa,* 182, and James Bruce, *Travels to Discover the Source of the Nile* (repr., New York: Horizon Press, 1964), 181.

18. "Les soldats éthiopiens sont convaincus de la versatilité des positions, et cette croyance contribue à les render cléments envers les vaincus. On voit de vainqueurs et des vaincus se reconnaîs, embrasser, s'informer avec solicitude de leurs récents adversaries ou s'interposer auprès d'un compagnon afin d'améliorer le sort de quelque ami." Arnauld d'Abbadie, *Douze Ans de Séjour dans la Haute-Éthiopie (Abyssinie)* (repr., Vatican: Biblioteca Apostolica Vaticana, 1980), 455. Translation mine.

19. Henry Dufton, *Narrative of a Journey through Abyssinia 1862–3* (repr., Westport, CT: Negro University Press, 1970), 134.

20. Tsegaye Tegenu, *The Evolution of Ethiopian Absolutism: The Genesis of the Making of the Fiscal Military State, 1696–1913* (Uppsala: Acta Universitatis Upsaliensis, 1996).

21. Heren Sereke-Brhan, "Building Bridges, Drying Bad Blood: Elite Marriages, Politics and Ethnicity in 19th and 20th Century Imperial Ethiopia" (Ph.D. dissertation, Michigan State University, 2002).

22. Haggai Erlich, *Ras Alula and the Scramble for Africa* (Lawrenceville: Red Sea Press, 1996), 161–96.

23. Scholler, "Open Air Courts."

24. Marilyn E. Heldman, "The Role of the Devotional Image in Emperor Zar'a Ya'eqob's Cult of Mary," in *Proceedings of the Seventh International Conference of Ethiopian Studies* (Uppsala: Scandinavian Institute of African Studies, 1984), 131–42.

25. Allan Hoben, *Land Tenure among the Amhara of Ethiopia: The Dynamics of Cognatic Descent* (Chicago: University of Chicago Press, 1973), 68.

26. Mehteme-Sillase Welde-Mesqel, *Zekra Nagar* [Recollection of Things Past] (Addis Ababa, 1962 [Ethiopian calendar]); a portion of this book is translated as "Portrait Retrospectif d'un Gentilhomme Ethiopien," in *Proceedings of the Third International Conference of Ethiopian Studies* (Addis Ababa: Haile Selassie I University Press, 1966), 63–64.

27. The manner in which these and other cultural norms are shared by all the major ethnic and religious groups in Ethiopia is the thesis of Donald Levine's controversial yet perceptive *Greater Ethiopia: The Evolution of a Multiethnic Society* (Chicago: University of Chicago Press, 1974).

28. Tadesse Tamrat, "Feudalism in Heaven and on Earth: Ideology and Political Structure in Medieval Ethiopia," in *Proceedings of the Seventh International Conference of Ethiopian Studies,* ed. Sven Rubenson (Uppsala: Scandinavian Institute of African Studies, 1984), 195–200.

29. Since the sixteenth century, Islam in Ethiopia taught similar practices. Moreover, studies of political and judicial practices in southern and

western Ethiopia, especially focusing on the Oromo Gada system of representation and compromise, suggested that non-Christian/Islamic social thought emphasized magnanimity, reconciliation, and traditions of restorative justice as much as in highland Ethiopia.

30. "Ethiopia: Former Regime Officials Plead for Clemency." www.irinnews.org/>IRIN/AnthonyMitchell, accessed March 1, 2004.

31. Ibid.

32. Tomaš Špidlík, *The Spirituality of the Christian East* (Kalamazoo, MI: Cistercian Publications, 1986).

33. John Sorenson, *Imagining Ethiopia: Struggles for History and Identity in the Horn of Africa* (New Brunswick, NJ: Rutgers University Press, 1993).

34. The figures are given by Harold G. Marcus around which a general consensus has emerged; see *The Life and Times of Menelik II* (Oxford: Clarendon Press, 1975), 173. It should be noted that about an equal number of Ethiopians died in the fierce fighting but as a percentage of the total fighting force the Ethiopian casualties were less devastating.

35. See ibid., 176.

36. Augustus Wylde, *Modern Abyssinia* (repr., Westport, CT: Negro University Press, 1970), 213.

37. See Matthew 18:23–35.

38. See Wylde, *Modern Abyssinia,* 213. Certainly as early as the Battle of Dogali (1887) the lines of enmity between Ethiopians and Italians and the *askari* who served them had been drawn; see Erlich, *Ras Alula and the Scramble for Africa,* 103–6.

39. Bahru Zewde, *A History of Modern Ethiopia, 1855–1974* (Oxford: James Currey, 1974), 120–28.

40. Harold G. Marcus, *Haile Selassie I: The Formative Years 1892–1936* (Lawrenceville: Red Sea Press, 1995), 24.

41. Gebre-Igziabiher Elyas Prowess, *Piety and Politics: The Chronicle of Abeto Iyasu and Empress Zewditu of Ethiopia (1909–1930),* trans. Reidulf Molvaer (Köln: Köppe, 1994), 367–73.

42. Critiques of truth commissions are growing especially in reference to South Africa, yet the allure of forms of restorative justice still appeals to African authorities charged with reconciling an abusive past. Although this paper argues that the Derg trials have not served the country or citizenry, Rosalind Shaw mounts an equally forceful argument that tribunals or other forms of retributive justice are better alternatives to truth commissions; see *Rethinking Truth and Reconciliation Commissions: Lessons from Sierra Leone* (Washington, DC: United States Institute of Peace, 2005).

43. Grude Bryant, former Interim Leader of Liberia, made the phrase "forgive but not forget" the cornerstone of his attempt to put closure on the

decades of Charles Taylor's civil war and bring about reconciliation by considering restorative justice through a truth commission.

44. Robert Rotberg and Dennis Thompson, eds., *Truth v. Justice: The Morality of Truth Commissions* (Princeton: Princeton University Press, 2000); Raquel Aldana, "A Victim-Centered Reflection on Truth Commissions and Prosecutions as a Response to Mass Atrocities," *Journal of Human Rights* 5, no. 1 (2006); and Lyn Graybill and Kimberly Lanegran, "Truth, Justice, and Reconciliation in Africa: Issues and Cases," *African Studies Quarterly* 8, no. 1 (Fall 2004).

CHAPTER 2

Making Peace with the Devil
The Political Life of Devil Worship Rumors
in Kenya

James Howard Smith

This chapter examines how contemporary conflicts are understood and acted upon through the prism of traumatic historical memories and historically entrenched structural conflicts. In
the process I analyze the religious dimensions of an apparently secular
state; the changing relationship between the secular and the religious
in neoliberal Africa; and the place of demonization in the creation of
imagined communities. I do this by focusing on the idea of *devil
worship*—a term that has come to refer, in Kenya, to ordered moral
chaos, as well as politically motivated and religiously inspired sabotage. Diverse and conflicting Kenyan political communities that seek
to ground themselves in reason or morality have used remarkably
similar, and symbolically resonant, ideas about devil worship as an
oppositional foil to conjure up and sustain their political visions. I
argue that discourse about the dangers of devil worship, originally
promulgated by Christian missionaries in Africa to characterize African minds and natures as vulnerable to evil and in need of being
saved, came to be explicitly politicized and integral to state governance during the colonial period. Colonial officials legitimated their
own violent actions and attempted to forge a coherent state image by
arguing that the Kenyan colony was threatened by irrational, demonic
forces brought about by the ravages of modernization on immature
African minds. *Devil worship* came to refer to the occult manipulation of primitive people unready for modernization (or, alternatively,

primitives who had been too quickly modernized) by educated Africans for political ends. The watershed moment in the early development of this political discourse was the colonial government's intellectual and physical war on the imaginary entity that its spokespeople called Mau Mau—which the government cast as a demonic religious movement—and the state's subsequent isolation and torture of the Kikuyu population. In this way, the state sought, with some success, to define itself as both Christian (rooted in values that were in some way Christian as opposed to being pagan or savage) and secular (predicated upon science—especially scientific agriculture, psychiatry, and cultural anthropology).

In the postcolonial period, Kenyan state officials continued to use the image of devil worship to rhetorically wage war on those who seemed to threaten state governance, including the lucrative and mostly untaxed private transportation industry (the youthful matatu touts) and, more recently, the Mungiki movement; they illegalized and frequently demonized publicly the alleged counter-state ritual of oathing, which had been made taboo by colonial state authorities reasoning in consort with anthropologists and senior African chiefs. At the same time, the idea of devil worship (now fed by an evangelical discourse coming from the United States, at the same time that ideas about multiparty democracy and economic liberalization were emanating from the same provenance) became popularized, and merged with historically enduring understandings of witchcraft; in this instantiation, *devil worship* referred to the sabotage of the transcendent, modernist state by unscrupulous powerful individuals—state officials, Kenyan businessmen, and international power brokers. And so the discourse morphed into a populist, at times even nationalistic, narrative mobilized against particular state figures, which retained the image of an ideal-typical modernist state, and mocked Kenya's actually existing state. In its various implementations and counter-implementations, the discourse of devil worship has profoundly shaped political and religious life in Kenya, and underpinned many acts of state violence, thus overflowing any imaginary or actual opposition between the secular and the religious in Kenyan life.

THE DEVIL DRIVES MERCEDES

The popular discourse about devil worship seemed to erupt suddenly in 1990s Kenya, when rumors of a secret, pervasive cult of elite devil worshipers (including President Daniel arap Moi and his cabinet) became a visible part of national popular culture and politics, and a new creative and pornographic genre emerged on the streets revealing, in vivid detail, the senseless acts of violence committed by alleged Satanists (Blunt 2004). The discourse led, ultimately, to President Moi establishing a presidential commission to investigate the spread of devil worship in the country. The national discussion was underwritten by the rapid proliferation of independent media (pamphlets, video, newspapers) and new Pentecostal-inspired churches, and was situated within the overall context of rapid social, political, and economic transformation, otherwise known as neoliberalism: in particular, state downsizing; multipartyism; renewed public concern about, and revelations of, ubiquitous state and popular corruption; the withdrawal of international aid; and the liberalization of the economy, which precipitated unprecedented inflation and loss of jobs and public services (Smith 2008). But, as we will see, this discourse has a long history, and has been thoroughly imbricated in what I have elsewhere called Kenyan tempopolitics (Smith 2008), or efforts to govern through the elaboration of the idea of divergent times in the same national space, and attendant state efforts to manage the flow, sequence, and experience of unilinear history through development projects, apartheid, indirect governance, and the like.

Consider these three, popularly cited vignettes. The first two are verbatim transcriptions of the insider confessions of professed devil worshipers, extracted from the *Report of the Presidential Commission to Investigate Devil Worship*, published in 1995; the third is my own condensed redaction of a confessional article published independently and readily available on the streets of Nairobi and elsewhere from the late 1990s until recently.[1] Though they are in some sense typical, and the themes are repeated in everyday discourse, they are privileged by the fact that they were responded to by a national governing body that tried to use them as a foundation for policy-making. They were also promulgated by print media, and the proliferation of these stories fed the sense of a spreading national problem, which in turn posited a national community compelled to act on this problem in a positive way.

Vignette 1: A Young Man Sheds His Skin, Twice

Sometime last year, as the boy was going to school, he met a beautiful lady who was accompanied by a man in a black Mercedes Benz. The two strangers introduced themselves to him and led him to a hotel in town, where they persuaded him to join the cult of devil worship. They informed him that the death of his father through a road accident in 1992 was a form of sacrifice, offered to the devil by his stepmother. This made him to suspect that the couple had been sent by his stepmother to recruit him. . . . Subsequently, he agreed to join the cult, after which he was given blood and meat to take. . . . Once he joined the cult he acquired mystic powers which would enable him to transform himself into a cobra. . . . He could also travel in spirit form, and in this respect he claimed to have visited several countries including Nigeria, South Africa, and India. He was also capable of going out through the school gate and sitting in staff meetings unnoticed. . . . He was given a black Mercedes Benz. . . . He was also given eyeglasses which had some supernatural powers, and a chain which he could use to cause road accidents just by squeezing it. He admitted to the Commission of having caused one such accident near his school, in which some passengers were injured. He also said that a road accident that involved the Lugulu Girls High School bus was caused by a former student of the school who was a devil worshipper. . . . The boy withdrew from the cult of devil worship when he received a letter written in blood asking him to offer his twin brother and a sister as a sacrifice and was unable to meet this demand. . . . [Afterward] the boy lost all the money he had mysteriously. He told the Commission that the devil worshippers keep visiting him at night, urging him with threats to rejoin the cult. (*Report* 1995, 49)

Vignette #2: A Bad Habit Is Acquired, Accidentally
The next case involved a young man who was a Mechanical Engineering student at Nyeri Technical Training Institute. He was introduced by a fellow student, to a person who owned a garage. . . . They entered the building through a low gate, and then downstairs into the basement. . . . He saw many people. . . . He noticed that the congregation was made up of Whites, Asians, and a few Africans. The activities that were conducted in the hall were completely bewildering to him. . . . The high priest marked their foreheads with some warm liquid, that turned out to be human blood. Some people came into the hall carrying a human body, which was roasted at the altar. . . . He had difficulty in drinking the blood as he found it very unpalatable. He was finally given some powder to lick, which triggered his thirst for blood. After this . . . he was a scary sight and his family members were afraid of him. He greatly surprised his family when he attempted to kill his brother . . . in the hopes of drinking his blood. . . . However, his church has been praying for him and he has been undergoing counseling by a seminarian in an effort to rehabilitate him. (*Report* 1995, 56)

Vignette #3: A Sadistic Entrepreneur in Non-Utilities Misses His Mother
An uneducated young mechanic barely able to feed himself and his even younger wife services the cars of a rich Cameroonian. Gradually he is recruited into being a courier for this man: he transports body parts that would seem to have no economic value (a baby's penis, tongue, and feet) from one wealthy person to another for reasons that are never clear to him or the reader. Over time, he witnesses many violent, seemingly senseless operations, all of which horrify him, but he continues because he desperately needs the money for his family. He is invited to go to various mansions and nightclubs for secret nocturnal meetings, where he participates in human sacrifice. He is given secret potions to drink that cause him to feel liberated; ironically, he stops caring about his family, and only wants to practice adultery and accumulate money. He becomes simultaneously inured and addicted to these

violent scenes, which he reproduces for fun: he picks up prostitutes, tortures them, and kills them; he forces children to have sex
with him, then decapitates them and soaks them in wine so he can
have a revitalizing drink, and so on. He continues performing
these violent acts, which he quickly lists as if they were routine,
without remorse. But eventually he begins to miss his family, and
feels guilty for not keeping in touch with them. One day he goes
home for a visit after many years, and finds that his mother has
been consistently praying for him all of this time, and is in fact the
reason he has recently felt this counteractive pull toward home.
From then on, he is saved. (Author summary, Anonymous 2000)

Certain key themes define this rhetoric, and enable it to function
as an inclusive moral-political discourse that fosters a sense of community by identifying dangerous moral threats to its existence. First is
the fact that vulnerable youth, usually but not always male, are the
victims of the cult, which reflects the fact that they have been disenfranchised from state-centered development and formal employment,
and are compelled to make their way in illegal and informal economies; they are also painfully aware of the relative prosperity of other
places and earlier times. Thus it is that these stories always commence
with a poor youth whose poverty is made crushing by the fact that
he is intimately aware of other people's often absurdly disproportionate wealth. This tantalizing exposure creates two problems: on the one
hand, the future victim feels unprepared and unworthy in the face of
this wealth, and so is not in a position to act with fortitude and resolve
later on. In addition, the victim is exposed to a desire that confounds
his capacity to distinguish needs from wants, causing something immoral to appear as moral: the victim needs money for his family
(and so kills for an arguably ethical reason), but later needs money because his natural desire has been perverted (often through some kind
of potion or ritual, but also through continuous exposure to and
participation in violent acts). His desires have been liberated from
control, and this threatens everybody with whom he comes into contact. Thus, the relationship between means and ends becomes confused and strangely inverted: the victim used to perform evil acts for a

social good (family) but now destroys the social good (kills, or tries to kill, family) so he can perform evil acts.

This confusion, or disconnection, of means from ends spills over into society as a whole, such that established institutions come to fulfill ends that negate their original intention: schools become recruitment training grounds for devil worshipers, and churches are covers for satanic conscription. Things, in short, do not mean what they are supposed to mean, signs are unleashed from referents, and a form of antidevelopment emerges that mocks and subverts normative Kenyan models of development, or *maendeleo* (movement forward, progress, and change). The popular discourse of devil worship implies that taken for granted understandings of development have been destructive—that many are dragged behind while a few race ahead, and that this putative development is often the consequence of the violent act of keeping, or "tying," others where they are (in extreme cases, by killing them). The rumors about the things devil worshipers accomplish (flying to global cities in the blink of an eye, battling with angels on the astral plane, visiting underground megacities where everything works impeccably, etc.) convert the utopian dream of development into a dystopian nightmare. People acquire some of the powers that are popularly associated with development by sacrificing authentic development (epitomized by the ideal of wealth in people, or the family), and so suggest a possible alternative path to development (for example, one based on reciprocity, a value Satanists are said to despise).

The idea of violence and images of violence are essential to the discourse: in particular, the desire to commit meaningless violence is unleashed as an unintended byproduct of the original desire to improve one's material conditions and social standing. Once it becomes its own end, violence becomes boundless and totally destructive, and so, importantly, relates only obliquely to any material condition or need. As a result, although participation in violence is precipitated by poverty, an improvement of material conditions alone will not solve the problem. More important, the hypothetical existence of this total threat provokes the people who imagine themselves to be threatened by it into action, and so the idea becomes a mechanism for community-building—it is as if the society that imagines itself as the inverse of this demonic agency calls itself into being to eradicate it but, as we will see, often ends up becoming the demonic image that it sought to destroy (as in the case of the colonial government's reaction to Mau Mau and the Kibaki regime's response to Mungiki).

Finally, the anti-religion is held to be organized by law and hierarchy, whose exact nature converts are only dimly aware of. As one saved preacher in Nairobi put it, "the devil worshipers will not give you everything [all knowledge]. They give one person a little piece of knowledge, and then another little piece to someone else." Satanism is therefore antidemocratic, and resisting it is often described as synonymous with supporting genuine national democracy. The organization is typically held to have originated outside the country, or it is governed by people with strong international connections. Moreover, this growing organism is said to be divided into cells whose far-flung members have no direct contact with one another (this aspect of the discourse can be traced back to Mau Mau); sometimes the organization is held to be so organized that the very idea of controlling it head on seems absurd (it is at times described as a "hydra," especially in official documents), and so the discourse posits an idealized picture of efficiency that normal society and government cannot hope to realize.

In this chapter, I draw attention to a few key moments in Kenyan history in which discourse about the devil informed state-society interactions and merged with state and public discourse about conflict and peace. Where exactly did this religious/political discourse come from? Is it mainly the product of globalization (such the spread of Pentecostalism together with press democratization and a "weakening" of the state), or, as I argue, part of a larger historical process of colonial and postcolonial state formation and transformation? I will map out a very preliminary genealogy of this continually changing discourse about the sources of violence and disorder and the moral failings of state-imposed order, or "peace."

ONE FOOT IN BARBARISM: NIGHTMARES OF DETRIBALIZATION IN LATE COLONIAL KENYA

Beginning in the late 1940s, white Kenyans spoke of the dreaded Mau Mau as a secret, hierarchical organization with branches all over the country, a highly organized recruitment system, and a chain of command with separated cells consisting of brainwashed converts. These alleged victims of possession were said to be disguised as humble servants and domestic workers, and were ready to strike at any moment. Although many scholars prefer the term *Land and Freedom Army* (or the unwieldy *Mau Mau Land and Freedom Army*) because rational ends and means are explicit in the title, the more mysterious term *Mau Mau* is still used to refer to the guerilla resistance movement of the early and mid-1950s, which scholars now recognize to have been both a Kikuyu civil war and an anti-colonial insurgency (see, for example, Berman 1991; Lonsdale 1994).[2]

The term *Mau Mau* has no meaning in Kikuyu or any other African language. Colonial settlers, administrators, and some Africans deployed it to reify a diversity of revolts, movements, and practices as part of a single, organized conspiracy that never obtained the seamless homogeneity it achieved in the colonial imagination. As historian Bruce Berman has put it, "What the British called Mau Mau, and by constant repetition imposed on both Kenya and the outside world, was not a singular entity, but rather a diverse and exceedingly fragmented collection of individual organizations and ideas out of which no dominant conception of Kikuyu national community had emerged" (Berman 1991, 199).[3] Regardless, the image of Mau Mau that came to be politically instrumental and, thanks to the role of international media, globally terrifying, was that of an anti-modern, anti-Christian cult invented by a frustrated, educated African elite that systematically deployed exhilarating and shameful oathing rituals to turn superficially civilized Africans into savage monsters. This brainwashed anti-community was held to represent "the complete negation of human evolution and the history of the human race" (Corfield 1960, 12) and "the last despairing kicks and struggles of superstition" against modernization (colonial secretary Oliver Lyttleton, cited in Lewis 2003, 31).

The demonization and animalization of Mau Mau was underwritten by the assumption that its putative members were committed to irrational violence—or violence as an end in itself—and the term has always concealed and mystified the issues that diverse groups of Kikuyu were struggling with, especially the alienation of land by white settlers. The struggle, rather, was ontological: Mau Mau was held to be a symptom of the psychological stress brought about by modernization (the demise of custom, the declining authority of senior men, the introduction of individualist values associated with commerce, urban migration, etc.). Kenyan government commissioner Frank Corfield put it succinctly in his *Origins and Growth of Mau Mau,* when he blamed Mau Mau on rapid modernization and the repressed desire, among Kikuyu, to return to a savage state: "This rapid transition [modernization] has produced a schizophrenic tendency in the African mind—the extraordinary facility to live two separate lives with one foot in this century and the other in witchcraft and savagery. This has often been noticed, but Mau Mau revealed the almost inexplicable lengths to which it could go. A Kikuyu leading an apparently normal life would, in one moment, become a being that was barely human" (1960, 9). Within this overarching colonial discourse, there were relatively enlightened variations: for example, liberal colonial figures like anthropologist and honorary Kikuyu elder Louis Leakey held that Mau Mau was created by partial economic and cultural development. In his view, colonial indirect governance and apartheid restrictions on urban migration and cash crop production had prevented African youth from sustaining themselves and developing self-respect through traditional means, at the same time as they were legally prevented from participating in the modern world as full citizens of the colonial Kenyan nation-state (Leakey 1953). For colonial theorists, the Kikuyu were problematic because they were neither traditional nor modern, but outside linear time, and their liminal status was pathological—they were personally experiencing nothing less than the strain of two epochs pushing inexorably against one another. Colonial psychologist J. C. Carothers, appointed by the government, alongside Louis Leakey, to make sense of and formulate policy regarding the Mau Mau menace, drew a parallel between Mau Mau occultism in 1950s Kenya and European occultism in the 1500s: during both historical moments there was rapid transformation and unprecedented inequality, which stimulated a desire that was immediately stifled by reality. In Carothers's words, early modern Europeans and contemporary Africans worshiped the devil because of a shared "desire to achieve some personal aim which they could not achieve within the righteous social framework of their time" (Carothers 1954, 15). But most colonial interpretations were not so generous, instead depicting Mau Mau as "lost in the haunted wilderness of superstition" (anonymous journalist's remark, cited in Anderson 2005, 117), from which an enlightened modernist colonial state was compelled to rescue them.

At the center of this colonial Mau Mau mystique was the oath, depicted as an extreme perversion of traditional Kikuyu ritual oaths, made more dangerous by the fact that it was implemented by youth, rather than by the upright senior males on whom the colonial policy of indirect rule depended; this interpretation was supported by anthropologists like Louis Leakey and by influential Kikuyu elders (Leakey 1953, 1954; Lonsdale 1990, 1992). The oath's gruesome features were elaborated on in a torrent of newspaper articles, professional and governmental reports, and heroic personal accounts of the violent struggle to save civilization from savagery. Colonial authorities described a ghastly and clearly nonexistent ritual: in the words of the government-commissioned Corfield Report, "an oath which, by combining magical forms with unheard of bestialities, has transformed a human being into a new frame of mind which has rarely, if ever, been witnessed before" (Corfield 1960, 163). Fusing secularist notions of mental perversion with modern Christian understandings of satanic possession, Oliver Lyttleton claimed to be genuinely frightened for his own soul: "The Mau Mau oath is the most bestial, filthy and nauseating incantation which perverted minds can ever have brewed. . . . [I have never felt] the forces of evil to be so near and so strong as in Mau Mau. . . . As I wrote memoranda or instructions [about Mau Mau] . . . I would suddenly see a shadow fall across the page—the horned shadow of the Devil himself" (quoted in Elkins 2005, 50).

Like the rites of initiation into the Satanic Church described in the press in the 1990s, and the Mungiki oaths of today (see below), the more advanced Mau Mau oaths were alleged to include group masturbation, sodomy, and bestiality—acts that utterly rejected all moral authority. Colonial administrators held that these rituals cast those who participated in them into a state of shock and shame, their self-worth destroyed (making it all the more easy for power-hungry African leaders to manipulate them). And so Mau Mau was psychological torture, and the modernist state was morally responsible for protecting its subjects from the cancer; as Corfield remarked, describing the alleged confession of a former insurgent who was captured by a settler, "when this confession was finished, he asked the farmer, in all sincerity and earnestness, to take him outside the hut and shoot him, as the world held no future for him" (Corfield 1960, 169). And, as the governor put it, "Mau Mau terrorism has almost completely shattered the average African's spiritual equilibrium" (Anderson 2005, 167). Thus, by hiring psychological and anthropological experts to discuss at length "the terrible effect [Mau Mau] had on their minds" (Corfield 1960, 35), the late colonial government tried to establish its image as a fragile vehicle of reason engulfed by a rising sea of savage violence and terror. Moreover, because this was spiritual and psychological terrorism aimed at acquiring tyrannical control over incompletely developed people, Mau Mau was not normatively political, meaning it was not rooted in material grievances; it was solely about the acquisition of power for its own sake. As the judge put it during the trial of Jomo Kenyatta, "Grievances have nothing whatever to do with Mau Mau, and Mau Mau has nothing whatever to do with grievances" (quoted in Anderson 2005, 67). This harmonized with the official line on Mau Mau, for "the British would not admit that this was a war; they would not even formally concede that it was a rebellion, fearing that to do so might imply that the Mau Mau fighters had rights under international conventions governing the treatment of prisoners" (Anderson 2005, 113).

While the oath was taken by Africans, the colonial authorities did not conceptualize it as African, but as a foreign perversion of a traditional cultural act, and so it embodied the dilemma that allegedly gave rise to it: the overly rapid exposure of primitive peoples to modern society and culture. Louis Leakey, who had written a three-volume ethnography of the Kikuyu, gave scientific and ethnographic authority to this belief in his two volumes on Mau Mau. Thus, like today's satanic initiations, the Mau Mau oath was made more dangerous by the fact that its source and secret purpose emerged from outside the nation/colony, and that it was spread by people who were ambiguously African. The oath's "broad outlines" were said to have been devised by a "highly sophisticated person" who probably had a working historical knowledge of sixteenth-century European occult practices like the devil's sabbat (Carothers 1954, 16). As Carothers put it, referring to Kenyatta's time studying anthropology at the London School of Economics, "Jomo Kenyatta is very certain to have made some study of European witchcraft; he had the opportunity, and it is easy to imagine more than one incentive" (Carothers 1954, 16). Because Mau Mau was caused by the oath, the colonial regime's strategy for dealing with the problem involved spiritual cleansing—most famously, the screening and quarantining of the Kikuyu population to prevent the spread of the Mau Mau disease to other ethnic groups, and the implementation of a counter-oathing campaign engineered by Leakey and carried out by government-salaried African witchdoctors. The stated purpose was to cleanse and reintegrate the insane Mau Mau into normal African society.

This idea of a monolithic, blood-thirsty Mau Mau had diverse political uses, which is one of the reasons it has had such an enduring life. During the war, insurgents often deployed and redirected aspects of this Mau Mau mythology to create a sense of irrational violence and terror. For example, General Kahinga Wachanga wrote a letter to Governor Evelyn Baring and General Sir George (Watkin Eben James) Erskine claiming that Mau Mau had built a factory in the forest to can the flesh of British soldiers in tin. Part of the letter reads, "Beware from now on, because we are going to eat all of your cattle, sheep, wheat, maize, and after finishing them, start consuming your flesh until the time of your last man" (Wachanga 1975, 66). But Mau Mau attitudes about what they were doing tended to be much more positive, and were epitomized in their ideas about oathing, which can be gleaned from their postwar autobiographies. These confirm that insurgents did take an oath (of which there were different types, of varying degrees), and that most viewed this ritual as the mechanism for the creation of a new political subjectivity and order.

Most of these insider references to the oath describe it as a kind of prayer involving the use and consumption of some combination of soil, goat blood, and stomach contents, combined with pledges of allegiance to the movement and to the Kikuyu god Ngai, but there were also stronger oaths. Kiboi Muriithi referred to the ritual as "the watershed of my life . . . the beginning of my manhood" (Muriithi

1971, 2); indeed, many *itungati* indexed the oath's transformative, and culturally authentic, power by referring to it as "circumcision." Ngugi Kabiro said that the oath made its adherents the "true sons of Gikuyu and Mumbi" (Kabiro 1973, 27), the mythical progenitors of the Ki-kuyu people, and Secretary General Karari Njama referred to being "born again into a new society with a new faith" (Barnett and Njama 1966, 120). Gucu Gikoyo argued that the oath was the opposite of devil worship: it made people "so converted to morality and obedi-ence that stealing was no longer a trait in them" (Gikoyo 1979, 55). At least one Mau Mau general had so much faith in the transformative power of the oath that he believed he could convert European soldiers and African Home Guards by secretly feeding them the oath's ingre-dients: "I told [the Mau Mau leaders] that we could not defeat the government unless we oathed them. . . . When the black lamb [to be shared with government soldiers under the pretext of surrender] was roasted we would pour the oath over the lamb. . . . The government would eat the lamb and become Mau Mau. . . . We went to meet the government with the "bottled oath." . . . When they ate the meat, they thought that we had become their friends, but we had not" (Wachanga 1975, 126).

SATAN IN THE STATE HOUSE: RUMORS OF SATANISM IN POSTCOLONIAL KENYA

Again, the colonial state's discourse of devil worship functioned by imagining a politically motivated terror that was culturally and temporally outside the modernist-Christian state that it threatened to consume. It developed alongside a parallel, popular African discourse about state vampirism, which accused state officials (firefighters, the police, hospitals) of stealing African blood and organs, and which sometimes held that this stolen value iconic of, among other things, family and community, was being used to finance the development of the colonial state (White 2000). This discourse built upon African un-derstandings of witchcraft, in which people are said to develop in power by spiritually and economically "closing" their victim, who re-mains "tied" behind; this is often accomplished through the secret theft of a part of that person (an article of clothing that touches the body or a lock of hair, for example). In the 1990s, this longstanding popular discourse achieved a new life with the proliferation of new independent media and new religious movements, which shaped people's understandings of and responses to dramatic political events.

In the 1990s, the popular mythology of devil worship developed alongside the first multiparty elections in nearly thirty years, and Moi's successful efforts to remain in power despite widespread opposition to his rule. One of the early sources of this new instantiation of the discourse was the conflict between Moi's regime and the mainstream churches, which condemned the state's violence against multiparty activists. Rumors proliferated when Anglican Bishop Alexander Kipsang Muge, a prominent critic of the Moi regime, was killed in a car accident in 1990 en route from Nyanza Province to Nairobi, only a few days after Kenya African National Union (KANU) MP Peter Habenga Okondo had warned him of stepping foot in that province, lest he "see fire" and die (Dauti Kauru 2003; "Bishop Muge's Legacy," *East African Standard,* December 3, 2003). But the public rumors of devil worship in the highest reaches of government really took off around 1992, when President Moi's ruling party, KANU, distributed more than a billion shillings in the form of gifts, donations, and beer during the campaigns preceding the elections, which nearly everyone predicted the incumbent would lose. In the words of one middle-aged informant looking back on that much anticipated election, "It was just too much money, and it was everywhere. We knew that Moi had to be getting that money through some kind of sacrifice [to a demonic agency]." Similarly, the author of the third vignette, cited above, claimed that he was first tempted by devil worshipers "in 1992, just before the elections, [when] there was a lot of money in circulation"; many held this very money to be cursed, and capable of enslaving its possessor in the growing international satanic cult (Anonymous 2000, 28).

In this popular discourse, the president and his inner cabinet were widely held to be converts to the international Satanic Church, and even Kenyan currency and state monuments were said to be encoded with satanic messages. As one *Nation* newspaper journalist wrote, just before the release of the government's *Report of the Presidential*

Commission of Inquiry into the Cult of Devil Worship, "That devil worship thrives in Kenya today is indisputable. That it is epitomized in strategic places is not. Do you know of snake signs at the parliament building? Of the morning star dangling at the entrance?" (*Kenya Daily Nation,* July 9, 1999). A student of Kenyan history has to appreciate the irony: in the colonial period, the state deployed the media to turn Africans into a retrograde satanic spectacle; now longstanding public rumors about the colonial and postcolonial state's involvement in the occult were projected to the national level through popular presses and pamphlets. Now, the rich and powerful were said to kill babies, consume human organs, and participate in satanic oaths, to the detriment of the derailed national development project, which was conceptualized as belonging to the public, not the state.

The colonial government had projected the discourse of devil worship outside itself and thereby tried to create an image of the state as transcendent, modernist caretaker. The new discourse of devil worship retained the ideal of the transcendent state, but argued that convivial patronage politics had rendered it farcical, and that the corrupt political climate was synonymous with Satanism. One prominent example was the imbroglio surrounding the 1999 sacking of the head of the civil service, Philip Mbithi. Mbithi was a sociology professor who rose to the ranks of vice chancellor of the University of Nairobi (President Moi was the chancellor) during the 1980s, many believed because he supported the president's draconian policies regarding university students. In the 1990s, he was appointed head of the civil service, and acquired an office in Harambee House, the civil service headquarters; he claimed to be isolated from the culture of Harambee House, with its graft and corruption, and said that he had refused to participate in the theft that had become the norm for everyone else. This refusal brought him untold metaphysical problems: Mbithi claimed that, during his tenure, he spent most of his time engaged in spiritual battles with demons sent by prominent politicians, including but not limited to President Moi. For example, after being fired in a humiliating fashion (he heard about it during a radio broadcast), Mbithi recalled that he "fought for one hour with a ghost that wanted to evict him from his office on the third floor of Harambee House, Nairobi," the headquarters of Kenya's civil service (*Kenya Nation,*

June 11, 2000). Later Mbithi found salvation in Jesus when he discovered that Harambee House, this once "revered, and almost sacred place," was possessed by demons (*Kenya Nation*, June 11, 2000).

Satanism also came to reference the total breakdown of Kenyan society under structural adjustment programs (SAPs), which were often depicted as part of a global satanic plot; all of the features of this collapse, from ethnicized political conflict to the declining value of education and schools, came to be seen, by many, as signs of satanic possession. For example, a series of school arson cases was interpreted as but one aspect of a larger conspiracy, redolent of Mau Mau attacks on schools: "Today students torch their colleagues in dormitories with abandon and the nation hurtles painfully over Bombolulu, St. Kizito [school arson cases that resulted in the loss of many lives], and other horrid kaleidoscopes of disaster which people link to devil worship" (Njau 1999b). The discourse also made sense of political violence, which intensified as the Moi regime developed ever more destructive ways of holding on to power, such as provoking Kalenjin attacks on Kikuyu farmers in the Rift Valley and torturing dissidents. Rumors—later confirmed to be true—circulated about the torture of government critics in the basement of Moi's signature building, Nyayo House; the secrecy of the place and the sadistic instruments of torture said to be found there became iconic of devil worship. After Mwai Kibaki took over from Moi in 2003, these spoken rumors began to emerge in the popular press. For example, a journalistic document called *The Devil's House: Nyayo House, Nazi Chambers, and Devil Worship—the Dark Link* (Kabande 2003) appeared on the streets of Nairobi, revealing the nature of torture in pornographic detail, while drawing a direct connection between Satanism and the terror. One chapter, entitled "How the Torture Squad Was Formed and Trained and Inducted into Devil Worship," claims that Moi's security forces were trained in Romania by Nikolai Ceausescu's government, which inducted them into Satanism so they could be counted on to "act like animals" (14); other pamphlet chapters include "A Woman Crushed My Balls with Pliers" and "The Python, Dead Body, and I in the Cell."

But the public discourse about devil worship had a positive, utopian dimension; it signaled the possibility of a different way of doing politics, an alternative to what Jean-Francois Bayart has referred to as the "politics of the belly" (Bayart 1993). In particular, it held that taken for granted social facts and moral values were false, and it insisted that African politicians and business leaders were satanic because they were principally motivated by banal, material interests. In this way, the discourse enabled people to criticize the state while invigorating the nation and the national interest, and retaining, for better or worse, the ideal of a universal, remote, and transcendent state standing above the fray of individual interests. When, in a video documentary on Satanism in Kenya, a Catholic priest asked a former devil worshiper-turned-Pentecostal preacher why politicians "would want to involve themselves in devil worship," the former Satanist responded, "Heaven is on high. There is nothing above heaven, and the devil cannot enter there, because he was kicked out. The devil is the master of things on earth. Politicians are concerned with wealth and things of this world, which is of the devil. This makes them very suitable for this cult." Similarly, as a Catholic bishop argued, "The devil can cause havoc on earth, and the United Nations cannot do anything about it," but those who look beyond the temptations of the moment can. As one man on the street in Nairobi put it in a video interview in 2001, "Politicians believe in material things, and once you believe in material things, you will become a devil worshiper. If you look at our parliamentarians, you will see there are no true believers there" (from the video, *Power of Darkness: Is There Devil Worship in Kenya?* [Ukweli Video Productions, 2001]).

This historically entrenched discourse about Satanism must be appreciated to fully understand the import of the elections of 2002 for Kenyans, when Moi was finally, and peacefully, removed from power, and of the apparently secular and universal rituals of democratic statehood that followed. For a time, Mwai Kibaki's government and the public seemed united in ushering in a new era of transparency, and this impulse took on manifestly religious overtones. It was widely understood to be a time of exposing and confessing the convoluted, satanic secrets of the previous regime, and so the transnational discourse of transparency and democracy was given a new, Kenyan twist. For example, immediately after the election, various former opposition politicians, now members of the new government, accompanied news reporters on a guided tour of the torture chambers in Nyayo House, and recounted their experiences with great emotion and drama. In so doing, the state publicly unmasked formerly secret rituals of state before television crews and transfixed audiences, producing not only publicity for themselves, but also a sense of healing.

REGULATING SATAN: THE PRESIDENT'S DEVIL REPORT

I highlighted above the popular deployments of this discourse, examining it as a form of critical social and political commentary. This circulating discourse was also picked up and redeployed by state authorities during this same period, however, culminating in a national investigation and a published government report on devil worship, extracts from which were quoted in the first section of this essay. The popular discourse about foreign devil worship dovetailed fortuitously with official state rhetoric about the pernicious influence of "foreign masters" spreading democratic ideologies ill-suited to Africa. It also deflected accusations that Moi was involved in Satanism, a fact that a suspicious public was quick to comment on. The *Report* claimed that Kenyan national culture was pervaded by a chaotic, potentially subversive polyphony that the state was morally compelled to control through the strengthening of the presidency and the extension of state power in the form of an occult police force (*Report* 1995, 65). The commission and its report were widely associated with the president, whose ability to open up the public's secrets in this way was presented, by the commission, as his sovereign right: "Once the President has so acted [to implement a commission] the issue cannot be inquired into by any person, court, tribunal, or authority" (*Report* 1995, 22).

The commission was headed by members of Kenya's mainline African churches, who interviewed the alleged victims of satanic initiation, most of whom were students. This was in keeping with the popular and official consensus that youth were the target of these troublemakers and the source of national hope and despair. Many of the interviewees were pubescent girls on the verge of social adulthood and reproductive promise who claimed to have been seduced into the cult with gifts of cash from wealthy "sugar daddies," and who then went on to seduce teachers and classmates with sex and drugs. After interviewing people for nearly a year, the commission ultimately wrote a report claiming that devil worship was a real threat to national society; to quote the commission's epistemologically strange claim: "The minute details of the stories given had such a consistency wherever we went that if they were not true, a great divergence would have been noted" (*Report* 1995, 46).

Not only did the cult exist, but its penetration of the school system through teachers "threatened to derail national objectives"; it had originated abroad, was linked to "drug abuse and other anti-social activities," and was led by elites: "membership of the cult is generally composed of wealthy people in the society, some of whom are said to own large commercial enterprises" (*Report* 1995, 42). The focus on schools reflected public concern about the current inability of education to provide sustainable employment for people and communities. As a journalist who had read the *Report* before it was available to the general public put it in an article entitled "Satan a Threat to Kenya Schools," "agents who recruit students to devil worship include senior students in Forms III and IV especially from rich families; beautiful girls and handsome young men who lure students when out of school; *matatu* (commuter taxi) touts, especially from Nairobi who use money, drugs and heavy metal music; wealthy members of the society who promise material gifts and wealth; and unscrupulous freelance preachers involved in miracle crusades" (Njau 1999b). Moreover, this religion was spread without people realizing it, for innocents were exposing themselves to demonic influence when they heard certain songs and bought particular articles of clothing (such as imported used clothes, which were at that time causing the national textile industry to collapse). And so popular Kenyan culture had become both globalized and satanic, a claim that actually harmonized with much public opinion.

The *Report* was a striking document, in part because it repeated the colonial state tradition of mobilizing the idea of modernism and science against satanic backwardness, and of attempting to define and regulate national culture in a period of state transformation (which partly accounted for the commission's firm commitment to presidential authority). Beginning with terms of reference such as *cult* and *devil worship*, the *Report*'s authors devoted an inordinate number of pages to establishing the legality of the commission and the admissibility of its findings, while also painstakingly describing, over eight single-spaced pages, the method of inquiry. In this way, the committee legitimated itself through the reasonable currencies of science and law, while adopting a tone of dispassionate reportage, shorn of alarm: it quoted Anton LaVey's *Satanic Bible* and provided a fairly detailed, if one-sided, history of the thought of Aleister Crowley, Madame Helena Blavatsky, Rudolf Steiner, and L. Ron Hubbard. In the back, a ten-page glossary explained the meanings of such occult terms as *hydromancy, kabbalistic, cephalomancy*, and *Antichrist,* and provided a compendium of occult signs and clues said to be "useful for crime investigations" (*Report* 1995, 65).

Like the colonial state discourse about Mau Mau, the *Report* depicted a highly organized underground movement possessing "a central authority with tight structures, philosophy, and lifestyle" (*Report* 1995, 35). It also depicted a national culture consumed by a singular menace that went by different names, which the state, acting in the form of the commission, interpreted and simplified for the national public. "Devil worship," the *Report* stated, "could find its way to individuals, institutions and society in general through the following": "1) matatu (mini bus) culture and music, 2) Golfing Society, 3) Freemasonry, 4) Transcendental Meditation, 5) The Church of Jesus Christ of Latter Day Saints, 6) Theosophical Society, 7) Medissage, 8) Rudolf Steiner Schools, 9) New Age Movement, 10) Communication Media (literature, films, TV, video)" (*Report,* 1995, 66). In response to such a widespread menace, the commission called for the expansion and strengthening of state institutions, including the establishment of "a national committee consisting of professionals, lawyers, social scientists, and clergy, to prepare a comprehensive national moral code of conduct which will regulate and govern the conduct of Kenyans, especially those in leadership" (*Report* 1995, 107). Again the state posed as a scientifically grounded defender of secular values and Christian values: like Mau Mau before them and Mungiki later on, Satanists, the

Report indicated, "fit a psychological profile" (*Report* 1995, 5), which needed to be identified and acted upon in the schools and churches. And the discourse was effective, in that it underpinned subsequent successful attempts to govern key places and industries; for example, the *Report* was followed by a series of interventions in the then un-regulated matatu (private minivan) trade, beginning with restrictions on dress, music, and matatu painting and design, and later extending to the regulation of routes and restrictions on the number of passengers. Ironically, these efforts at regulation were mostly accomplished through youth gangs sponsored by politicians; these gangs would later refer to themselves as Mungiki, and would develop ritualized recruitment mechanisms that state officials and the public condemned as satanic. More recently, the discourse has had a role in legitimating and popularizing government bans on outdoor and public smoking, which has ironically become a mechanism for police to acquire revenue in the form of bribes from smokers, in lieu of salary increases.

Notwithstanding the public criticisms, this state-driven discourse had a nationalist, anti-globalization dimension that appealed to a public burdened by the inflation and job losses associated with SAPs and neoliberal reform. For example, in his public commentary about the *Report,* the chair of the commission, Catholic Archbishop Nicodemus Kirima, argued that Satanism was synonymous with neoliberal economic policies. In an interview with a journalist from *The Nation,* Kirima laid bare the moral consequences of putatively amoral structural adjustment:

> Devil worship has been introduced into Kenya by the international community as part of their campaign to drain Africa of her resources, Nyeri Catholic Archbishop Nicodemus Kirima claimed yesterday. The cult, the prelate said, had been brought into the country in a gradual process under the guise of the New World Order "which has completely changed our system to suit the needs of the devil." The Archbishop continued, "In the New World Order, the Western countries first brought capitalism, which came with poverty. Then today we have liberalization and

computerization which have left our nations poorer and a clique owning the state." Archbishop Kirima asserted that "these impositions have forced Africa to privatise her public enterprises, which are being bought by a minority rich." (*Kenya Daily Nation,* August 15, 1999)

Kirima concluded that since the nation was now in a state of "perpetual poverty," Kenyan citizens, who found it "hard to survive in the liberalized economy," would be challenged to "resist the Devil." But before giving into temptation, he said that Africans "should ask themselves why the Western countries are using so much money to bring changes in our society."

The *Report*'s final release to the public in 1999 was met with an outpouring of interest and commentary, some of it supportive and expectant, much of it scathing in its criticism of the commission's interests and motivations. Many claimed that the released report, which said much about youth movements, Rastafarianism, matatu touts, yoga, and the Lucifer Golfing Society, while commenting little on high-level corruption and saying nothing of prominent public officials, was not the "true" devil report, which was imagined to exist somewhere else. Almost every letter to the editor of the *Kenya Daily Nation* reaffirmed the reality of Satanism in Kenya, and many urged the president to save the country by releasing the "true" report. Debates about the veracity of the devil report congealed and catalyzed larger concerns about the convoluted nature of social and political life in contemporary Kenya, and the difficulty of discerning the true nature and distribution of power. As one writer to the newspaper put it in a missive entitled, "Devil Report is Unrealistic" (Kioi 1999): "Talk of loud music in matatus, inverted crosses and Nazi chains [all associated with Satanism in the commission's report] does not hold water. Wealth can be gained through different sources. . . . People who organize mass murders like the tribal (political) clashes, those who grab toilets [a reference to politicians who have public land allocated to them by paying off government officials], road reserves and forests and looters of public money should have been included in this report."

MAKING PEACE WITH THE DEVIL: THE MUNGIKI UPRISING
AND THE ATTEMPT TO REESTABLISH STATE HEGEMONY IN
THE POST-MOI ERA

During this period of political and economic collapse, many historically valued things came up for critique in Kenya—including the
moral authority of Christianity, the religion from which Kenya's political elite has drawn its moral and cultural legitimacy. Moreover, the
whole idea of unilinear progress was questioned, and many Kenyans
sought moral grounding in repressed religious and cultural traditions.
But in Kenya, as in much of Africa, dabbling in the past is fraught
with danger, because it means conjuring up forces that have long been
associated with darkness, sin, and chaos—and for some decades the
relative prosperity of the Christian-educated elite gave credence to
this belief by manifesting relative prosperity and civility on a daily
basis. And so any attempt to revitalize the past ends up also dredging
up repressed violent memories, which nowadays are usually fed by
underpaid news journalists who write their stories with a view to a familiar national cultural script—such as the idea of an underground satanic cult with multiple independent cells and ghastly, dehumanizing
rites of initiation.

But, in the 1990s, young men marginalized from the dominant
development paradigm were launching a counter-state development
project rooted in received understandings of traditional values. On
the outskirts of Nairobi, a neo-traditionalist Kikuyu religious movement called Mungiki (the exact meaning of which is debated, but
whose best translation is something like "the activated public"), became popular and powerful in the city of Nairobi and some large Kikuyu towns in the Rift Valley; while Grace Nyatugah Wamue-Ngare
discusses her research with the original group that formed Mungiki in
this volume, in the following pages I focus on the national spectacle of
Mungiki and its consequences. Originally, Mungiki was made up primarily of impoverished young urban men, and had complicated origins. The desire to pinpoint these origins of this group, like that of
Mau Mau and the Satanic Church before it, has dominated Kenyans'
discussion of the movement: who is really behind it, and what do they

really want? Is the movement autonomous, or is it controlled by invisible state and international figures? Like the 1950s Mau Mau movement, which its members emulate, Mungiki has never been a uniform
social movement, although there have been central figures behind it,
or behind factions of Mungiki, throughout. Nonetheless, as Wamue
argues, many who identify as Mungiki have fabricated a cohesive and
strict set of behavioral practices rooted in received understandings of
traditional Kikuyu religious beliefs and practices in their effort to purify the national consciousness from the bottom up.

The movement was defined, above all, by its commitment to vernacular democracy. The original founders and members claimed to be
the inheritors of Mau Mau practice and ideology, and at times they
verbally attacked the government for its enslavement to foreign interests, specifically naming the World Bank and the International Monetary Fund (IMF). They mocked the government's, and middle-class
Kenya's, commitment to Christian rectitude, and argued that the
Christian elite had corrupted Kenya by making the foreign values of
individualism part of the common sense of the nation. In the year
2000, these urban youth famously marched on the president's house
and the Masonic church (President Moi had long been rumored to be
a member) and threatened to expose the links among national elites,
foreign financial backers, and secretive religious cults. Their self-
avowed leader echoed a national sentiment when he declared that
"Kenya today is controlled by the International Monetary Fund, the
World Bank, the Americans, the British, and the Freemasons. It can't
initiate its own development and has sold all its properties to Westerners in the name of liberalization" (*Kenyan Daily Nation,* October 23, 2000). Waruingi claimed that they wanted to burn down the
Masonic church because "it promotes devil worship," and he challenged the government before the press: "Why did an individual push
the [real] Kirima report on devil worship under the table instead of
making it public?"

Early newspaper reports on Mungiki were derisive and whimsi-
cal, with titles like "Why Won't the State Clip Them Dreadlocks?"
although even early on Mungiki were accused of worshiping the devil
(see, for example, "Mungiki Devil Worshippers: Kuria Calls for Probe
into Sect," *Kenya Standard,* October 1, 2000). There was, from the

beginning, a general sense that the demons of Kenya's history were repossessing the social body: "Fifty years later [after Mau Mau], Kenya's history seems set to repeat itself. Mungiki—a shadowy movement—has been organising itself quietly and systematically as the Government downplays its threat" (*Kenya Daily Nation*, October 23, 2000). By 2002, the media, the government, and much of the public converged to blame Mungiki for most gangster activities in Nairobi's slums, where some Mungiki pitted themselves against rival ethnic gangs and raided police stations to free captive members. During this time, immediately preceding the elections of 2002, journalists echoed Mau Mau with titles like "Three Killed in Orgy of Mungiki Violence" (*Kenya Daily Nation*, October 11, 2002).

The majority of Kenyans were appalled by Mungiki's apparent desire to return the country to its dark past, and they wondered aloud whether this group was engineered by powerful politicians (perhaps President Moi himself) to create chaos and confusion. Many held that Mungiki members were a new type of witch: in 2003, people in Nairobi told me that you could easily tell the difference between a Rastafarian and a Mungiki adherent by closely examining their dreadlocks (Mungiki's were frayed), and their eyes (Mungiki had insane eyes, for they were possessed by demons). Police reports explicitly invoked colonial government studies of the "cult" of Mau Mau from the early 1950s, when they described such pornographic Mungiki atrocities as "organ theft, drinking human urine, eating a human being's umbilical cord, sniffing tobacco and burning scents" (Kwamboka 2004). After Moi stepped down, the new government, presided over by the Kikuyu Mwai Kibaki, attempted to demonstrate that the days of unscrupulous and mysterious politics, as well as the era of "moving backward," were over by declaring war on the backward-looking Mungiki, and jailing many adherents. In jailing Mungiki, the government repeated the Emergency-era war on Mau Mau as farce, while conflating the Moi era with a mythic, savage past.

But the media was helping to create a spectacle that spiraled out of control, and that soon lost its moorings in the neo-traditionalist group that founded it. In March 2007, matatu operators in central Kenya refused to pay a costly "tax" to gangs that referred to themselves as Mungiki, and the gangs responded by beheading matatu operators; for months beheadings were reported every few days. The government formed a special police force to deal with the gangs, and thousands of suspects and alleged oath-takers (including school children) were arrested (later, many locals claimed that these were just idle, unemployed youth that the police arrested randomly). The movement was reported on daily in the national and international press, and in the month of June alone titles included "Back to the Shrine—How a Peasant Farmer and His Sons Created a Violent Cult" (*Kenya Standard,* June 13), "They Might Drink Your Blood, but Otherwise they Are Not Bad Guys" (*New York Times,* June 22), "Night of Terror as Mungiki Gangs Take Revenge" (*Kenya Standard,* June 23), "Body Parts Found at Mungiki Camp" (*Kenya Standard,* July 4), "Kenya Government Admits Wiping Out Mungiki Not Easy" (*Kenya Standard,* July 9), and the very telling (because it shows how, as in the case of Mau Mau, the reduction of social groups to demonic animals enables the state to violently annihilate them), "Dialogue with Mungiki Sect Ruled Out" (*Kenya Daily Nation,* July 10).

In 2007 and 2008, I traveled around the Rift Valley and Central Province asking people about Mungiki, and found that, in each community I visited, Mungiki was said to be something different. In Nairobi and nearby towns like Banana, it was a transport and utilities racket sponsored by politicians who stayed in the background while their minions chopped off heads; in the town of Banana, several people claimed that murders allegedly tied to Mungiki were actually committed by private individuals—including a well-publicized case of infanticide. In these areas, there was a genuine fear of transport mafia gangsters who had allegedly been transformed by gruesome oaths into people who could decapitate others without remorse. Some young men, who claimed to be former members, spoke nervously about being possessed by the spirits of angry ancestors from the past, and sought out various forms of cleansing from traditional healers. In Nakuru, where violence between Kalenjin and Kikuyu over land has been promoted by politicians with nothing else to offer, Mungiki were held to be the Kikuyu terror gangs that chased Luo and Kalenjin from their homes. In Murang'a and other towns near the Aberdares, where Mau Mau was fought, Mungiki were said to be the descendants of Mau Mau insurgents who had fought for freedom and never received their land. The declared war against Mungiki by Minister of Security John Michuki, a former colonial home guard whose father was an anti–Mau Mau chief, represented the continuation, in the present, of a decades-old conflict between Kikuyu insurgents and Kikuyu home guards, or loyalists, in the former African Reserves. In much of Central Province, Mungiki was seen as a misunderstood, peace-loving religious movement that had simply grown dissatisfied with Kenya's dominant cultural values of individualism and greed. As the father of one of the founders put it to me, "This is just a church. We discovered that God cannot hear you praying when you're inside—he wants you outside, under a tree. And he wants to smell roasted goat. It pleases him. And he doesn't want money—that's for the devil." As far as I could tell, none of these Mungikis had anything to do with each other; there was certainly no way that the poor religious practitioners in Nyahururu had any direct connection to the terror gangs in Nairobi.

For the police, Mungiki seemed to be an excuse to detain or murder anyone for any reason; the Kenya National Commission on Human Rights (KNCHR), a state organization, estimates that five hundred alleged Mungiki were killed extra-judicially by the police in 2008 alone, and the Oscar Foundation, a Kenyan legal aid clinic devoted to defending poor clients, puts the number at eight thousand between 2002 and 2008 (Mulama 2009; Oscar Foundation 2008). KNCHR claims that the police now kill suspect Mungiki by beating, bludgeoning, or strangling their victims, so that it appears that Mungiki is the perpetrator (KNCHR 2008). For the journalists with whom I spoke, Mungiki was a profitable pornographic tale that they perpetuated with a certain amount of guilt and private skepticism. As a judge in Nakuru put it to me, "I believe there is a Mungiki somewhere, but we have not seen it yet. The real Mungiki is too clever, too secret. These stories we are seeing, they are just that. The police kill someone and say it is Mungiki and they tell this to the journalists, who write it down because they don't want trouble and anyway Mungiki is a good story. But these are just idle youth being arrested. And idle youth are everywhere!" In one small town near the Aberdares forest, where Mau Mau insurgents formed and launched their attacks, the newspapers reported, in 2007, that the police had discovered and shot a handful of Mungiki members while participating in a dreadful oathing campaign. When I arrived at the village and spoke with people, they told me that, in fact, more than fifty people had been slaughtered while performing a coming-of-age rite in the forest; the police had allegedly opened fire without warning. Those with whom I spoke claimed the victims were the descendants of Mau Mau insurgents. Throughout the region, I spoke with aspiring politicians and prominent people who claimed that their rivals had told the police they were Mungiki, and who claimed to have been harassed or threatened with death while participating in a benign non-Christian rite. And so it soon became clear that Mungiki as it is represented in the national media did not exist—there were many Mungikis and no Mungiki; but there were certainly many different variants of the idea of a demonic evil, of a kind of devil worship, each suited to the circumstances affecting the community in question, and each shaped by a state and media that poached images from a troubled past.

CONCLUSION

In this essay, I have examined a historically dense and layered discourse about devil worship with multiple imprints—a palimpsest. This discourse contains within itself memories of a whole history of traumatic state betrayal and violence dating back at least to the colonial state's war against Mau Mau (although, as I have suggested, we would have to go back farther, to early missionization, to find the real origin of this discourse). The discourse comments on the destructive, chaotic consequences of violence and poverty for subjects and communities, at times bemoaning capitalism's abuses and the sabotaged promise of national development. The discourse shapes the culture of politics and state-society interactions, while fueling the national imagination by conjuring up a vision of future possibility from a traumatic and violent history. But the discourse of devil worship also legitimates senseless state violence and offers up personified sacrificial scapegoats for complex social problems, including the growth of illegal economies and spiraling inequality.

The point of this essay's title ("Making Peace with the Devil") is that, at various moments in Kenyan history, diverse agents have used the idea of the devil to conjure up peace by obliterating an imagined evil menace that is soon personified in very real individuals and social groups. While this imagined threat often incites regimes to violent acts, this discourse about evil is also infused with hope and possibility, pointing to a new possible social order—one where there is no corruption, for example, and where there is something that could be called democracy. The devil is thus a harbinger of a kind of peace, or rather a fraught and violently imposed social order. For the enforcers of state control, peace means winning a total war against alleged terrorist malcontents whose indebted souls are wholly given over to meaningless violence (Mau Mau, matatu touts, Mungiki). For much of the public that has appropriated key elements of the discourse (and remade themselves as a public through it), the peace promised by an end to devil worship is synonymous with the total transformation of how elites and state officials think and do business (the culture of corruption that spreads throughout society). In all cases, community is imagined in relation to an image of violence and conflict that is culturally resonant. This image of violence, projected onto others, sometimes incites actual acts of violence against the image and the people who personify it, while also temporarily creating social cohesion and enthusiasm among the perpetrators of violence (whether we are talking about Mungiki gangs or state actors). Clearly, waging a total war against a demonic other can only create a very tense, temporary, and violent peace. But the Kenyan discourse about devil worship also cajoles Kenyans to face their demons, to realize that it is in fact their history that possesses them, and to come to terms with the local and global sources of conflict, inequality, and violence in their haunted nation.

Notes

1. The titles are my own invention.

2. The British claimed that eleven thousand Africans were killed during the war, but more recent data on deaths in the camps and fortified villages suggest that the number might have reached more than seventy thousand. In contrast, thirty-two European civilians were killed by Mau Mau during this period, fewer than died in traffic accidents during that period (Elkins 2005).

3. While the actual origins of Mau Mau are disputed by scholars, the total war on the so-called Kikuyu terrorists that the colonial regime called the State of Emergency, or simply the Emergency, began in October 1952. The Emergency was precipitated by rumors of Kikuyu oathing (at least some of which were based in reality) and various individual acts of violence and protest from 1947 until 1952; the assassination of Senior Chief Waruhiu in October 1952 was the final and decisive event leading to the declaration. The organized resistance movement achieved momentum after the declaration of a State of Emergency, when thousands of mostly young, male Africans in central Kenya evasively entered the forests of the Aberdares and Mount Kenya, many of them intending to fight the colonial regime.

REFERENCES

Anderson, David. 2005. *Histories of the Hanged: The Dirty War in Kenya and the End of Empire*. New York: W. W. Norton and Company.

Anonymous. 2000. *Satanism: How the Devil Is Trapping God's People* [subtitled *Devil Worship in Kenya: The Untold Story*]. Nairobi: Pawak Computer Services.

Barnett, Donald, and Karari Njama. 1966. *Mau Mau from Within*. New York: Monthly Review Press.

Bayart, Jean-Francois. 1993. *The State in Africa: The Politics of the Belly*. London and New York: Longman.

Berman, Bruce. 1991. "Nationalism, Ethnicity, and Modernity: The Paradox of Mau Mau." *Canadian Journal of African Studies* 25:181–206.

Berman, Bruce, and John Lonsdale. 1992. *Unhappy Valley: Conflict in Kenya*. Vol. 2. London: James Currey.

Blunt, Robert. 2004. "'Satan is an Imitator': Kenya's Recent Cosmology of Corruption." In *Producing African Futures: Ritual and Reproduction in a Neo-liberal Age*, edited by Brad Weiss. Leiden: Brill Press.

Carothers, Dr. J. C. 1954. *The Psychology of Mau Mau*. Government Printer.

Comaroff, J., and J. L. Comaroff. 1991. *Of Revelation and Revolution: Christianity, Colonialism and Consciousness in South Africa*. Chicago: University of Chicago Press.

Comaroff, J., and J. L. Comaroff, eds. 1993. *Modernity and its Malcontents*. Chicago: University of Chicago Press.

Cooper, Fred. 1988. "Mau Mau and the Discourses of Decolonization." *Journal of African History* 29(2):313–20.

Corfield, Frank. 1960. *The Origins and Growth of Mau Mau: A Historical Survey*. Sessional Paper No. 5 of 1959/1960. Government Printer.

Elkins, Caroline. 2005. *Imperial Reckoning: The Untold Story of Britain's Gulag in Kenya*. New York: Henry Holt and Company.

Furedi, Frank. 1989. *The Mau Mau War in Perspective*. London: James Currey.

Geschiere, Peter. 1997. *The Modernity of Witchcraft: Politics and the Occult in Post-Colonial Africa*. Charlottesville and London: University Press of Virginia.

Gikoyo, Gucu G. 1979. *We Fought for Freedom*. Nairobi: East African Publishing House.

Kabande, James, and Mburu wa Mucoki, eds. 2003. *The Devil's House: Nyayo House, Nazi Chambers, and Devil Worship—the Dark Link*. Nairobi: Immediate Media Services.

Kabiro, Ngugi. 1973. *Man in the Middle*. Richmond, BC: LSM Information Center.

Kauru, Dauti. 2003. "Bishop Muge's Legacy." *East African Standard*, December 3.

Kenyatta, Jomo. 1965. *Facing Mount Kenya*. New York: Vintage.

Kioi, Samuel Ng'ang'a. 1999. "Devil Report is Unrealistic." *Kenya Daily Nation*, August 27.

KNCHR. 2008. *The Cry of Blood: Report on Extra-Judicial Killings and Disappearances*. Nairobi: KNCHR.

Kwamboka, Evelyn. 2004. "How Mungiki Trains Killers." *Kenya Daily Nation*, March 8.

Leakey, L. S. B. 1953. *Mau Mau and the Kikuyu*. London: Methuen.

———. 1954. *Defeating Mau Mau*. London: Methuen.

———. 1977. *The Southern Kikuyu before 1903*. 3 vols. London: Academic Press.

Lewis, Joanna. 2003. "'Daddy Wouldn't Buy Me a Mau Mau': The British National Press and the Demoralization of Empire." In *Mau Mau and Nationhood: Arms, Authority, and Narration*, ed. E. S. Atieno Odhiambo and John Lonsdale, 227–50. Oxford: James Currey.

Lonsdale, John. 1990. "Mau Maus of the Mind: Making Mau Mau and Remaking Kenya." *Journal of African History* 31.

———. 1992. "The Moral Economy of Mau Mau: Wealth, Power, and Civic Virtue in Kikuyu Political Thought." In *Unhappy Valley: Conflict in Kenya*, vol. 2, edited by Bruce Berman and John Lonsdale. London: James Currey.

———. 1994. "Moral Ethnicity and Political Tribalism." In *Inventions and Boundaries: Historical and Anthropological Approaches to the Study of Ethnicity and Nationalism*, edited by Preben Kaarsholm and Jan Hultin, 131–50. Roskilde: International Development Studies, Roskilde University.

Maclean, William. 2003. "Banned Kenya Sect Dismisses Crackdown, Wants Jobs." Reuters, January 12.

Mamdani, Mahmood. 1996. *Citizen and Subject: Contemporary Africa and the Legacy of Late Colonialism*. Princeton: Princeton University Press.

Mbembe, Achille. 1992. "The Banality of Power and the Aesthetics of Vulgarity in the Postcolony." *Public Culture* 5(1).

Mulama, Joyce. 2009. "Kenya Cannot Fail to Prosecute Extra-Judicial Killings." Inter Press Service.

Muriithi, Kiboi, with Peter Ndoria. 1971. *War in the Forest*. Nairobi: East African Publishing House.

Mutua, Makau. 2000. "A Scandal That Could Topple Kenya's Shaky Democracy." *Boston Globe*, June 17.

Ngugi wa Thiong'o. 1987. *Devil on the Cross*. London: Heinemann.

Njau, Muteji. 1999a. "Posh Lifestyles of the Satanists." *Kenya Daily Nation*, August 5.

———. 1999b. "Satan a Threat to Kenya's Schools." *Kenya Daily Nation*, August 6.

Ombuor, Joe. 2000. "Is Devil Worship Real in the Country?" *Kenya Daily Nation*, March 27.

Oscar Foundation. 2008. *The Veil of Impunity*. Nairobi: Oscar Foundation.

Report of the Presidential Commission of Inquiry into the Cult of Devil Worship. 1995. Government Printer.

Rosberg, Carl, and John Nottingham. 1961. *The Myth of Mau Mau: Nationalism in Kenya*. New York: Hoover/Praeger.

Smith, James. 1998. "Njama's Supper: The Consumption and Use of Literary Potency by Mau Mau Insurgents in Colonial Kenya." *Comparative Studies in Society and History* 40(3):524–48.

———. 2008. *Bewitching Development*. Chicago: University of Chicago Press.

Throup, David. 1988. *Economic and Social Origins of Mau Mau*. London: James Currey.

Wachanga, Kahinga. 1975. *The Swords of Kirinyaga: The Fight for Land and Freedom*. Nairobi: Kenya Literature Bureau.

White, Luise. 2000. *Speaking with Vampires*. Berkeley: University of California Press.

PART II

NEW RELIGIOUS MOVEMENTS,
ENDURING SOCIAL TENSIONS

CHAPTER 3

The Mungiki Movement

A Source of Religio-Political Conflict in Kenya

Grace Nyatugah Wamue-Ngare

The chimerical neo-traditionalist Gikuyu religious and political organization known as Mungiki captured local and
international news headlines in 2002 and 2003 after a rash of violence
that left dozens of people killed throughout the Rift Valley Province
of Kenya and in the capital city of Nairobi. Outsiders have been unclear about the origins, intentions, and beliefs of the Mungiki. Indeed,
the nature of Mungiki is elusive, and it has been characterized vari-
ously as a social movement, criminal group, ethno-religious political organization, traditionalist religion, and fundamentalist sect. Although members of Mungiki insist that they are peaceful, they have
been labeled by the government as dangerous and violent, intent on
disrupting Kenyan society and enhancing the position of the Gikuyu
at the expense of other ethnic groups. What is clear is that the movement, which has remained largely mysterious to both Kenyans and
outsiders, is focused on rejecting the trappings of Western colonialism
and returning Kenya to indigenous African, and specifically Gikuyu,
traditions and values. Particularly notable is their vehement rejection
of Christianity and a call for traditional forms of governance, albeit
with a privileging of youth.

This essay seeks to better illuminate the origins, teachings, and intentions of the enigmatic Mungiki movement, and to assess its role in
violent conflict in Kenya. Without excusing the violence that Mungiki
members have committed, I hope to provide greater perspective on
the motivations behind their actions. Mungiki is not, as has been

claimed by the government, many Christian groups, and some scholars, simply an apolitical and basically criminal group with no constructive agenda. Rather, while the movement itself is relatively young, originating in the late 1980s, it is rooted in a much longer process of anti-colonial traditionalist revival, with connections to the Mau Mau rebellion of the 1950s and indigenous religious movements of the 1960s. The challenge to Gikuyu customs, values, and peoplehood, along with economic grievances blamed on government policy, adverse environmental conditions, and globalizing markets, have fueled the discontent that has fed the movement. Mungiki has mobilized this discontent and inserted itself into the political sphere, opposing certain government policies and figures and endorsing other candidates, but it has not organized into a political party per se.

While Gikuyu ethnicity, economics, and politics are all integral elements of Mungiki identity and goals, at its core the movement is religious. It exhibits certain characteristics of what has been called fundamentalism with an ideological reaction to modernity and the marginalization of religion, selective retrieval of texts and traditions, a kind of moral dualism, apocalyptic millennialist myths, sharp boundaries between insiders and outsiders, and a prescribed code of behavioral requirements (Almond, Sivan, and Appleby 1995). Without understanding its deeply religious origins and ethos, it is impossible to fully comprehend Mungiki; to characterize it as merely economic, political, or ethnic is to miss the heart of the movement.

This essay considers the origins and impact of the Mungiki movement in Kenyan society. I sketch out various narratives of its beginnings, particularly in the context of the conflicted milieu of post-independence Kenya. I then go into some depth regarding Mungiki beliefs and rituals, demonstrating the religious content at the heart of the movement. I examine Mungiki's role in Kenyan politics, including the use of violence by some of its members to achieve their goals. Finally, I consider the future prospects of Mungiki and under what conditions the group might contribute to greater peace, stability, and justice in Kenyan society and government rather than fomenting conflict and violence.

ORIGINS

Mungiki probably began in 1987, although this date is debatable, as the movement's origins are controversial. In all likelihood, there is no single origin, as multiple narratives have been constructed regarding its beginnings. Mbataru (2003, 4) argues that Mungiki was a splinter from the Tent of the Living God (Hema ya Ngai wi Muoyo) movement, which drew upon Gikuyu traditional values as alternatives to the materialism of the mainstream Christian churches. The Tent movement is comprised of several hundred young men who worship the Gikuyu deity Ngai by raising their hands to Kirinyaga (Mount Kenya), the second highest mountain in Africa and mythological birthplace of the Gikuyu people, Kenya's largest ethnic community. The Tent rapture started in the 1960s, when the founder, a young man named Ngonya wa Gakonya, began questioning the validity of his parents' Christianity. Gakonya saw himself as a crusader destined to salvage Gikuyu culture by reviving and revamping the laws and values of his forefathers. He learned this knowledge by talking with senior males in the rural areas and participating with them in rituals and sacrifices. Ngonya engaged in rigorous public campaigns, which were banned in 1990 following a mass rally held at Kamukunji grounds in Nairobi, after which he was arrested and imprisoned for two years. The Tent of the Living God movement continues to have many supporters in Central, Nairobi, and Rift Valley provinces. By 1990, adherents numbered in the thousands, and a distrustful government began to clamp down on it, first by leveling accusations of tribalism against the movement, and then by banishing it entirely. Gakonya, now deceased, spent much of his last decade in jail.

The established Mungiki leadership provides an account of their origins that is not so closely connected to the Tent movement. According to them, Mungiki dates back to 1987 when, in keeping with the traditional Gikuyu understanding of visions, Ndura Waruinge and Maina Njenga, who were not members of the Tent of the Living God, each had separate but identical visions in which they returned the Gikuyu people to their cultural roots. After receiving the revelation, the youngsters consulted area elders about their perceived prophecy, and the old men approved of their plans to form a new religion. But it was not until the beginning of 1992 that Mungiki came into the limelight through the local media. Not coincidentally, 1990–92 was a turning point in Kenyan politics, a period characterized by massive riots carried out by multiparty activists calling for serious change (Waruhiu 1994, 96).

Though they have assumed different roles—self-appointed national co-coordinator and spiritual leader, respectively—Waruinge and Njenga have been the movement's primary public faces. Of the two, Waruinge (who has since converted first to Islam, then Pentecostal Christianity, and so has detached himself from the appellation Mungiki) is better known, because of his prominence at the Mungiki rallies and in confrontations with the police. Several adherents of the movement link this period and the inspirations of their leaders with Ngai's call. They argue that God had finally heard the cries of his people and was fulfilling his promises to Gikuyu, the founder of the ethnic group, by using these militant youth to liberate them from the oppression of the government and their rival ethnic group, the Kalenjin.

Waruinge claims that he co-founded Mungiki with his friends when he was a fifteen-year-old high school student at Molo High in Nakuru District. Nakuru is the administrative capital of the massive Rift Valley Province, and was at the center of the government-encouraged Gikuyu-Kalenjin ethnic violence that tore the region apart during the early and mid-1990s. Notably, Waruinge and his friends hailed from a very poor neighborhood, and their school, like most district schools, ranked in the bottom tier of Kenya's school system; indeed, most students dropped out before they completed the four-year program. By being in a district school, rather than the more elite national and provincial schools, Waruinge and his friends were thus effectively closed out of mainstream Kenyan society, and precluded from joining the now-entrenched Gikuyu middle class, who had for some time pursued outwardly Western styles, language, education, and mannerisms.

According to current Mungiki adherents, Waruinge's original motive was to curb violence, as well as to fight for freedom and justice in the conflict-ridden Rift Valley Province. The movement began literally as a spark ignited by disgruntled youths ultimately guided by what some Mungiki leaders today refer to as a "peace-building process." However, it is more accurate to say that Mungiki's initial political goal was to resist and counteract the violence being perpetrated on Gikuyu in the Rift Valley Province, and it is therefore doubtful that the original aim was indeed to promote peace, except insofar as they sought autonomy from the government as a prerequisite for peace. Given the controversy surrounding the movement today, and the fact that it has been banned by the government, it is understandable that followers would go to great lengths to justify the "peace agenda" as an original impetus.

Mungiki was therefore born, and has since spread and thrived, in the hostile environment of the Rift Valley Province, inflamed by official propaganda about ethnic and political divisions. Since those humble beginnings, shrouded in memory and hearsay, the original movement has become something else indeed, transformed by a range of forces external to it, including the machinations of Kenyan political leaders and opportunists. In the name of Mungiki, multitudes have carried out violence, crime, and other atrocities, such that the term has become synonymous with chaos. Kenya's most wanted criminal, Simon Matheri, alleged to be a member of Mungiki, was gunned down by police on February 20, 2007. The youths who created Mungiki clearly did not anticipate the ultimate outcome of their actions and ideas, which have now become so closely related to criminality and violence.

Some scholars see Mungiki as an apolitical movement made up of simple-minded youths without any specific agenda or direction. Although many of their activities seem, on the surface, to confirm this view, this does not mean that Mungiki practices and beliefs are instrumental, disingenuous, or epiphenomenal. Indeed, their beliefs and ritual practices are fertile sources of social-political commentary and critique, which not only bind members together but also influence national politics and build on widely held sentiments and values. Mungiki's original inspiration was arguably more social and religious than political, in the formal sense of the word, because they primarily sought to transform Kenya's blighted moral order from the bottom up, by focusing on everyday behavior and belief. Because most "recruits," as they are called in the media, have been jobless and uneducated, they have been vulnerable to various power brokers who have sought to hijack them for their own purposes. Consequently, the movement has strongly influenced the dynamics of youth voting, and of political processes in general, causing Mungiki to take on the character of a political youth gang, something quite different from its original inspiration.

Today, the movement is polymorphous, without any commonly defined purpose, and so one can speak of numerous splinters of Mungiki or, perhaps more appropriately, a brand-name that different youth gangs have either taken on themselves or had thrust upon them by others, often by the government. At one time or another, all manner of criminals, including rapists, gangsters, and carjackers, have taken on this banner and have been encouraged by sensationalist press and a government ill equipped to curb crimes, such that Mungiki has over time become increasingly criminalized. Youth crimes across the country have been attributed to the group, in much the same way as colonial authorities blamed all forms of political resistance on the allegedly barbaric and satanic Mau Mau movement in the 1950s, a process which—then as now—directed public opinion away from underlying social problems and placed it instead on this alleged embodiment of backwardness and chaos.

While many Mungiki adherents have been associated with crime, we cannot rule out the existence of remnants of the original group which, though changed over time because of persecution, may not be directly involved in these criminal factions or gangs. After all, there is a high rate of crime among all urban Kenyan youth, most of whom are not Mungiki followers. Considering that Mungiki is exclusively a Gikuyu affair, and that Kenya has criminal elements drawn from literally all other communities, the recent national habit of linking Mungiki with every youth crime is not only erroneous, but also dangerous. This way, the Mungiki movement is used as a scapegoat for the government's inability to curb crime, while also allowing it to expand its authority. Both Kenyans and outsiders do not seem to understand who Mungiki followers are, their mission and objectives, or their place in Kenyan socio-economic and political history. This essay seeks to remedy some of these false conceptions of Mungiki.

Mungiki Religious Beliefs and Practices

The term *Mungiki* is based on the word *muingi,* and implies coming together for some objective, mission, or purpose. Mungiki is made up of young Gikuyu males and some females who worship what they view as the traditional god of the Gikuyu people, Ngai, and who perform recovered indigenous Gikuyu religious rituals. After receiving the revelation of the Mungiki, the youngsters claim that they consulted the elders about their "call," seeking to understand the meaning of Gikuyu indigenous rituals and shrines. Over time, Mungiki followers have also borrowed insights and information from a variety of ethnographic and literary texts, including Jomo Kenyatta's ethnography, *Facing Mount Kenya,* and Ngugi wa Thiong'o's renowned novels concerning Mau Mau.

Kenyatta demonstrated that religion shaped social identity among the Gikuyu, and he sketched out the basic beliefs and rituals of their worship. He argued that Ngai took no interest in individuals save at key moments of life such as birth, initiation, marriage, and death— and then only if the person's family group was involved in the ritual (1938, 234). Kenyatta sought to inform Europeans about the religious traditions of Gikuyu, and his book was meant as a kind of bridge between competing cultures and religions. He associated the loss of land and livelihoods by the Gikuyu with a spiritual pauperization driven by a deprivation of connections to the ancestors (1938, 213). *Facing Mount Kenya* was thus a call for freedom through the recovery of land, and it made a return to traditional morals and religious practice a precondition of regaining sovereignty. The Mungiki have taken Kenyatta's words to heart, and see themselves fulfilling his call to recapture true independence through the restoration of indigenous practices.

Mungiki beliefs reiterate the Gikuyu concept of a monotheistic god who resides and manifests his might by dwelling on Mount Kenya. The Gikuyu have historically known him through oral traditions, which are passed on *agu na agu* (generations to generations). Mungiki view the Bible as a collection of obscure stories about a particular people (the Israelites) and their God (Yahweh). Referring to it as the *Gikunjo* (tying, binding, imprisoning, enslaving) from which all

Kenyans must free themselves, they make reference to the Bible only
when it affirms their beliefs and practices. For example, Mungiki men
bar women from preaching by quoting 1 Corinthians 14:34–35: "let
your women keep silent in the churches, for they are not permitted to
speak; but they are to be submissive, as the law also says." They similarly insist that women should not dress in trousers, as this demonstrates a desire for sexual equality (Mwangi Githendu, October 12,
2002). Despite their selective appropriation of Bible references, in
general Mungiki members tend to see this book as the major weapon
in the mental colonization of the Gikuyu people (Wamue 2001), a position that probably also reflects their resentment of literacy as a form
of power from which they are excluded. Many of the nation's Christians view Mungiki's criticism of the Bible as open blasphemy (Mu-
tava Musyimi, April 10, 2001). Similar sentiments have been echoed
by the Catholic archbishop of Nyeri and the Anglican bishop of
Kitale, thus putting the authority of the Christian Bible at the center
of one of the major ideological conflicts between Mungiki and Christians in Kenya.

Mungiki's teachings are also centered on their belief in the power
of the ancestors, with a specific focus on the legendary Gikuyu and
Muumbi, the mythical original parents of the Gikuyu. Gikuyu and
Muumbi are interpreted and deployed as genealogical and moral alternatives to Adam and Eve, who fell from God's glory due to their
immorality. According to Mungiki's teaching, Adam and Eve are not
Gikuyu ancestors, but rather ancestors of the Jews (Kimani wa Mungai, June 30, 2002). Any Mugikuyu who claims such ancestry is men-
tally colonized and confused; perhaps borrowing from Bob Marley,
they call this bondage to the beliefs and rituals of another culture
mental slavery (*ukombo wa meciria*), which in turn requires mental
liberation. In a fascinating inversion of religious mythology, the Mungiki use Christianity's most sacred text and doctrine as a means of undermining its own universal authority and as providing an indictment
of its impurities: thus, many Mungiki see Christian depravity as originating in the Garden of Eden; here, paradoxically, they invoke the
Bible. Thus, the Christian faith is rooted in sin, which the Europeans
(*athungu*, plural; *muthungu*, singular) passed over to unsuspecting
Africans. Ironically, this inherited Christian-based immorality has

defiled the land, thereby turning the Gikuyu away from Ngai (and vice versa), resulting in severe economic, social, and political woes. A major aim of many Mungiki, therefore, is to restore their own spiritual purity and hegemony (*kigongona*) by ritual cleansings of Africans and through public denunciations of Christianity and Westernization, all of which is seen as a sine qua non of economic recovery.

Moreover, many Mungiki see the Christian equation of Jesus Christ with God as a false belief that was foisted on African Christians. They argue that Jesus is merely a human ancestor—for that matter, a Jew from Joseph's family—and therefore socially and culturally unrelated to Africa and Africans. Moreover, Jesus had a mother (Mary) and a father (Joseph), and therefore cannot be God's Son, unless God had kin, which he cannot (Kimani wa Mungai, June 30, 2002). Jesus also loses credibility because, if he had no wife or children, as the Bible portrays him, he could not be an ancestor. According to Gikuyu beliefs, ancestors are elders who have completed all rites of passage, including marriage and childrearing, and after death have been elevated to high ranks in the ontological order.

In Mungiki worship, prayers are directed to Ngai, who dwells on Kirinyaga (Mount Kenya). All adherents face the holy mountain, and in so doing, they invoke the spirits of the ancestors (Mukebe, May 14, 2002). As the members raise their hands toward Kirinyaga, they remove shoes, watches, ties, bracelets, belts, and practically anything that seems to physically bind them and interfere with the prayers (*guthahia igongona*). These are all items associated with foreigners, and this ritual practice reiterates Mau Mau rituals of the 1950s. "Unbinding" a member through the removal of the above items is perceived to be a form of ritual cleansing (*gwitheria na kwiohora*) from what Mungiki call *mathahu ma ageni* (unclean foreign rituals), brought by *athungu*. Once all members perform this small ritual, they declare themselves ritually clean, free, and ready to indulge in the frenzy of certain traditional songs and dances (*mumburo*), before they face Kirinyaga and chant their prayers. These songs combine Gikuyu traditional songs with Mau Mau protest songs and their own compositions, most of which describe Mungiki's heroic battles with the police in different parts of the country.

The Mungiki initiation rite, referred to as *igongona ria mat na mwa*ki (baptism by water and fire), involves an explicit denunciation of foreign cultures and Christianity. The ceremony involves baptism in a selected river, dam, or any other water mass. The candidate then denounces the things Mungiki recognizes as foreign, in particular, Christian teachings, including the initiate's Western name. After the water ritual, novices go through smoke derived from a nearby fire. They are then sprinkled with olive oil and a mixture of milk, meat, and honey, signifying their purification. Once a person undergoes this ritual, he or she publicly declares his or her commitment to the movement, becoming a recognized full member ready for what is referred to as "the cause" (Mukebe, May 14, 2002). Afterward, the initiate must give this conversion "testimony" every time he or she meets other members. For example, one introduces oneself as so and so (only Gikuyu names are used) of this and this family (*nyumba*), lineage (*mbari*), clan (*muhiriga*), and age-set (*riika*), back to the fifth generation. The initiate also learns certain codes, greetings, and other marks of identification, such as mode of dress, hairstyle (dreadlocks), amulets, and body tattoos. Most of these are acquired as the person enters crucial hierarchical guilds (*njama*) within the movement. Unity among these guilds is emphasized, with members of the *njama* referring to each other as *kiawa* (comrade, age-mate), *awa* (father), and *maitu* (mother). In case of a dispute among the members of the *njama*, "elders"[1] sit together to reconcile them, and this must be done immediately to avoid *thahu* (ritual uncleanness) within the *njama* (Kimani wa Mungai, June 30, 2002). Many Mungiki followers also take snuff as part of this initiation, which they prefer to cigarette smoking, claiming that this causes cancer, while snuff cleanses the brain by stimulating the mucous membranes. They say that its strong taste reminds them of hardships created by political and economic situations in Kenya that have subjected followers to absolute poverty. Wearing dreadlocks and taking snuff demonstrate oneness among members and serve as marks of identification, comradeship, and solidarity.

Mungiki philosophy is represented in their flag. The green background represents African people in their own land, and the black horizontal stripes depict the fractious effects of Christianity and

Westernization on Africa and Kenya. They identify the consequences as bloodshed in the form of violent robberies, ethnic clashes, fatal car accidents, cattle rustling, HIV/AIDS, cholera and malaria epidemics, terrorist attacks, and floods, all of which have been on the rampage in Kenya, especially in the last decade. Notably, the movement attributes all these problems to Christianity and Westernization, which, according to them, have divided Kenyans so much that they cannot worship as a unified group as they once did. To reunite the people and consequently liberate the Gikuyu and all other Kenyans from this bloodshed, Mungiki see a return to the indigenous shrines as crucial and inevitable. In their philosophy, peace, signified by the color white at the bottom of their flag, will only be attained once the country is rid of foreign ideologies, beliefs, and practices that have confused Africans.

Mungiki's concept of peace, though central to the story it tells others about itself, is based on a particular patriarchal vision of Gikuyu society, which not only conflicts with the reality of contemporary Kenya, but also with the very presence of women in public life. It is commonly believed within the movement that women are more prone to immoral behavior, such as premarital and extramarital sex. Other proscribed behaviors include the common practice of women either preparing food for their husbands or sharing beds with them while menstruating. This behavior is perceived as *mugiro* (taboo), and women in this condition should have minimal interactions with men. Women are subjected to similar restrictions after giving birth, whereby the husband stays at his hut (*thingira*) for up to seven weeks without sleeping with her. It is perceived to be a taboo for the couple to sleep together before cleansing. In addition, women are not supposed to use contraceptives for family planning, for this is perceived to be equivalent to murder. The assertion of these traditional beliefs and practices, along with others such as polygamy and separate houses for males and females, is particularly challenging in contemporary Kenya, where they are seen to defy more modern notions of gender equality.

The government insists that Mungiki uses violence to impose itself on followers, a claim that their leaders constantly deny and that is by and large unfounded. As mentioned earlier, Mungiki came into the limelight amid major socio-economic frustrations, especially among the Gikuyu within the ethnically divided and violent Rift Valley Province. Conflict begat disillusionment and desperation, and as a result, many Gikuyu turned to anything that seemed to offer them hope. In this desperation, Gikuyu indigenous beliefs and practices served as a unifying bond, and attracted the people who constituted the first generation of Mungiki followers. Rather than being coercive, the movement provided answers and solidarity in the midst of difficult circumstances. Over time the values of the movement have shifted, and it has become increasingly attractive to large masses of youth, but recruitment appears to remain voluntary.

SOCIAL BACKGROUND TO THE MOVEMENT

The popularity of this movement can only be appreciated with respect to the political and economic conditions of the place where it began. The people in the part of the Rift Valley Province from which these youths hailed are very poor, even in comparative terms, the majority being former squatters in the colonial government or former Mau Mau freedom fighters or their descendants. Many of the inhabitants either lived and operated from the forests during this epic struggle, or worked as squatters on settler farms, where they served as servants in the former "White Highlands." Many others are recent Gikuyu immigrants from the congested Central Province.

With independence in 1963, many of these people were rendered landless, since land was demarcated when they were in the forests fighting, if it had not already been expropriated by the British. To ameliorate this potentially volatile situation, the first independent government, led by Jomo Kenyatta, began resettling these people in the Rift Valley Province through large land-buying companies. Of particular infamy was the Ngwataniro-mutukanio company organized by a renowned Kenyan, the late Kihika Kimani. In this arrangement, the company, owned by rich Kenyans, purchased large tracts of land from both the former settlers and the government. This land was then subdivided and redistributed to individuals through self-help cooperatives, in which each person received a small share of two to three acres. Most of the people who were trying to purchase this land were very poor, so the process was tedious and fraught with obstacles, due to their meager incomes and corruption in the allocation process (Njau wa Kamau, Njenga wa Mumira, and Mary Muthoni, December 12, 2001). In most cases, individuals seeking land deposited money in intervals over many years, often receiving nothing, and typically waiting for years before any land was allocated.

With European settlers, indigenous pastoralist communities, immigrants from other parts of Kenya, and ex-Mau Mau all competing for the same resources, land issues in the Rift Valley Province remain a critical challenge for the government. Spiced by ethnic politics and seasoned corruption, the issue has continued to spark serious tensions, leading to destruction of property and loss of life and perpetuating cleavages along ethnic lines. The churches have often taken a stand against corruption in the government and upper echelons of the bureaucracy (Ahluwalia 1996, 179). This combination of corruption along with the unwillingness or inability of the government to address grievances of small landowners and the poor has plagued modern Kenya and aligned large segments of the people against the government. Land was the commodity most prized in the revolt against the British, and many of the problems articulated by the freedom fighters remain in Kenya today.

Having suffered great "opportunity costs" in terms of alienated land, time, and education when they were involved in Mau Mau, Gikuyu in this region continue to feel betrayed by a system they helped build (Kanogo 1987, 162–71). It is now widely known that the people who reaped massive benefits after the Mau Mau were mostly those Africans, Gikuyu included, who supported the British during the war, and thus, according to the freedom fighters, betrayed the cause by not participating in fighting. These people were in a better position to acquire large tracts of land after independence, because they had money by virtue of being beneficiaries of colonial education and formal employment (Ahluwalia 1996, 109).

Due to the settlement patterns both before and after independence, the massive Rift Valley Province is a multiethnic region, with virtually all major Kenyan communities represented, including the vast majority of the country's Kalenjin people, President Daniel arap

Moi's ethnic group. Ethnic tension in the Rift Valley intensified as the result of the withdrawal of foreign aid after 1989 and the demand from foreign donors that Kenya democratize its political institutions by promoting multiparty democracy, a policy that threatened to remove the president and destabilize the tenuous and far from complete dominance of his small ethnic group. Moi categorically equated political pluralism with ethnic tension and tribal animosity, placing principal blame on the Gikuyu, and argued that Kenya was not politically mature enough for a multiparty system.

Moi's close associates took advantage of existing political differences created by multiparty politics to create or rekindle already existing conflicts among Kenyans, especially in the Rift Valley Province. At the onset of multiparty elections in the early 1990s, Moi and his Kenya African National Union (KANU) Party sought to exclude the Gikuyu from carrying this region, particularly as the constitution mandated that an aspiring president must gather majority votes in five out of the eight provinces (Waruhiu 1994, 80–81). During the 1980s and 1990s, "Gikuyu-bashing" became a key tactic for many aspiring politicians. A number of candidates made provocative comments about "these flat-nosed, pot-bellied people with brown teeth," imploring their constituents to "cut the Ibos of Kenya down to size," and to "lie low as envelopes" (*Daily Nation,* July 3, 2004). These and other calumnies against the Gikuyu community fed a kind of collective paranoia, which gave added fuel to neo-traditionalist movements like Mungiki. Moi's strategy was probably designed to prove the point that tribalism, as displayed by the Gikuyu, would be the inevitable consequence of multiparty democracy. Ethnic rivalries had always been present, but had previously been managed relatively effectively (Grindle 1996, 68), so the higher level of animosity was the sign of a new arithmetic.

The 1992 repeal of section 2A of the Kenyan constitution, which had made the single-party state mandatory, precipitated a mushrooming of opposition parties. In August 1991, a group of KANU leaders from the Rift Valley Province held a series of meetings in Nandi, Kericho, and Narok, ostensibly to affirm their loyalty to KANU and the president. The leaders were led by Nicholas Biwott, by then a powerful and influential minister in Moi's cabinet. In their speeches, they declared the extensive Rift Valley Province a "KANU Zone" from which opposition parties should be banned from soliciting votes and influence. The meetings threatened to forcefully evict members of opposition parties if any "set their foot in the Province." The targeted opposition was in fact the Gikuyu underclass, many of whom had at least some genealogical link to the Mau Mau struggle. Soon afterward, ethnic clashes broke out when Kalenjin began attacking Gikuyu farms in patches of the Rift Valley Province, as well as in Western, Nyanza, and Coast provinces (Wachira 2001, 28).

Many people lost their property, including land, which was often grabbed by the politically connected. The Moi government could neither give an explanation nor halt the clashes, and so there were accusations and counter-accusations concerning who was causing them. Certainly, the fact that it was Kalenjin who launched first attacks made the government's claim that the Gikuyu were the protagonists seem absurd. While the government was accusing the opposition forces, the latter was accusing the government. As a consequence, a twelve-member task force consisting of opposition parties, other pressure groups, and the National Council of Churches of Kenya (NCCK) set out on a fact-finding mission on ethnic clashes. The committee noted, in part, that "the president has lost control of the country; that people trained in military warfare were taking part in ethnic clashes; that senior members of the provincial administration, senior cabinet ministers and KANU officials were involved on the side of the Kalenjin warriors" (*The Nairobi Weekly Telegraph,* June 1992, 130). Furthermore, the Justice and Peace Commission of the NCCK, responsible for intervening and fact-finding, accused the government of complicity: "Having carried out detailed extensive thorough investigation in the affected areas, we have clearly observed that certain influential personalities in the government were directly involved in fanning tribal sentiments that led to acts of lawlessness and hooliganism against innocent citizens. There should be no link between pluralism and violence and what we need is responsible leadership which educates the people on participatory democracy" (*The Nairobi Weekly Review,* March 13, 1992, 19). The infamous ethnic clashes left many Kenyans dead, displaced, and maimed. The Kenya Human Rights Commission (1996, 43) said, "the violence was not purely on 'land' clashes for there were largely conflicts brought about as a result of incitement of the poor by greedy politicians who misunderstood multiparty democracy to mean the end of their political and economic clout in the country."

In addition to these politically motivated struggles over land, the conflict has been fed by economics. The Gikuyu are the primary growers of coffee and tea in Kenya, and were disproportionately affected by the declining price for these commodities on the world market after the mid-1980s. Gikuyu youth like Waruinge saw their position as a kind of double jeopardy, for they had lost not only their grandparents' land through colonialism but also their parents' lands through ethnic clashes. At the same time, the value of their land had declined due to macroeconomic forces that were outside their control, but which they linked to the government. Mungiki resistance to the government was thus fed by grievances related to their uncertain place in the economy and the disproportionate toll that global market conditions had taken on their primary form of livelihood.

Recruits to the movement were initially people of the same socioeconomic, regional, and educational backgrounds, namely, the poor and disenfranchised Gikuyu of the Rift Valley Province. However, as the movement spread elsewhere in the province and to other parts of the country, in particular Nairobi and Central provinces, more educated and socioeconomically advantaged people joined. Irrespective of these differences among Mungiki followers, members seem to share similar values, ideals, and views, and they are subsequently bound together by the same rituals and history. As more educated members joined the movement, they brought with them a greater diversity of religious experiences and textual sources. For instance, in one research encounter with followers in Rift Valley, I discovered Mungiki followers with texts by Marcus Garvey and Kwame Nkrumah, in addition to the nostalgic literature of Ngugi wa Thiong'o on neocolonialism. Moreover, political scientists, politicians, and human rights activists were influential on the movement, and Mungiki often shared platforms with such people at political gatherings, thus slowly changing through association. This kind of mingling was to have a profound effect on the direction the movement would take, especially in regard to Kenyan politics.

Recent Developments

As the 1990s proceeded, Kenya entered a downward spiral precipitated by the withdrawal of international aid. Most Kenyans became completely disillusioned by joblessness, escalating crimes, and failing infrastructure. The situation was especially bleak for youth, leading to nostalgia for an age of mythical prosperity they never experienced. This nostalgia was encouraged by their forefathers, who grew up as squatters but still reminisced about a golden past. For the youth who formed the Mungiki, the blame for the country's poor economic conditions fell on the educated elite, Christians, and senior government officers, who were the purported sources of suffering from colonial times.

On the surface it appears absurd that young people living in modern times, often in urban places, would resort to an imagined traditional past and rural economy in their efforts to revolt against the country's leadership. Given this, many people see Mungiki's beliefs and practices as disguising a more real and sinister intent (see, for example, Anderson 2002). Although Mungiki's return to traditionalism may appear vague and absurd to outsiders, their practices, such as their ritual surrender of material objects, is partially a reaction to the upwardly mobile accumulative philosophy that characterizes other popular youth movements, like Pentecostalism. It is a form of social critique bred of a combination of alienation and hope that suggests something in the making, and is worthy of further attention.

By the 1990s, Mungiki adherents numbered in the thousands, and a distrustful government began to clamp down, leveling accusations of tribalism. In the end, Mungiki was banned. Both President Moi's and, more recently, President Mwai Kibaki's governments have dismissed the movement as tribalistic, antigovernment, satanic, and violent. This view is vehemently opposed by the movement's leadership. They willfully continue to violate the law by holding illegal assemblies, which they claim are prayer meetings but are in fact suffused in a political agenda. Yet the movement has always taken great pains to explain that it is a "peaceful" religious movement, with the idea of a Gikuyu (and African) cultural essence based on civic cooperation, egalitarianism, and peace being central to its teachings.

Although Mungiki's initial position may have been well intended, in fact the group has changed its orientation over time. While their philosophy appears clearly peaceful and constructive, either the leaders underrated the volatile natures of their youthful followers, or the "mission" became too complicated over time. On the other hand, due to the amorphous nature of the movement, current Mungiki members (whether self-professed or accused) may not be very clear as to the original objectives of the movement. Whatever the explanation, Mungiki has ceased being a "peaceful" religious movement, as their leaders still insist it is, and many of their activities have become criminally oriented. In truth, Mungiki was criminalized by political power brokers, who took advantage of their numbers and influence. Not all Mungiki followers are criminals, and many persist in practicing the original religion. However, because many youth have engaged in crime, and because most young people are declared by the media and the government to be a Mungiki, this fact is invisible to Kenyans.

Part of the issue lies in the nature of their religious beliefs, for this is not a complacent belief system, but a politicized religion that seeks to transform the world by changing people's daily practices, and which cuts against the grain of modern life. It is also not traditional in any simple sense, because it is carried out by youth acting autonomously, often against their elders. For example, in Mukurwe-ini Division of Nyeri District, Central Province, a son teamed up with his peers and circumcised his own mother in the name of upholding traditions (Lucy Njeri, April 23, 2002). Interview information indicated that the boy's father became enraged and killed his son in revenge. Further interviews with the people from the area confirmed that these things happen quite often, but no one wants to report them due to the shame they bring to the victims. Such errant behavior belies any genuine or positive Mungiki intentions. Noting that no indigenous practices would allow any male, especially a son, to circumcise his own mother, or any female for that matter, one wonders which traditions Mungiki are reviving, and whether indeed such abhorrent acts are central to their teachings. Such cases, even if isolated, are used by the media, the churches, and the government as ideal weapons to completely dismiss the movement.

In other incidents, clashes between the movement's followers and members of the public or police have been sparked by a dispute over the control of the private minibus (matatu) business in some parts of Nairobi. According to police reports, many people have died in matatu-related clashes between the owners and the Mungiki. In addition to the running battles with the police, alleged Mungiki members have also been involved in other antisocial acts. Among these are stripping women wearing miniskirts and trousers in public, forcibly imposing female circumcision, and raiding police stations to free their own members under police custody (*Daily Nation,* February 5, 2008). In the recent past, the criminals described as Mungiki followers have been assuming a new modern face, using AK-47 assault rifles instead of clubs, machetes, and swords.

Due to such controversial acts, which some members may be committing in isolation of the movement's main objective or which may have been done by criminals claiming to be Mungiki, it is no wonder that Ken Ouko (*Daily Nation,* January 5, 2003) suggests that Mungiki is the political/military wing of a religious organization that deploys religion as a camouflage. However, as my research found, these are isolated cases, and rarely is the mainstream Mungiki movement involved. The majority of the followers equally condemn such acts as sacrilegious (Mukebe, May 14, 2002).

Although the leadership of Mungiki may have become interested primarily in controlling matatu stages and operating as racketeers, the interest in traditionalism and return to the values of the past is widespread, even among people who do not identify with Mungiki. Many of those involved in Mungiki believe strongly in these ideals, but are nevertheless forced to deal with real material contingencies, like the need to make a livelihood in a relentlessly difficult urban setting. It is important to point out that although Mungiki's political activism may be materially motivated, leaders are careful to justify it in terms of Gikuyu customary religion. For example, Mungiki insist on a reversion to indigenous methods of governance, based on the Gikuyu age-grade system. They understand this system in terms of parliamentary process, whereby rulers stayed in office for a specific period of time, and handed over power through a ceremony referred to as *itwika* (Leakey

1977, 1278–83); their interpretation of this is probably informed by Jomo Kenyatta's *Facing Mount Kenya*, in which he draws a parallel between *itwika* and British governance. Gacheke (June 30, 2002) refers to *itwika* as the "radical" philosophy of Mungiki, as it is interpreted by Mungiki to mean that a bloody revolution must happen to bring the liberation that the Kenyan youth desire, in which the older generation relinquishes power to the youth. This millenarian ideal, though very unclear in terms of methodology, is central to their teachings, and is even evident in the ideology inscribed on their flag that there must be bloodshed before attainment of peace. Most followers of the movement contradict one another in the notion of this ideology, some saying there has been enough bloodshed, which signifies the revolution is due, others claiming that blood has to be spilled for the revolution to take effect. In the end, there is no clear explanation of how this *itwika* ceremony would be carried out.

This interpretation of tradition has motivated, or at least legitimated, Mungiki members' seemingly inconsistent political actions. For example, in the succession debate preceding President Kibaki's ascension to power, Mungiki was at the forefront of backing Jomo Kenyatta's son Uhuru Kenyatta, whom President Moi—the Mungiki's antagonist—also supported as his successor. The aged Moi's announcement of stepping down in favor of a young contender was seen as a fulfillment of the philosophy of the youth taking over power and hence completing the *itwika* revolution. For Waruinge, requirements for the next leader included being a Gikuyu not more than forty-five years of age, being a proponent of a nationalist outlook, and being acceptable to most Kenyans. Consequently, Uhuru Kenyatta was thus the most ideal candidate for presidency.

THE FUTURE OF THE MUNGIKI

Prior to the December 2002 general elections, Mungiki had come under fierce attack from members of the public over its alleged atrocities. Among these were the bloodbath in the sprawling Kariobangi North slums that left more than twenty-three residents dead, and the alleged threat of forced female circumcision in parts of Kiambu

District. In addition, the new National Rainbow Coalition (NARC) government that came to power in early 2003 placed a strict ban on all groups perceived to be security threats, forcing Mungiki underground. The movement's open support for the KANU candidate Uhuru Kenyatta in the general elections may also have led the new government to repress Mungiki. Indeed, they appealed to Mungiki members to surrender, whereby a large number of youths came forth and claimed to denounce the movement. Though a few leaders allegedly supported surrendering, leading the NARC government to claim that it had quashed the movement, most opted to go underground. The pressure to surrender came with the euphoria that characterized Kenya at the wake of NARC victory over KANU, and the desire to return to some kind of peaceful "normalcy."

The reemergence of thousands of Mungiki members eight months later shocked not only the government, but Kenyans as a whole. In September 2003, the group, which had been carrying out its activities in hiding, resurfaced at a political rally in Limuru in Central Province, sparking fresh fears of its existence. This large rally, attended by outspoken political leaders, proved to all Kenyans that Mungiki was still a vibrant movement. It appeared that its members had responded to the ban by simply changing their external appearance and strategies of operation, at least temporarily. But the political potency of "traditional" Gikuyu symbols proved too compelling and politically charged for Mungiki to abandon completely; while most followers had cut off their dreadlocks and stopped sniffing snuff in public when the movement went underground, to the surprise of the government and many Kenyans, many donned dreadlocks and took snuff openly during the rally. They even went as far as offering some to their "guests," including the attending MPs.

Many observers had claimed that Mungiki was a small, marginal, and even Machiavellian movement that would disappear with a firm threat from the government (see Anderson 2002). Clearly, this view underestimated the appeal of the movement, which continued to attract many youth long after its supposed defeat. Unless youth problems, and unemployment in particular, are addressed in Kenya, Mungiki is likely to continue to attract followers. Several reasons account for this. First, the precarious socioeconomic situation in Kenya attracts unemployed and uneducated youths searching for survival and something to believe in. Mungiki members openly discuss these issues in their heated religious-cum-political assemblies. In these meetings, leaders talk about the socioeconomic and political situation in Kenya, often criticizing the government for neglecting the youth in these matters. The group thus easily shifts back and forth among religious, political, and economic discourse. It is in these forums that Mungiki openly criticize the institutions of church and state, which in their view have led to the unfavorable economic circumstances in Kenya, as well as the nation's deep-seated corruption and immorality. More than 60 percent of the followers I encountered insisted on having joined the movement out of being inspired by Mungiki's teachings against the state, Christianity, and Westernization.

Second, Kenyan youth have been indoctrinated through the home and school systems into anticipating a bright future after completing their education. In particular, children who grew up in postindependence Kenya were constantly reminded that they would be future leaders, and were promised that the so called *matunda ya uhuru* (fruits of independence) would soon flow. Unfortunately, the Kenyan situation offers nothing close to this dream to young people. Instead, there is pervasive hopelessness arising from poverty caused by landlessness and joblessness, all of which leave many youths maladjusted. Most youth blame the government for not responding to their plight.

Mungiki leaders lead the youth in protesting against the government's neglect and incompetence in handling state affairs, and youth issues in particular. Mungiki attributes all of the problems facing the youth—including joblessness, idleness, HIV/AIDS, and poverty—to political and religious leaders who have let the youth down by abandoning indigenous values (such as the *itwika* ceremony in favor of the adoption of foreign worship). Consequently, the solution to all these problems lies in a return to what the elders have abandoned: the "indigenous shrines." Unfortunately, although Mungiki leaders are clear in spelling out the afflictions of Kenya's youth and blaming the government for incompetence in handling the problems, they do not offer concrete proposals or programs to remedy the situation. To the contrary, in heaping blame on others, they transfer the problem from themselves, thus inciting some of their followers to violence.

In this sense, David M. Anderson (2002) is correct when he observes that whatever Mungiki may once have been on the distant farms of Laikipia, it has been transformed into a radically different movement in the urban estates and slums. Mungiki members are youths looking for sense and meaning in life. They are an indictment of Kenyan society—an index of failure—and they easily fall prey to political and economic machinations. In Kenyan cities crying out for security, Mungiki found easy jobs as vigilante groups protecting small traders and extorting money from those who needed protection against thugs and even against business rivals. While Anderson concludes that Mungiki is now basically a criminal group, in fact Mungiki youth do, by and large, see themselves as a force for good, claiming that they will salvage the country from the precarious situation it is in. The government's repeated association of nearly every criminal act with Mungiki says more about its own inability, or unwillingness, to address the root causes of youth crime than it says about the nature of Mungiki.

The best approach to the movement is dialogue, since trying to hunt them down only aggravates the problem. This view has been highlighted by Patrick Mbataru (2003), who observes that "Mungiki is not dead. . . . This movement is not just 'a family affair' or 'a thing of the past,' as Internal Security Minister Chris Murungaru says. And it is, of course, not going to die soon. This is not to defend Mungiki. But by not studying the deeper sociological issues behind this movement, we would be aping the philosophical ostrich. We cannot just wish it away."

CONCLUSION

Like many other religions, Mungiki manifests both constructive and destructive elements. Many sectarian groups suppress believers by isolating them from other influences, consequently forging strong bonds of cohesion. Members thus conform to the psychology and politics of isolation, viewing other religions as outside forces that they must protect themselves from. Mungiki see Christianity and modernity as new forms of slavery, blaming them for all of Kenya's social, economical, and political problems. This has translated into waging a rhetorical and at times physical battle on Kenyans as a whole, since the vast majority of the nation's citizens self-identify as Christians and modern.

The Mungiki movement claims to be a nationwide party. In reality, Mungiki is purely an ethnic movement, with only Gikuyus as followers, and therefore advocates for ethnicity at the expense of a fragile national unity. Their claim to be promoting systemic national peace thus appears questionable. In addition, Mungiki's confrontations with the law have often led to bloodshed, sometimes of innocent bystanders who may be caught in the melee. These and many other aspects of the movement, if unchecked, may eventually take the path of ethno-religious militance, which has proven destructive in many other locales, from Nigeria to Bosnia to Sri Lanka. As mentioned above, Kenyan leaders often take advantage of the group solidarity found among Mungiki followers to promote their interests, in particular during political campaigns. In some cases, this has led to significant destruction of property and loss of life.

On the other hand, there is a positive social vision in Mungiki thought, although it is generally disconnected from the harsh and unjust realities of daily life. For example, Mungiki advocate and practice hard work and self-reliance. Moreover, Mungiki's strict ideas concerning teenage sexuality and family values can be positive, and can be used to teach youth about the HIV/AIDS menace afflicting the country. In addition, Mungiki preaches against drugs and alcohol abuse, while emphasizing peer counseling. Though there is no evidence that Mungiki followers have effectively put any of these doctrines into practice, since many of them have been associated with drug abuse, violence, and unemployment, the fact that their teachings are often positive suggests that they might deter youth from engaging in criminal activities. In addition, in their outspoken stand on bad governance, corruption, and constitutional change, the group has often served as a social and political watchdog. In sum, despite the devolution of some movement members to criminality, Mungiki beliefs draw on widely held Kenyan values, such as kinship, community sharing, and personal dignity, all of which are indeed positive and reflect many Mungiki youths' genuine desire for social change.

NOTE

1. Unlike traditional Gikuyu society, where elders who settled disputes were people above a certain age (typically not less than sixty years), Mungiki elders are young men, some between the ages of twenty-five and thirty-five. This demonstrates how predominant young people are in the movement.

REFERENCES

Ahluwalia, D. P. 1996. *Post Colonialism and the Politics of Kenya*. New York: Nova Science Publishers, Inc.

Akuar, W. V. 2001. "International Conference on Religion and Conflict in Sub-Sahara Africa." Seminar paper presented in a workshop on "Religion and Conflict in Africa," Utrecht, Netherlands.

Almond, G. A., E. Sivan, and R. S. Appleby. 1995. "Fundamentalism: Genus and Species." In *Fundamentalisms Comprehended,* edited by M. E. Marty and R. S, Appleby, 399–424. Chicago: University of Chicago Press.

Anderson, D. 2002. "Vigilantes, Violence and the Politics of Public Order in Kenya." *African Affairs* 101(405).

Assefa, H., and G. Wachira, eds. 1996. *Peacemaking and Democratization in Africa*. Nairobi: East Africa Educational Publishers.

Barot, R., ed. 1993. *Religion and Ethnicity: Minorities and Social Change in the Metropolis*. Kampen: KOK Pharos Publishing House.

Barret, A. J. 1998. *Sacrifice and Prophecy in Turkana Cosmology*. Nairobi: Paulines Publications Africa.

Bascom, W. R., and M. J. Herskovits. 1970. *Continuity and Change in African Culture*. Chicago: University of Chicago Press.

Bourdillon, M. 1990. *Religion and Society: A Text for Africa*. Harare: Mambo Press.

Cagnolo, C. 1933. *The Akikuyu: Their Customs, Tradition, and Folklore*. Nyeri: Mission Printing School.

Carlston, K. S. 1968. *Social Theory and African Tribal Organization: The Development of Socio-Legal Theory*. Urbana: University of Illinois Press.

Clothey, F. W. 1981. "Ritual." In *Abingdon Dictionary of Living Religions,* edited by K. Crim. Nashville: Abingdon Press.

Cox, J. L. 1996. *Expressing the Sacred: An Introduction to the Phenomenology of Religion*. Harare: University of Zimbabwe Publications.

Des Forges, A. 1999. "Leave None to Tell the Story." In *Genocide in Rwanda*. Paris: Human Rights Watch.

Fashole-Luke, E. 1978. *Christianity in Independence Africa*. London: Indiana Printing Press.

Feeders, A., and C. Salvador. 1988. *Peoples and Cultures of Kenya*. Nairobi: Trans-Africa.

Grindle, M. S. 1996. *Challenging the State: Crisis and Innovation in Latin America and Africa*. Cambridge: Cambridge University Press.

Hinga, T. M. 1998. "Christianity and Female Puberty Rites in Africa: The Gikuyu Case." In *Rites of Passage in Contemporary Africa*, edited by J. L. Cox. London: Cardiff.

Idowu, E. B. 1973. *African Traditional Religion: A Definition*. London: SCM Press Ltd.

Johnstone, R. L. 1988. *Religion in Society: A Sociology of Religion*. Upper Saddle River, NJ: Prentice Hall.

Kagwanja, P. 2003. "Facing Mount Kenya or Facing Mecca? The Mungiki Ethnic Violence and the Politics of the Moi Succession in Kenya, 1987–2002." *African Affairs* 102(406).

Kang'ethe, K. 1981. "The Role of the Gikuyu Religion and Culture in the Development of Kenya: Religio-political Movement, 1900–1950 with Particular Reference to God and the Rite of Initiation." Unpublished Ph.D. thesis, University of Nairobi.

Kanogo, T. 1987. *Squatters and the Roots of Mau Mau 1905–63*. London: James Currey.

Kenya Human Rights Commission. 1996. *Ours by Right, Theirs by Might: A Study on Land Clashes* (KHRC Report).

Kenyatta, J. 1938. *Facing Mount Kenya*. London: Seeker and Warburg.

Kibicho, S. 1972. "The Kikuyu Conception of God and Its Continuity into Christian Era, and the Question It Raises for the Idea of Revelation." Ann Arbor, MI: University Microfilms International.

Leakey, S. B. 1977. *A History of the Kikuyu*. Nairobi: OUP.

Lonsdale, J. n.d. "Jomo Kenyatta, God, and the Modern World." Unpublished paper presented at Cambridge University.

Magesa, L. 1998. *African Religion: The Moral Traditions of Abundant Life*. Nairobi: Paulines Publications Africa.

Marty, E. M., and R. S. Appleby. 1993. *Fundamentalism and the State: Remaking Polities, Economies and Militancy*. Chicago: University of Chicago Press.

Mbataru, P. 2003. "Taking 'Mungiki' Lightly Will Be a Mistake." *The Daily Nation*, May 8.

Mbiti, J. S. 1969. *African Religions and Philosophy*. London: Heinemann.

———. 1993. Peace and Reconciliation in African Religion and Christianity." In *Dialogue and Alliance*. Vol. 7, no. 1. New York: International Religious Foundation.

Miller, E. 2000. "Re-traditioning: Revival of Kenyan Religions." *The Daily Nation,* May 3.

Mozorewa, G. H. 1985. *The Origins and Development of African Theology.* Maryknoll, NY: Orbis Books.

Mutua, Makau. 1999. "Returning to My Roots: African 'Religions' and the State." In *Proselytization and Communal Self-Determination in Africa,* edited by A. A. An-Naim. Maryknoll, NY: Orbis Books.

Mwikamba, C. 1993. "Conflict and Social Changes in Kenya." In *Dialogue and Alliance.* Vol. 7, no. 1. New York: International Religious Foundation.

Otunnu, A. O. 1995. "The Dynamics of Conflicts in Uganda." In *Conflict in Africa,* edited by Oliver Furley. London: Tauris Academic Studies.

Phombeah, G. 2003. "Kenya's Secretive Mungiki Sect." BBC News Online, http://news.bbc.co.Uk/l/hi/world/africa/2745421.stm.

Platvoet, J., and K. van der Toorn. 1995. "Ritual Responses to Plurality and Pluralism." In *Pluralism and Identity: Studies in Ritual Behavior,* edited by J. Platvoet and K. van der Toorn. Leiden: E. J. Brill.

Rosberg, C. G., and J. Nottingham. 1966. *The Myth of Mau Mau Nationalism in Kenya.* Nairobi: East Africa Educational Publishers.

Sandgren, P. 1976. "The Kikuyu, Christianity and the African Inland Mission." Unpublished Ph.D. thesis, University of Wisconsin.

Schmidt, R. 1988. *Exploring Religion.* Belmont, CA: Wadsworth Publishing Company.

Smith, D. E. 1974. *Religion, Politics and Social Change in the Third World.* London: The Free Press.

Specht, J. 2000. "Rebels & Soldiers: Religion and Healing in Contexts of Armed Conflicts in Africa." Geneva: International Labour Organization.

Wachira, J. M. 2001. "The Upsurgence of the Gikuyu Traditional Religion: A Case Study on the Mungiki Movement." Unpublished paper, Tangaza College of The Catholic University of Eastern Africa, Nairobi.

Wamue, G. N. 2001. "Revisiting Our Indigenous Shrines through Mungiki." *African Affairs* 100:452–67.

Wanjohi, G. J. 1997. *The Wisdom and Philosophy of the Gikuyu Proverbs.* Nairobi: Paulines Publications Africa.

Waruhiu, S. N. 1994. *From Autocracy to Democracy in Kenya: Past Systems of Government and Reforms for the Future.* Nairobi: Author.

Welbourn, F. B. 1965. *East African Christian.* London: Oxford University Press.

CHAPTER 4

Magic as Identity Maker

Conflict and Militia Formation in Eastern Congo

Koen Vlassenroot

When naked Mayi-Mayi fighters temporarily took control of the border post between Goma (eastern Congo) and Gisenyi (northern Rwanda) in 1997, it was the first time they revealed themselves to the outside world. For most observers the images of these fighters were bitter proof that the eastern parts of Congo were descending further into anarchic violence, day by day bringing the region closer to Joseph Conrad's "heart of darkness." It was as if many wanted this remote area to be exactly this way: a representation of the darker side of humanity or another civilization with no links at all to the civilized West. In line with Robert Kaplan, it was argued that the "blind rage" of these Mayi-Mayi fighters had nothing to do with politics, labeling their actions instead as massive criminal behavior.[1] The naked Mayi-Mayi fighters were seen as an expression of a backlash or re-primitivization of African society, pushed into their rebellion by demographic pressure and ecological decline. This approach served a clear interest: it supported the widespread calls for international disengagement and at the same time legitimized the declining interest in African crises.[2]

One of the elements that attracted particular attention from Western observers was the use of magico-religious elements by these Congolese fighters. The Mayi-Mayi militias' practice of sprinkling water, which was supposed to render these fighters invulnerable, and uttering the "water cry" when entering a village (to protect villagers from the enemy), lent them a distinctly exotic cast. Reinforcing the image of an atavistic movement rooted in traditional beliefs, these elements suggested a historical path of irrational resistance based on magic and rituals. Indeed, the Mayi-Mayi rituals echoed the beliefs and traditional magic of the Simba rebels that operated in the eastern parts of Congo in the 1960s. Similar practices could be traced during the Maji-Maji uprising between 1906 and 1909 against the German occupation of the western parts of Tanganyika[3] or during the anti-colonial uprising of "Mad Mollah" Mohamed Abdille in British Somaliland in the 1920s.

Rather than interpreting the Mayi-Mayi's religious practices as evidence of a re-traditionalization of Congolese society,[4] this essay argues that, during the first years of their appearance, ritual and magic were deployed in response to highly contemporary transformations. The spiritual rituals functioned as a token of membership and forged a social bond between the different individuals involved, allowing militia groups to mobilize youngsters.[5] Because these rituals were based on existing belief systems, the Mayi-Mayi militias offered these youngsters not only an escape from poverty but, even more important, a recognizable yet alternative model of identification in an environment of war that has produced a deep sense of disorientation. Becoming a militia fighter and relying on rituals and beliefs that find their origin in local tradition was, therefore, not only an attractive alternative to economic despair, but also an effort to make sense of shifting social realities.

The rebellion of the Mayi-Mayi expressed a major transformation taking place within eastern Congolese society. Thirty years of patrimonial rule by President Mobutu had led to a deep economic crisis, destruction of the educational system, and social exclusion. In eastern Congo, the frustration caused by this exclusion was shared by many young Congolese, who were the main victims of Mobutu's destructive rule. Beginning in the early 1990s, these youngsters showed a growing willingness to act against what they perceived as the roots of their marginalized position. Banned from any meaningful political, economic, or social participation, these young Congolese were easily attracted by the efforts of local strongmen to institute armed groups for the defense of local communities or private interests. Accordingly, they joined the ranks of militias that presented themselves as guards protecting local communities but at the same time hoped to obtain some semblance of social integration and access to economic benefits. The presence of Rwandan troops on Congolese soil since 1996 provided these militias fresh legitimacy and popular support.

The impact of these militias on local society, however, should not be underestimated. Initially, local customary chiefs considered the Mayi-Mayi an instrument to protect their position of control over land allocations. Recurring conflict has reshaped these militias from traditional brigands into war profiteers who thrive in a context of disorder. Even if the Mayi-Mayi militias have never turned their actions directly against customary chiefs, their presence and actions have had the effect of weakening the powers of traditional authorities. Another consequence of the rising influence of militias is that the state has lost its monopoly on violence, as violence became a legitimate strategy of not only collective actors but also of individuals. Because the young combatant has been able to reposition himself in local society as a powerful actor in the modern context, he has become a strong model in the imaginary of other youth.

All of this raises questions as to the meaning of violence in present eastern Congolese society and the impact of the Mayi-Mayi militias on the local social order. Therefore, this essay considers in some detail the process of militia formation in the Kivu provinces. Rather than regarding the Mayi-Mayi as a purely religious movement, the resurgence of these militias only makes sense within the dynamic of social exclusion that enabled it. These armed groups did not direct their struggle at achieving mystical or transcendental goals, but aimed at protecting their own communities or the interests of their sponsors while offering new modes of integration to their members. The first section of this essay outlines the background of militia formation in the Kivu provinces by investigating the historical dynamics of resistance. The second section illustrates the dynamic of militia formation since the early 1990s and interprets these forms of violence as reactions against growing economic and social marginalization. The final section deals with the personal motivations of the Mayi-Mayi combatants, the uses and meanings of magic and ritual, and the impact of the choice of violence on the wider social environment.

LOCAL HISTORY OF CONFLICT AND REBELLION

The eastern parts of the Democratic Republic of the Congo (DRC) have long been a breeding ground for the formation of resistance movements that have drawn on local culture and tradition to motivate their resistance and have made use of magico-religious rituals to explain their actions.[6] Since colonial times, a number of movements have arisen to resist foreign occupation. A brief historical account of this local resistance helps to explain the genesis and proliferation of militias since the early 1990s.

One of the first famous examples of rebellion against the colonial administration and the expropriation of land by its members was the Binji-Binji revolt of the Bashi, the dominant ethnic community in the Bukavu region. The revolt started in 1931, near Nduba, when Ngwasi Nyagaza, a local healer and former plantation laborer, suddenly began speaking the language of Lyangombe, a sixteenth-century magician whose religiously inspired ideology centered on radical ideas of equality and the elimination of social cleavages. The Bashi maintained a strong belief in *bazimu*, or the spiritual transformation of a man after his death, and believed that the spirit of Lyangombe could, after his death, possess people through initiation rites (*kubandwa*).[7] Once possessed by the spirit of Lyangombe, Ngwasi Nyagaza was called Binji-Binji. His prophecies of food sent from heaven and great herds of cattle that would be distributed freely among the people thrilled the Bashi community. Binji-Binji ordered the Bashi to leave the plantations and told them of a great vision he had that all whites would soon be driven out of Bushi (the land of the Bashi), ending forced labor and returning the people's land to them. All this was more than enough to alarm the plantation owners, missionaries, and the colonial administration. The army was sent in, and the leaders were given jail sentences.

On the one hand, the Binji-Binji revolt must be considered a largely ethnic upheaval, reflecting a parochial view of the world, with the liberation of the Bushi region as the ultimate purpose. But its heavy reliance on traditional rites, initiations, prophetic leadership, and the cult of invulnerability also lent the movement a distinctly religious ethos. While they concentrated on the achievement of seemingly limited and localized goals, such as land and the promise of cows, their strategy was to seek unarmed victory through moral and spiritual superiority. In their minds, their political and economic objectives were inseparable from their religious tactics.

During World War II, mainly due to the heavy burdens of colonial rule, the spirit of resistance rose again in the Kivu, leading to the outbreak of the Kitawala rebellion in Masisi-Lubutu (northern Kivu).[8] The first historical record of a Kitawala movement in Congo dates back to the 1920s. Originally linked to the Pennsylvanian Watch Tower movement, its first African roots were in Rhodesia in 1897, from which it spread to Tanganyika and finally to Congo. From its onset and until its shift to a purely religious movement during the 1950s, the Kitawala could be seen as a religious revolutionary movement that aimed mainly at limiting the power of the colonial powers— violently if need be. Kitawala ideology revolved around three central premises: first, that Africans and Europeans were equal; second, that colonial rule and exploitation of local resources should end; and third, that until "God's rule" was installed, the people should refuse to follow the dictates and education of the colonial administration. From Katanga, the Kitawala rebellion spread farther north and east. In 1937, it arrived in Kivu (Lubutu), where its leaders helped mobilize the miners working at the colonial campsites. Kitawala flourished throughout the region until, in 1944, Bushiri took the lead of a local rebellion against colonialist abuses at the local rubber plantations. Under the leadership of this new prophet, all activity at the plantations stopped and three Europeans were tortured. Once again, repression and a total ban of the Kitawala by the colonial administration were the answers to rebellion.

The next, and most serious, expression of resistance developed during the 1960s, and came to be known in eastern Congo as the Simba rebellion. While outsiders frequently portrayed the conflict as a localized expression of global tensions, the players at the grassroots level had their own rationales and agenda.[9] Although national and international issues were largely a guise for local arguments over land and cattle, the spread of violence during this rebellion was considerable. Youngsters who joined the struggle for personal gain, called *la jeunesse,* acted under no command structure and were feared everywhere for what was perceived as their random brutality. The internationalization and privatization of the conflict also exacerbated violence, as Western, Soviet, and Chinese intelligence services all operated in the region and sent in arms, Belgian troops and advisors intervened, and mercenaries were hired from around the globe. In fact, one gets the impression that two battles were being simultaneously fought: one on the international chessboard concerning the future of the country, and the other involving local issues.

The Simba rebellion was described by one scholar as a "magic- and religion-accompanied revolutionary attempt to rectify certain of the 'neo-colonialist' conditions by which large segments of the population felt oppressed four years after Independence, and to realize the promised goals that Independence was supposed to, but failed to bring."[10] Although independence was enthusiastically welcomed initially, dissatisfaction vis-à-vis this new political context and the new state soon ran high. Many Congolese were supporters of independence "not because they knew where they wanted to go, but because they did not like where they had been."[11] None of their expectations were met, and instead of going through a honeymoon period, people went through an extremely violent nightmare. Political opportunism overshadowed work for the common good among many political leaders, and violent rebellion became a means of achieving power in the transitional state.

Infighting among different ethnic groups (particularly between the Bafulero and Babembe, the core groups within the rebellion) and divided interests began to fracture the rebellion. This internal degeneration made it difficult to control the rank and file and to connect with rural populations, which had been the backbone of the movement's support. What began as a military campaign to liberate the country turned into a curse on the population, as in many cases the rebellion offered a convenient excuse for those who wanted to settle scores or simply loot the local populace. A year after the rebellion started, the rural population no longer knew whom it had to fear the most.

One crucial element needs further attention: the vital role played by magical and religious beliefs and practices. The underlying rationale of the rebellion was largely based on elements of local belief systems, which were often portrayed erroneously as constituting a rejection of the existing political order and a return to indigenous tradition. Rather, historically and culturally entrenched symbolic elements were appropriated and deployed to change the existing social order. In this sense, the religious rituals mobilized by the Simba had the aim of rallying local youngsters and offering new ways to transform the world. These rituals also served to motivate the youngsters in combat and to strengthen their inner commitment to the cause. Traditional rituals and elements of local war magic were rigorously reproduced by the Simba. Mostly women from Kindu and Kisangani were believed to possess special powers and became magico-religious specialists, or *monganga*. Their role was to produce the *dawa,* or magico-religious powers designed to confer invulnerability, strength, protection, and victory and to ensure the immunity of the rebels against bullets.[12] The initiation required the sprinkling of lustral water followed by scarification of the forehead and the insertion of special powders in a scratch made by the *monganga*. The *dawa* not only protected the warriors themselves and produced internal cohesion but was believed to also persuade their enemies, as well as the local population, of the Simba's immunity from bullets. When a Simba warrior was injured or killed, this was attributed to the loss of powers of invulnerability because of the impurity of the warrior, usually explained by a failure to follow prescribed norms and taboos.

Even though traditional elements had a strong influence on the behavior and social organization of the rebel movement, during the rebellion the traditional culture underwent a deep shock. For the Simba rebel movement, magico-religious elements were of crucial importance as these not only helped to explain to the outside world what they were fighting for but also served a number of objectives during battle. From the use of magico-religious elements, however, it cannot be concluded that this rebel movement was fighting for the protection of the local, traditional order. Rather, it was campaigning against the impact of decolonization and nation-building on local power structures. By employing a number of local traditional values and symbolic

elements the rebels sought an alternative to the newly introduced political order. Even if there was a genuine commitment to traditional
forms, which were accommodated to the realities of modernity, the
use of traditional rituals was largely outside customary power structures. Their desire was to create a new socio-political order, without
subverting the power of the traditional chiefs yet at the same time
without integrating these authorities into their structures.

New Dynamics of Militia Formation

Since the early 1990s, eastern Congo has faced resistance of a new
type. Even though there is some continuity with the historical examples we just considered (one element suggesting this continuity is
the use of magico-religious rituals that are similar to those mobilized
by the Simba), the former cases could be explained as attempts to prevent the subsumption of local society by alien global structures. By
contrast, recent militia members reacted against their position of exclusion and demanded right of entry into the international system.
This did not prevent most militia members from following a very
local agenda. Most of these militias were directly related to a particular ethnic background and were struggling for the improvement of the
position of their own ethnic community. Composed mainly of school
dropouts and socially excluded youth, these armed groups were opportunities to escape from further alienation. Because the dynamic of
militia formation in eastern Congo during the 1990s was part of a social process that—in the rejection of the current institutional order—
was creating a rationality of its own, it was a very flexible phenomenon
with shifting goals and objectives. Several references were made by
these militias to local belief systems, mainly as part of a larger process
of self-definition of its members, in which several local cultural elements (including religious rituals) were fused with global referents in
order to give meaning to the changing socioeconomic environment in
which they had to survive.

The existence of these rural militias is the result of a crisis of the
existing patrimonial order combined with a number of regional dynamics of conflict. For many of its members, these militias were in the

first place an alternative to desolation: their ethnic ideology and violence could be interpreted as a reaction to the effects of a long process of social deterioration and political destruction. Thirty years of Mobutism not only led to the destruction of the Zairean state and the collapse of the national economy, it also pushed large parts of the Zairean society into a position of total impoverishment. One strategy to deal with the effects of marginalization was to develop an alternative system of economic development that completely escaped state control. Another strategy was armed resistance. As Mobutu's economic resources were dwindling, his rule was leading to increasing political and military fragmentation and a loss of political control to the advantage of alternative, local centers of authority that included traditional authorities and business elites. These local centers, which mainly developed in the border regions, could secure their control over local resources through clandestine trade networks. As part of their strategies of dominance, they also increasingly challenged the state's monopoly on the (legitimate) use of violence, which explains why, in the early 1990s, the eastern Zairean border regions provided a continuous breeding ground for militias and nonstate armed groups to proliferate in the absence of a rigid single (state) framework of protection. These groups, which would later be labeled "Mayi-Mayi," were instituted spontaneously by rural youngsters opposed to Mobutu's political system and had very limited impact on the regional power game. With the further collapse of the Zairean state and intensified political and economic competition, these youth became attractive targets for local strongmen in their search for political and economic power. This explains why the term *Mayi-Mayi* came to refer to a variety of groups, including both well-defined militias with clear political agendas and looser gangs of "streetlords"[13] using the name *Mayi-Mayi* to prey on the rural population.

The first militias to erupt were the Kasindien and the Ngilima.[14] The Ngilima were based in the northern areas of Beni and Lubero, while the Kasindien were a border militia, with their headquarters located on the slopes of the Ruwenzori Mountains. While their origins were connected to attempts of President Mobutu to destabilize Uganda (the area of operation of these militias was the Zairean-

Ugandan border region of the Ruwenzori Mountains), the Ngilima and the Kasindien soon started operating for their own cause and even began opposing the Mobutu regime. A few years later, a new generation of rural fighters started operating in several parts of northern Kivu.[15] Local politicians and traditional authorities played a crucial role in the recruitment and arming of these fighters, which explains why their main target shifted from the established Mobutu administration to the local Banyarwanda communities (who have their roots in neighboring Rwanda and are composed of Hutu and Tutsi populations). After 1990, and the official start of the democratization process, a coalition of autochthonous politicians and traditional authorities, afraid they would lose political power if these Banyarwanda were to be registered as Zairean nationals and participate in elections, started a campaign to exclude the Banyarwanda from political participation. A first wave of interethnic violence erupted in March 1993, when militia members killed several people at a local market and autochthonous militias attacked Banyarwanda in the Masisi District (northern Kivu). At the time, *Mayi-Mayi/Bangilama* came into currency as a loose term to describe any local armed youth group, suggesting, somewhat prematurely, the unification of all these local groupings.

The fragile settlement between the different communities in northern Kivu, eventually forged at the end of 1993, lasted until the arrival of more than one million Hutu refugees from Rwanda and the settling of the former Rwandan Army elements and Interahamwe in the different camps in eastern Zaire. The presence of the Rwandan refugees had some major effects on the local security situation. Given the particular position of the Zairean state, the influx in 1994 of more than one million refugees who were armed and resourced from the outside created the opportunity for future conflict, putting the Rwandan Hutu-Tutsi antagonism at the heart of local struggle. Local antagonism between autochthonous and Banyarwanda communities was now altered by a new coalition of local Hutu-Banyarwanda, the refugee leadership, and local Mayi-Mayi militias that aimed at tracking down the Zairean Tutsi-Banyarwanda populations.

The start of the Allied Democratic Forces for the Liberation of Congo/Zaire (ADFL) rebellion in October 1996 was the next turning point in the history of the Mayi-Mayi. In communities previously untouched by militia formation, rural armed groups started to mushroom. Particularly in southern Kivu, newly formed local militias became important components of the local political and military balance of power. After some initial hesitation, these armed groups joined the ADFL campaign against Mobutu, but turned against this rebel movement when the Tutsi dominance became apparent.

After the start of the Rally for Congolese Democracy (RCD) rebellion in August 1998, the local political and military landscape once again underwent a total reshuffling. The changing political environment also had a strong impact on the Mayi-Mayi militias, because the new context of war and state implosion linked grassroots realities directly to regional political dynamics, via informal militarized networks. The new conflict gave the Mayi-Mayi movement a fresh legitimacy in its struggle against Rwandan and Tutsi dominance. The state of disorder also created the necessary conditions for the formation of new militias and for the spread of informal militarized social and economic networks. As the local balance of power and the existing alliances drastically changed, Mayi-Mayi leaderships were forced to assume new political and military positions. Their resistance against what was locally percieved as a foreign occupation (the RCD rebels were backed by the Rwandan and Ugandan regimes) resulted in growing popular support and gave them new symbolic backing. The attempts of some Mayi-Mayi leaders to unify the different ethnically embedded armed groups and support from the Congolese regime led to a serious increase in military capacity and control over large parts of eastern Congo's hinterland. What initially could be considered bottom-up violence in response to social and economic marginalization eventually took on the appearance of a rural-based movement for civil defense. The downside of this process, however, was that these armed groups became attractive resources for local strongmen in their search to consolidate their control over informal trading networks. At the same time, the growing importance of armed youngsters led to a further militarization of local society, as the image of a strong fighter mobilized an increasing number of young armed men into profit-seeking through violence.

Understanding the Mayi-Mayi

Even if the Congolese conflict encouraged the formation of armed groups, the proliferation of the Mayi-Mayi militias in eastern DRC should be understood in the first place as a reaction of rural young-sters against the harsh effects of a long process of social deterioration and political marginalization. Becoming members of a militia and re-sorting to violence in a context of intensified conflict could be ex-plained as part of a strategy to reject the existing socio-political order and to improve their social and economic position. As Luca Jourdan has pointed out, "young combatants use violence to their own profit, in order to renegotiate and improve their social status. In this sense, violent practices have a political value because they manifest a will to undermine the social order, promoting at the same time new forms of organization."[16] Becoming a member of a militia not only improved the combatants' social position, it also rewarded them with a new identity, defined by their position as fighters. Mayi-Mayi militias re-lied on a well-defined set of values and beliefs, which not only strengthened the internal cohesion of the movement and protected the militia members in battle, but also defined the fighters' new iden-tity. After being initiated, fighters found themselves in a totally new environment, characterized by a different order and authority struc-ture than the society in which they originated. Their recourse to magico-religious elements and the introduction of new codes of social conduct were sources of reassurance, yet they also produced internal cohesion within the armed band. In the end, these values and codes of conduct strengthened existing social boundaries, and gave new meaning to notions such as egalitarianism and social solidarity.

In the chaotic and disorderly context of eastern Congo, however, militia formation not only offered attractive alternatives to local youngsters but also further divided local society, as it produced vi-olence and disorder. During the Congolese war, a strategy of violence clearly served a number of functions. Besides offering a new social position, violence also gave easy access to economic resources. Given the very harsh living conditions of being a farmer or a miner, being a combatant was the best possible position one could reach. In this sense, "the goal of violence seems to be . . . self-affirmation and the affirmation of one's right to be recognized as a social subject."[17] Mayi-Mayi militias, therefore, served a double function: they offered a new identity and social position while giving meaning to the outside world, and they provided the necessary means by which to improve one's economic position. In the remainder of this essay, we explore these two elements, which are crucial to a better understaning of the dynamic of militia formation in eastern DRC. I analyze the motivations and objectives of the Mayi-Mayi in further detail, then examine the use and meaning of magico-religious elements within the movement, and finally offer some insights on the use and impact of violence in the wider social environment.

Guided by Ideology, or Driven by Greed?

Marginalization is only part of the explanation for militia formation in eastern DRC. Since the start of the first Congolese war in 1996, the dynamics of militia formation was given new fodder. Since then, most militia fighters have put their struggle against the foreign occupation of Congo at the center of their discourse. The specific content of this discourse strongly varied from group to group, while largely depending on the origins and the social setting of the specific militia. As mentioned earlier, the original objective of the first generation of Mayi-Mayi groups (those created before October 1996) was to protect their customary lands from the growing influence of the Banyarwanda communities. After 1996, however, the objectives of these groups shifted to a struggle against the presence of the ADFL—and RCD—rebel groups and its Rwandan supporters on Congolese territory. These forces were blamed for the suffering of the local population; the overall protection of their communities came to be the undisputed binding element between all the armed groups. The Mudundu 40, which operated around Bukavu, stressed that it wanted to "defend the Bushi territory against outside aggression, to protect the customary heritage, to protect the personal property and land of the inhabitants of the Bushi, to act against human rights abuses, to restore peace in the region and to reconcile the people of the Great Lakes Region."[18] Other groups attached a more radical aim to their actions. For instance, some Bembe and Bafulero in southern Kivu not only stressed that the Rwandan forces had to leave the country immediately, but also sought to expel the Banyamulenge population (Congolese Tutsi of Rwandan origin), which had become subject to repeated attack.

Ideology, however, was not always the only guiding motive on the ground. In some cases, local disputes were linked to regional politics and short-term economic objectives became the main guiding force. A number of Mayi-Mayi militias, under a banner of resistance against foreign occupation, were not fighting for the protection of the Congolese territory but primarily aimed at defending their own ethnic community. The slogan of the Mayi-Mayi around Fizi (southern Kivu) was *ebalo ese, ese ebalo* ("our land, our heritage"). Even if the security concerns of their own community was a driving force of many groups, economic interests were one of the main reasons for the existence of certain other groups. In Luindji (southern Kivu) in late 1996, local youngsters were supported by some members of the Bembe community in setting up a militia group in what seemed to be an attempt to get access to local mining sites or to land that was controlled by Banyamulenge pastorals, rather than to combat the Rwandan forces.[19] The same Bembe leaders tried to unify several local militias around Mwenga and Kamituga in what was locally believed to be an effort of the Bembe to extend their control over non-Bembe parts of the region. While some militia leaders aimed at gaining control over the local exploitation of natural resources, for others the only raison d'être seemed to be looting and pillaging. In the Beni-Butembo region, several armed groups operating under the banner of Mayi-Mayi were mobilized by local economic actors to protect their businesses or came to be directly involved in the exploitation and trading of natural resources.

In other words, two different forces led to the formation of local militias. Although resistance against foreign occupation was the common denominator for most of these armed groups, in reality it was difficult to distinguish patriotic militia leaders from warlord-type actors.[20] Of course, the dynamic feature of local militia formation goes a long way in explaining the confusion. Yet, as demonstrated, the different social settings of these militias offer a more valuable explanation for the strong dissimilarity in objectives and motivations, as well as for their shifting nature.

The Use of Rituals

One element that attracted particular attention from outside observers was the use of magico-religious rituals by militia fighters before going to battle. These rituals and symbols were used by these combatants as part of a larger process of self-definition, a process that fused global and local cultural referents in order to give meaning to the rapidly changing outside world. These rituals clearly symbolized that the fighter's social environment no longer corresponded with his former social background and that his enrollment in the militia provided him with a new social identity. Through the use of violence and the mobilization of hybrid religious rituals, Mayi-Mayi fighters tried to renegotiate their status and to gain within society a social space from which they were normally excluded because of their young age. In the situation of social and economic collapse that characterized the eastern Congo, the new generations experienced a deep sense of disorientation: on the one hand, the traditional culture and the traditional forms of social organization were no longer able to give sense to and to organize reality; on the other hand, the idea of modernization and the theology of development completely failed, producing only disillusion and frustration. In this context of widespread uncertainty, many youngsters tried to redefine their identity, and violence guided by rituals and symbols provide an alternative model of identification as well as an opportunity to affirm their own subjectivity or self-assertion.

In many regards, the rituals of the Mayi-Mayi resistance reproduced the beliefs and traditional magic of the Simba rebels of the 1960s. The belief systems and use of magico-religious elements had a clear purpose in the dynamics of militia formation in eastern Congo. The spiritual dimensions of the movement served a number of important functions: providing the militia members with a new social identity; delimiting boundaries between the in-group and the wider social environment; increasing the internal cohesion of the militia; giving the warriors a sense of divine protection; and confusing the enemy by creating an image of invincibility and protection by supernatural powers. As a Mayi-Mayi member in Uvira stated, "We are a little superstitious. We believe in the forces of plants and vegetation. But we could also easily demonstrate that a banana tree leaf that is treated with ritual water can resist a bullet or grenade. For a combatant, the effect is similar, except when he has not respected our prescriptions and code of conduct."[21]

After being initiated, Mayi-Mayi fighters lived in a totally new environment, characterized by a different order and authority structure than the society in which they originated. For these fighters, the concept of ritual purity was of particular importance because it offered them protection when fighting, which assured them victory over their enemies. The first step to purity was the initiation through a ritual celebration, which bestowed specific and powerful forces on the newly recruited (male) members. The initiation rituals included the insertion in an incision above the right hand of a medicine developed by the militia doctor and the sprinkling of the new recruit with divine water.[22] The preservation of ritual purity and its attendant powers was dependent on the warrior's observance of certain norms and taboos. New codes of social conduct were created, for which the traditional social organization was the main point of reference, even though this type of organization was transformed to comport with their own perceptions of the outside world. Some norms were part of most local traditions, while other prescriptions only existed in particular local traditions or were newly created. It seems that these prescriptions were developed in Mayi-Mayi groups that were related to ethnic communities with a strong magico-religious tradition and that were held together through initiation rituals (such as the Batembo and the Bembe) or a tradition of hunting (such as the Hunde in Masisi).

Some behavioral proscriptions defined the nature of contact with the outside world, including relationships with women: taboos against hugging people when meeting them; taboos against directly giving something to someone (the object first has to be put on the ground); abstention from eating food prepared by women and from sexual relations with women; and avoiding crossing the path of women. Other proscriptions aimed at strengthening unity within the movement: abstention from eating particular foods (such as vegetables); the obligation of sprinkling holy water over food before eating it; and abstention from shifting plates on the table (these need to be lifted). The last group of prescriptions was directly related to military activities, including abstention from any military action against the population and the obligation to sprinkle the local villages with water to temporarily protect the population. When these prescriptions were transgressed, the rituals were void and the fighter lost his protection. As for the Simba rebels, death of a Mayi-Mayi fighter during combat was explained by the loss of his ritual purity. In no instances were the rituals questioned.[23]

In the end, the rituals also symbolized the militia fighter's passage to a social environment that no longer corresponded with his former social background. Enrollment in the militia provided him with a new social identity that enabled him to cope with the effects of the use of violence. The impact of these new social identities should not be underestimated, as the identity of young combatant became a strong model in the youth imaginary. In essence, the strategies developed by local youngsters during the Congolese war all expressed the desire to reverse the existing social structures and to impose their own rules. This explains why the daily experience of the young combatant was embodied: "tattoos made by Mayi-Mayi, amulets around ankles and wrists, extravagant uniforms, hats from cowboy style to bandana, sun glasses and body postures that recall Hollywood action movies. A list that could be very long and that cannot leave out the Kalashnikov—the rebels' gun par excellence which, because of its continual presence and ostentation, seems almost to represent a prosthesis of the combatants' bodies."[24]

Violence in Its Social Context

What impact have these militias had on the wider social environment in eastern Congo?[25] Most militias tended to emerge from, and to rely on, ethnic differentiation. In resisting state collapse and armed foreign interventions, rural and urban youth, however, have tended to combine older traditions with newer influences, reflecting patterns of mobility in their interpretation of customary and national defense. Rather than mobilizing around traditional emanations of authority, the crisis in the social fabric meant a shift of power toward the combatants themselves and their use of violence. For several years, in some remote areas the armed groups have been the only representatives of any authority structure, even if this structure was based on violence, and several Mayi-Mayi leaders have become the true leaders of the regions under their control. This shift of control was not limited to the leadership of communities but also affected lower levels of authority.

With the war in the DRC, the monopoly on violence has definitively shifted from the state to individuals and armed nonstate groups. Contrary to the prewar situation, the Mobutist pact between citizens and the state has thus been broken. As a result, the *débrouillardise,* or the principle of fending for oneself, has gradually lost its character of social pact to finally become the unconditioned rule of individual behavior. Within this context, violence has become the most important instrument for affirming personal interests and the interests of one's community. The Congolese peace process, which started in 1999 and concluded with an inclusive peace agreement in 2003, sent out a message in this respect that has not been misunderstood. The troubled course of the Lusaka (1999) and Sun City (2003) peace agreements demonstrated that violent behavior provides a profitable formula: leaders and rebel movements relying on the use of violence have consistently been rewarded and gratified through the offering of political posts. The message sent out to noncombatants is that violence works in Congo. In eastern DRC, this offers part of the explanation for the continued military activity of armed groups that were refused access to the benefits of the transition process. Several regions are still faced with armed groups that continue to roam the countryside and obstruct the mobility of the rural population.

The real danger of this tendency is that in the absence of a social contract, this violent behavior also risks becoming the unconditional rule of individuals, while in a situation of enduring poverty and exploitation, everyone ultimately becomes an opportunist. Proof of this tendency is the impact of the Goma peace process, which in early

2008 aimed at finally resolving deep-rooted causes of conflict in the Kivu provinces. Rather than paving the way toward sustainable peace, this process has caused the revival of demobilized armed militias and has engendered new processes of mobilization.

CONCLUSION

Contrary to most observers, I have tried to understand the Mayi-Mayi militias in relation to local dynamics instead of as a local reaction against the presence of foreign troops. Categorizing these militias in terms of their own self-description would be as misleading as condemning the naked militia fighters at the border gate in Goma as a manifestation of social deviance, encouraged by their Rwandan or Tutsi enemies. Rather than defining the Mayi-Mayi fighters as a resistance movement driven by nationalistic ideals, I have tried to present their rebellion as a reaction to marginalization and exclusion and as an alternative to despair. Even though many youngsters have been attracted to the anti-Rwandan discourse of their leaders, reference to this discourse helped to mobilize young recruits and gave it its necessary ideological underpinning. At different moments some Mayi-Mayi leaders made reference to traditional elements as a source of their behavior. On the one hand, a number of recent Mayi-Mayi militias were based on localized historical dynamics and have to be understood as a continuation of existing traditions of rural resistance. As the historical analysis of these traditions demonstrates, reference to elements of traditional belief systems was a crucial part of these groups' existence, even if these elements have been reshaped by these militias. On the other hand, other more recently created Mayi-Mayi groups also have relied on these elements, partly because it served the clear purpose of guaranteeing the internal cohesion of the militia and of mobilizing and motivating its combatants. In this last group of militias, reference to traditional belief systems diminished after these groups had become better militarily organized and came to be integrated into larger military structures.

The large proliferation of rural militias during the Congolese conflict has had a considerable impact on local social environment. Not only the Mayi-Mayi groups but also other armed groups in Ituri, Maniema, and Katanga triggered a shift in authority to the advantage of those in charge of armed groupings and has provoked a fierce competition between a new generation of militia leaders and local traditional authorities. This is not a new phenomenon. It was already one of the guiding forces of some militia members in the 1960s. Recently, however, some Mayi-Mayi leaders replaced the traditional authorities, becoming the true leaders of the regions under their control. The conscious denigration of these representations of authority often carried an element of power inversion to the advantage of systems of private protection, in which the perpetrators of violence took over the symbols of local authority. The power of these traditional authorities was eroded even further by efforts of militia leaderships to consolidate their power position within those communities that they were protecting. Alliances with outside supporters aimed at strengthening their control over local economic transactions and increasing their local independency eventually further reduced the need to remain socially embedded.

This explains why Mayi-Mayi militias eventually shifted from being protection movements to being predatory forces. While in origin, initiation rituals transformed young recruits into guards protecting their community (yet at the same time cut the existing links with their former social environment) the local "protection force" evolved into actors that, even when claiming to defend collective interests, became a burden to the population that it wanted to defend. Even if the official discourse remained one of ethnic protection, the taxation of economic and social transactions (which were explained as *efforts de guerre* and therefore in origin met hardly any resistance of the local population), as well as the alternative systems introduced by the rebels to administer their territories of control or to deal with impunity and restore justice, moved toward mechanisms of extortion and repression.

In other words, even if marginalization and exclusion are the main causes for the existence of and enrollment into militias, the bitter end result is that these militias have helped to reinforce the view that violence is a legitimate strategy of defense or of bringing about change, as well as of constructing identity and of improving one's social position. The processes of demobilization and reintegration as part of the peace process might therefore turn into arduous efforts, as their success depends on the ability to break the cycle of violence that has become part of the daily life of so many Congolese militia fighters.

NOTES

Any attempt to understand movements such as the Mayi-Mayi should include close contact with its members, either by interviewing them or accompanying them during their operations. In the context of conflict, both research strategies are severely limited. Some Mayi-Mayi groups are extremely difficult to approach, while identifying true members of other groups sometimes requires fieldwork skills, personal relations, and an understanding of the security risks this entails. Therefore, this presentation and analysis of the Mayi-Mayi militias is mainly based on interviews with local observers, contacts, or relatives of militia members and, where they could be identified, local Mayi-Mayi members. A second difficulty is in explaining movements and behaviors that from different external viewpoints are dismissed as parochial barbarism. Rationalizing what is generally believed to be irrational creates a perception that the researcher is justifying rather than explaining the research subject. Finally, because of the extreme heterogeneity and the many subgroups that exist today, it is impossible to present the different Mayi-Mayi militias as one movement of the result of the same dynamics.

    1. R. Kaplan, "The Coming Anarchy: How Scarcity, Crime, Overpopulation, Tribalism, and Disease Are Rapidly Destroying the Social Fabric of Our Planet," *The Atlantic Monthly*, February 1994.

    2. M. Duffield, *Global Governance and the New Wars: The Merging of Development and Security* (London: Zed Books, 2001).

    3. For an account of the Maji-Maji, see T. Sunseri, "Statist Narratives and Maji Maji Ellipses," *International Journal of African Historical Studies* 33, no. 3 (2000): 567–84.

    4. See Patrick Chabal and Jean-Pascal Daloz, *Africa Works: The Political Instrumentalization of Disorder* (Bloomington, IN: International African Institute in association with James Currey and Indiana University Press, 1999).

    5. In this sense, the Mayi-Mayi militias are reminiscent of Alice Lakwena's Holy Spirit movement (HSM) in northern Uganda. After initiation, the HSM fighters could change stones into exploding grenades, and bees and snakes would be transformed into allies, while the fighters themselves were protected against the bullets of the enemy. Sprinkling with holy water and

anointment with shea-butter oil were central rituals to obtain the status of "invulnerability." See H. Behrend, *Alice Lakwena and Holy Spirits: War in Northern Uganda 1985–97* (Oxford: James Currey, 1999).

6. Part of this section is based on K. Vlassenroot, "Violence et Constitution de Milices Dans L'Est Du Congo: Le Cas des Mayi-Mayi," in *L'Afrique des Grands Lacs, Annuaire 2002–2003,* ed. F. Reyntjens and S. Marysse (Paris: L'Harmattan, 2003), 115–86.

7. L. Cenyange, "L'origine de Lyangombe d'après les Bashi," in Lyangombe: Mythes et rites, UNAZA-ISP, Actes du 2ème colloque du CERUKI, 10-14 mai 1976 (Bukavu: Editions CERUKI, 1976), 129–33.

8. See J. E. Gerard, *Les fondements syncrétiques du kitawala* (Brussels: CRISP, 1969); I. Ndaywel è Nziem, *Histoire générale du Congo. De l'héritage ancien à la République Démocratique* (Brussels: CGRI, Duculot, 1998), 421–26; M. Lovens, *La révolte des Masisi-Lubutu (Congo-Belge, Janvier–Mai, 1944)* (Bruxelles: CEDAF, 1974); M. Merlier, *Le Congo, de la colonisation Belge à l'indépendance* (Paris: Maspéro, 1962).

9. Even if the rebellion led by Mulele started in western Congo, it soon spread to the east, where it is better known as the Simba rebellion. Although the Bukavu-Goma-Uvira area played no decisive role in the national power game, this region also witnessed a very turbulent period. From one point of view, the conflict between the leftist government in Stanleyville (Kisangani) and the Mobutu-led forces in the capital was an expression of a worldwide conflict, radical versus moderate nationalism, East versus West, and the like.

10. R. Fox, *The Intelligence behind the Mask: Beliefs and Development in Contemporary Congo* (Cambridge: Harvard University Press, 1970), 59.

11. G. Wada and J. C. Davies, "Riots and Rioters," in *Why Men Revolt and When,* ed. J. C. Davies (New Brunswick, NJ: Transaction Publishers, 1977), 57.

12. Fox, *The Intelligence behind the Mask.*

13. This notion was introduced by Timothy Raeymaekers. See K. Vlassenroot and T. Raeymaekers, eds., *Conflict and Social Transformation in Eastern DR Congo* (Ghent: Academia Press, 2004).

14. Some observers suggest the existence of a link between these first militia groups and the bandits who between 1986 and 1988 were active in the same region and were headed by the son of a former leader of the Simba rebellion in the 1960s, Marandura. See G. de Villiers and J.-C. Willame, "République Démocratique du Congo. Chronique politique d'un entre-deux-guerres," *Cahiers Africains,* nos. 35–36 (1998).

15. These fighters were known as Basimba (around Congo-Manday), Batiri (mainly composed of Hunde recruits from Masisi), and Katuku (originally Nyanga recruits, but also later found among the Batembo in Bunyakiri).

16. L. Jourdan, "Being at War, Being Young: Violence and Youth in North Kivu," in *Conflict and Social Transformation in Eastern DR Congo*, ed. K. Vlassenroot and T. Raeymaekers (Ghent: Academia Press, 2004), 162.

17. Ibid., 163.

18. H. Romkema, *Research Report: Democratic Republic of Congo, Eastern Region* (Uppsala: Life and Peace, 2001).

19. Personal communication, Bukavu, May 1999.

20. This phenomenon has been documented in numerous civil conflicts. See Mats Berdal and David M. Malone, eds., *Greed and Grievance: Economic Agendas in Civil Wars* (Boulder, CO: Lynne Rienner Publishers, 2000).

21. Mayi-Mayi fighter from Uvira, cited in L. Tormaquenaud, "Une guerilla de voisinage," *Libération*, May 29, 2000.

22. For these rituals, the militia has its own doctor or is dependent on the doctor of other Mayi-Mayi groups, while the incision is usually made by Bembe women from Fizi. In Bunyakiri, I was told that the traditional authorities are consulted during the ritual as well as before every battle. I also learned that the local doctor developed a product in 1997 that makes the recruit invincible for a period of about twelve years and gives him the powers to thunder down airplanes and transform wild animals into allies.

23. Personal communication from Mayi-Mayi fighters, local inhabitants, and visitors of their camps around Bunyakiri, Bukavu, May 1998 and April 1999.

24. Jourdan, "Being at War, Being Young," 163. In this sense, the parallel with life in the artisan mining centers becomes all too obvious. In these centers, the rush for gold or coltan not only has replaced the traditional safety nets related to their rural livelihoods; it also provides the youngsters involved in this activity with a new sense of identity, which is largely based on the external features of a new and modern capitalist lifestyle. This new identity visibly combines the traditional elements of male initiation with the excessive spending and luxury that is associated with urban livelihoods. The young miner or militia member has thus become a role model, a new ideal that has become the ultimate expression of individual positioning in the social hierarchy. Although still referring to their rural backgrounds, male youngsters active in the gold sector increasingly copy the lifestyle of soldiers and militia members, who in turn imitate fictional heroes like Rambo or Jean-Claude Van Damme whom they see in the local cinemas. In this sense, the strong and fortunate *orpailleur* or *garimpeiro* has gradually become a role model for these youth, who sometimes make direct references to these diamond diggers in their search for social standing. This economy of desire is mostly associated with massive drinking, the buying of masculine articles, and the "consumption" of women. At a deeper level, this fast prosperity also demonstrates

the limits to the *garimpeiro* lifestyle. In a context of daunting physical and economic insecurity, the symbols and assumptions of modernity (of which the access to dollars forms one of the essentials) often stand in sharp contrast to the miserable and isolated livelihoods of these young miners or militia members.

25. Parts of this chapter are derived from Vlassenroot and Raeymaekers, eds., *Conflict and Social Transformation in Eastern DR Congo.*

CHAPTER 5

Religion, Politics, and Gender in Zimbabwe

The Masowe Apostles and Chimurenga Religion

Isabel Mukonyora

In 2000, Zimbabwean President Robert Mugabe announced the beginning of the third chimurenga, a war of liberation aimed at reclaiming ancestral land. The first and second chimurengas, which took place from 1893 to 1896 and from 1965 to 1980, reflected the desire of Zimbabweans to take back land that had been seized by British settlers. Mugabe, whose declaration of the third chimurenga was a way of strengthening his hold on power, argued that there remained vestiges of the colonial enemy holding on to land in postcolonial Zimbabwe. Soldiers, police, veterans from the second chimurenga, and bands of youth called the "youth militia" saw themselves as carrying out a just war in which the people (re-)occupied the land held by white commercial farmers that Mugabe said rightfully belonged to them. Thousands of migrant laborers from Malawi and Mozambique, who could not use the same arguments about reclaiming ancestral land as the native Shona people, became homeless and even poorer than they had been as cheap farm laborers. Mugabe thus added violence to the corruption, drought, poverty, and AIDS that already ravaged the nation. At the end of 2010 at least two million black and white Zimbabweans lived in exile in South Africa. An additional half a million Zimbabweans were said to live in the United Kingdom at the time of the publication of this book.[1]

This essay focuses on the religious obstacles to peace-building among people ruled by a regime embracing militant ideas from earlier wars of liberation. In this country where strong adherence to Christianity combines with fidelity to ancestors, Mugabe capitalized on the combined appeal of religious ideas about Mwari as the creator of land owned by the ancestors of the nation under the ZANU/PF government. This essay shows how a political dispute over land became a religious reason for reinforcing beliefs in the third chimurenga. One of the constituencies that supported Mugabe's campaign was made up of a widespread indigenous religious sect called the Masowe (Wilderness) Apostles weChishanu (Friday). This popular church, whose leaders claimed independence from the three million followers of the prophet Johane (1914–73) spread throughout southern and central Africa,[2] was led by male preachers who embraced the martial spirit of the third chimurenga. The Masowe Apostles weChishanu combined Zimbabwean nationalism with a militant interpretation of the biblical quest for redemption. The Masowe Apostles weChishanu thus added a well known Judeo-Christian language of liberation to Mugabe's fight. The same religious militancy resulting from the eagerness to prevail also reinforced a gender hierarchy and sexist behavior. Women did not always react. When they felt too offended, they complained to the church elders, or joined other congregations of Masowe Apostles. Otherwise, as shown below, many women reacted against sexism by expressing their quest for redemption in terms of ceremonial acts of healing and a language about God's love for all his children.

Two of the most prominent Masowe weChishanu male prophets who encouraged their followers to support Mugabe were Border Gezi and Nzira. Gezi interpreted Mugabe's political promise of land distribution in light of Masowe hopes of redemption associated with traditional biblical teachings regarding the chosen people inheriting the promised land. Gezi was an active member of Mugabe's political party, the Zimbabwe African National Union and the Patriotic Front (ZANU/PF), and rallied support for the third chimurenga in his religious meetings. When he died in a car accident in 2001, Mugabe added him to a list of "heroes" buried in a special place on the outskirts of Harare. Gezi was not alone in fusing religion with national reclamation politics. Nzira, freed from prison in January 2011, where he was serving time on six charges of rape, was another popular prophet and leader of the Masowe Apostles weChishanu Church during the same period as Gezi. Nzira, who entertained ZANU/PF party officials at prayer meetings, led crowds of up to eight hundred people in generating fervor for the repossession of ancestral land in the countryside as the way to end an exile with three generations of Masowe Apostles wandering around southern and central Africa.

Nzira encouraged the members of his church to join Gezi's followers in dressing in white robes and singing praises to Mugabe at political rallies organized by ZANU/PF. Under such leadership, the religious beliefs and rituals of the Masowe Apostles WeChishanu became militantly political, nationalistic, and patriarchal.[3] The militancy was such that women were constantly under verbal attack in nine out of ten of Nzira's sermons. He frequently used the rhetoric of chimurenga not only to attack people who opposed Mugabe's regime as agents of Satan, but also turned sermons against witchcraft and sexual immorality into attacks on women. Nzira combined Masowe language of fighting for land and defeating Satan with conceptions of women as evildoers.[4] While it proved difficult to contest Nzira's misogynistic interpretation of Masowe theology, there were limits to this behavior in other groups of Masowe prayer meetings in the same city of Harare. Many other male preachers abused their roles by turning sermons into opportunities for targeting women as the leading examples of sinners in society, but nonetheless acted with greater self-control. Furthermore, while women were almost always treated as subordinate to men in sermons that only men were allowed to deliver, women were not always passive when male preachers attacked them. In many groups, up to 70 percent of the Apostles attending prayers were women and children. Women could use song and prayer to remind the male preachers that God's purpose for the community was to bring about peace, justice, and harmony among people who were equal before him; in this way men's sexist preaching gave way to more sexually egalitarian expressions of Masowe religious thought. Singing, sharing experiences of displacement, expressions of love toward children, and interpersonal counseling transformed the church into a mechanism for building harmonious relationships among all the believers. Arguably, women's actions had the potential to transform Masowe prayer meetings into schools of democracy and justice where the work of peace-building could be done.

Chimurenga Mentality in Zimbabwean Nation-Building

Two chimurenga wars preceded Mugabe's declaration of the third chimurenga in Zimbabwe at the beginning of 2000. In the first chimurenga (1893–96), Shona people reacted against the expropriation of their land by British colonists. The Shona viewed the actions of the British South Africa Company police in hoisting flags and building forts and settlements around the country as an offense to their ancestors and their high god Mwari. The uprising was fueled by spirit mediums representing ancestral figures of hereditary rulers proclaiming the voice of Mwari admonishing Africans to keep strangers out of Zimbabwe.[5] The resistance ended when white settlers arrested two spirit mediums, a woman named Nehanda and a man called Kaguvi, and sentenced both to death for encouraging Zimbabweans to resist colonial conquest. Today, portraits of Nehanda and Kaguvi grace the walls of the Houses of Parliament of Zimbabwe, and their statues can be seen in the National Archives in Harare. Shona religion thus features prominently within the anti-colonial narratives of the first chimurenga, which became a point of pride for many Zimbabweans.

The second chimurenga took place between 1965 and 1980 against an army of Rhodesians defending white supremacy after the British colonial government withdrew from the country. Anthropologist David Lan observed that guerillas saw themselves as acting in the name of the ancestors and Mwari, whom spirit mediums promoted as the ultimate proprietor of the land.[6] Throughout the second chimurenga, bands of guerillas relied on the assistance of these spirit mediums scattered throughout rural Zimbabwe. The spirit mediums warned the guerillas of the dangers posed by Rhodesian soldiers, reminded them of the need for discipline, and highlighted the religious meaning of fighting the white settlers. Like the first chimurenga, the second chimurenga was fueled by reviving indigenous beliefs in ancestral spirits and especially Mwari as the ultimate source of power. The conflict associated with the second chimurenga was valorized in both the national anthem, which refers to the "heroes' sacrifice" in dying for freedom from colonial control, and the national flag, which featured black stripes to remind Zimbabweans of their forebears who died in the liberation struggle. Mugabe took part in this second chimurenga, gaining the popularity that ultimately fueled his rise to the position of president.

At the start of the third chimurenga in 2000, Mugabe made ancestral land and the rural population all-important and, drawing from the country's national and religious heritage, felt justified in engaging in wars to simultaneously protect land rights and solidify his own power. He placed the third chimurenga in the broader context of the first two chimurengas and thus created a narrative of a long struggle for equality for Zimbabweans against land-grabbing foreigners and elites from Britain. The soldiers, war veterans, and notorious youth militia who perpetuated violence against fellow Zimbabweans believed their actions to be commensurate with protecting the interests and honoring the sacrifices of the ancestors; indeed, shedding blood in the name of the ancestors became expressive of the loyalty expected of all citizens. Mugabe's political ambitions and military campaigns were thus baptized in both civil religion and traditional religion, forging an ideology that worked powerfully on Zimbabweans. The Shona religious dimension of chimurenga created in people a sense of righteous obligation to allow Mugabe to lead this fight for land.

The people who stood to gain the most from Mugabe's policies, and the ones he expected to understand and support him most fervently, were the four-fifths of Zimbabwe's population who speak Shona and whose forefathers' homesteads were occupied when British settlers invaded the country since the first chimurenga. Even if the rural lifestyle of their ancestors lost its attraction to the majority of modern Zimbabweans, the third chimurenga was popular because it made fighting in the name of one's ancestors and hereditary rulers difficult to disapprove. When it came to Shona religion, Mwari was viewed as the creator of the land and people on it.[7] However, Mugabe's policies led to violence and threatened thousands of people with displacement, including the approximately 15 percent of Zimbabweans who speak Ndebele. These people migrated from the Zulu homeland in South Africa and settled in southwest Zimbabwe shortly before the British arrived in the 1890s. Although they were relatively new neighbors of the Shona when the British army began its conquest of the Shona, Ndebele people resented the British for defeating them in a battle for their land, and joined the Shona in the first chimurenga. They similarly participated in the second chimurenga under the leadership of Joshua Nkomo (1917–99), the Ndebele man known as the father of nationalism in Zimbabwe. Despite their contributions to the nation's liberation, the Ndebele suffered greatly within a few years of Mugabe's ascent to power. In the mid-1980s, Mugabe sent a group of Shona soldiers to the homelands of the Ndebele people to eliminate all traces of opposition to his regime, killing hundreds of innocent people in the process; even Nkomo was forced to flee the country. Mugabe's violent movement against the Ndebele was an early sign of the problems that would arise with his third chimurenga, especially as he associated anyone who opposed his political party with colonial (and thus inherently anti-Shona) interests. Other non-Shona groups marginalized by Mugabe's chimurenga included the approximately 100,000 white citizens of Zimbabwe, 23,000 Asians, some 10,000 people of mixed race, and thousands of migrant workers from neighboring Mozambique, Zambia, and Malawi.

In 1980, the majority of people expected peace and justice to prevail after the conclusion of the widely popular second chimurenga. But the third chimurenga, a reaction against continuing injustices associated with colonialism, increased divisions among the citizens of Zimbabwe along the lines of rights to ancestral land, race, class, and gender.[8] According to Mugabe, the third chimurenga was a war against white commercial farmers who occupied land that was seized from indigenous people during the colonial area. In the rural areas, Mugabe's regime used violence to seize land from some of the white farmers, arguing that indigenous people with ancestral connections to the land were the rightful owners. Hundreds of white farmers left the country, either to rebuild their lives overseas or to market themselves as professional farmers in neighboring countries such as Mozambique and Zambia, an exodus that contributed to the collapse of the economy and a skyrocketing poverty rate among Zimbabweans.

The majority of people who provided white farmers with cheap labor were not Zimbabweans by birth but children of migrants from neighboring countries. Mugabe's supporters ignored the human rights of these migrant workers by harassing them and forcing them to run away or enter refugee camps. To make matters worse, Mugabe and his regime used violence to force the poor out of urban areas. In June 2005, the Zimbabwe Human Rights Forum documented the violence caused by Operation Murambatsvina ("saying no to filth"), pointing out how soldiers destroyed the homes of thousands of poor people and forced them to flee from the outskirts of Harare. Mugabe's aim was to compel the Zimbabwean poor to live as peasant farmers in rural areas.[9]

Mugabe's third chimurenga was thus a means of realizing his dream of replacing the capitalist society created by white settlers with a socialist society built on the backs of peasant farmers. But by declaring this war a third chimurenga, Mugabe stood to gain from people who believed in the connection between Mwari's territorial power, the spirits of their ancestors, and rural homelands. Here we have an example of a political leader using religious rhetoric to mobilize the masses in a political and economic conflict. In order to counteract this phenomenon, peace-builders need to focus on transforming the direction of religious zeal from divisive violence to unifying community-building and social justice.

MASOWE RELIGIOUS LANGUAGE AND ORIGINS

Chimurenga politics resonates with the way that many of the Masowe Apostles practiced Christianity, particularly in the variant preached by Border Gezi and Nzira. A characteristic practice of the Masowe Apostles, and several other related groups, was to gather for open-air healing ceremonies or vigils (*pungwe*). These meetings lasted seven to ten hours, with male prophets and preachers proclaiming the gospel in terms of warfare against Satan, whose demonic presence Masowe Apostles generally claimed to exorcise through the power of the Holy Spirit. As the men preached, they drew on Old Testament narratives to give their listeners the impression that they were children of God lost in a biblical wilderness; they sometimes dramatized this by jumping around like men waging a war against a forceful enemy.

The rhetoric of Masowe preachers went beyond the purely spiritual realm, however. Border Gezi's recapitulation of the biblical exodus, a story that includes the promise of land and opportunities to rebuild lives, made Mugabe's policies for land distribution plausible, like the offer of a practical answer to prayers of people whose daily existence is a struggle. Furthermore, the theme of spiritual warfare against Satan was applied to the chimurenga, or fight over the actual possession of land. Even their choice of space to perform their rituals was telling: rather than assembling in the city, where the landscape was dominated by missionary churches built by European colonists, they prayed barefoot in the open air, thereby rejecting colonialism and embracing offers of land. The language of spiritual warfare also became an avenue to express hostility toward women, whose subordinate status was taken for granted by the male leadership. Meanwhile, the Masowe women, who constituted the vast majority in most worship services, directed their prayers to a quest for redemption that corresponded with their need for greater peace and equity in society.[10]

According to anthropologist Clive Dillon-Malone, Johane Masowe ("John of the Wilderness"), founder of the Masowe Apostles, was in his early twenties when he began preaching the gospel during the 1930s.[11] He grew up under the family name of Shoniwa Masedza Tandi Moyo, and adopted the Shona translation of the name John the Baptist. Like the biblical prophet, Johane Masowe prayed outdoors, usually on the edges of lands where people lived or worked and, sometimes, farther away in *matongo* (forests). He baptized his followers in rivers and lakes that he called Jorodanis, emphasizing the biblical foundations of his theology. Masowe was raised in a village called Gandanzara ("a land of hunger"), a name that illustrates the displacement of Africans from their traditional lands. The location of this village in Makoni District was, like many parts of Zimbabwe during the 1930s, a place where colonial administrators had forced Africans to move and become squatters. By pushing indigenous people to the fringes of the land that their forefathers had owned while the white settlers occupied large tracts of fertile land, the colonial regime fueled the feelings of displacement Johane Masowe addressed through his preaching.[12]

Dramatically dressing in a white robe and making the borders of white-controlled areas his venues for prayer, Johane Masowe, accompanied by his followers, made plain the experiences of injustice after the colonial takeover of African lands. His hopes for redemption in

Christ were expressed in terms of a longing to regain control of the promised land seized by the white invaders.[13] Memories of the take-over of ancestral land and the first chimurenga uprising would have been fresh during the 1930s. His group's ritual behavior expressed the hopes for redemption of people whose marginality Johane Masowe made public by emulating John the Baptist, the biblical "voice crying in the wilderness" (Mark 1:2–4). Johane led people to pray outdoors in *masowe,* a wilderness made sacred by suffering and oppressed people's prayers for healing and longings for redemption.

Nengomasha, one of Johane's early followers, explained his leader's prophetic status as if writing an updated African Bible: "In 1914 Johane Masowe was born. This shows that God remembers us at that time. As the scriptures say, 'in the last days, the house of Ham, the race of Kush will be remembered by God.' This means that now is the time of our race, the race of Kush, and so God came to us."[14] Nengomasha's statement is significant not because it gave the date of Johane Masowe's birth, which was otherwise unknown,[15] but because it linked his advent with the onset of the Great War that convulsed Europe and involved its African colonies. Nengomasha, like many biblical commentators, associated the house of Ham and the race of Kush with Africans, whom he called *vanhu vatema* (black people), in order to draw attention to white colonial oppression as the cause of a conflict that would end through divine intervention on behalf of the marginalized but chosen race. Nengomasha relied on the logic of oral tradition to provoke his audience into seeing itself as a people at war, with God on their side as the oppressed *vanhu vatema.*

Masowe's teaching fits the context of millennial sects from Europe and America that sent missionaries to the African continent spreading beliefs in an imminent apocalypse. Watch Tower preachers sent by Jehovah's Witnesses, who gained currency in southern Rhodesia during the 1920s and 1930s, taught that 1914 marked the beginning of the world's end, a time when violence was to be expected.[16] Such preachers traveling far and wide in southern and central Africa posed a threat to authorities because their millennial message found a ready audience among colonial subjects.[17] When anthropologist and church historian Bengt Sundkler met a group of Johane Masowe's followers during the 1940s in South Africa, then under apartheid rule, he concluded that the Masowe Apostles were religious people "inspired by a hatred of whites"; in his view, the entire movement relied on "an apocalyptic consciousness of the imminence of the Day of Judgment" against white colonial authorities.[18]

Gezi and Nzira were popular leaders of the Masowe Apostles weChishanu in Zimbabwe around 2000. The third chimurenga reminded them of the history of displacement and struggle for the possession of land by a regime that was criticizing British colonialism. The chimurenga language used connected African Christians of the Masowe variety to a past where the people of Zimbabwe were forcibly displaced on account of the expropriation of land by colonialists. Conflict over land thus became part of a broader spiritual struggle. It is no wonder that the Masowe Apostles I met during fieldwork in and around Harare during the 1990s often imagined themselves as going into the wilderness to fight Satan in the form of ancestral spirits.[19]

Drama is an important medium of communication in Shona culture, functioning to draw attention to the supernatural realm and narrating the conquest over evil.[20] Male Masowe preachers insisted on their official leadership role over their communities as preacher or evangelist. So they led dramatizations of the fight with Satan in the *matongo* where ancestral spirits very often transformed into agents of Satan were said to hover, tempting believers to sin.[21] Upon entering the forest, Masowe Apostles sprinkled each other with holy water for protection. The men who dominated prayer meetings acted like commanders of a battle carried on through the power of the Holy Spirit against the spirits of the dead they viewed as agents of Satan. Participants in the ritual fell down, acting as if they were struck by lightning, cried at the top of their voices, behaved as if they suddenly lost the power of speech, shook in fear, and spoke in strange voices, only to stand up and sing and dance in jubilation a few moments later. Exorcism rituals were conducted in the name of God whose Holy Spirit believers used to reclaim the wilderness from the ancestral spirits.

When I attended the Masowe rituals, one woman warned me about mentioning my surname in the forests, or anywhere the Apostles gathered to pray. She explained that doing so could enable ancestral spirits to come back to control me and the wilderness that had been cleared of their power. For these Masowe Apostles, converting to Christianity means turning away from a concept of people as members of families established through the lineage and benevolence of the ancestors, and turning instead toward the God of the Bible who made promises of land to his chosen people. The Masowe Apostles I met hoped to regain jurisdiction over the land, not by appealing to the ancestors who claimed control of it, but rather by expelling their spirits through ritual and appealing instead to the Christian God who they believe will grant them their inheritance in the promised land. This shift in the view of the ancestors had significant bearing on how those Masowe Apostles who followed Mugabe and tried to connect their religious aspirations with his political agenda. Again, the rhetoric of Mugabe's chimurenga was that reclaiming the land was a way of giving honor to the ancestors who fought in previous wars to liberate it from white colonialists. The original Johane Masowe Apostles, on the other hand, rejected the ancestral spirits, whom they associated with sin and misfortune for losing the land in the first place, and connected themselves to biblical promises instead.

The early followers of Johane Masowe talked about him as someone gifted with power to defeat their own lineage ancestors. Johane worshiped outdoors to make visible his protest against all kinds of oppression, including not only white expropriation of Shona lands but also the oppression that the Shona people allowed to happen through ignorance and fear of the lineage ancestors. One of the popular stories about Johane refers to his approaching a village to expel the spirits: "At midnight, there was a roar of thunder on earth from east to west. Cattle bellowed as they looked towards the east. Cocks crowed and dogs barked as they looked towards the east. There was noise everywhere. Many people were awakened by the sound." As Johane Masowe, the messenger of God, approached, "the spirits knew that time for their departure had come" and they bade noisy farewell, leaving the people to turn to God. They dared not wait for further humiliation by a man filled with the Holy Spirit who taught people to denounce the ancestors before they could be baptized.[22]

The male preachers counted on being able to demonstrate that the God sought by believers is victorious over forces of evil. The preachers expressed their triumphant hope for redemption using idioms that dramatized both dread of Satan and confidence in the awesome power of God. They perpetuated the belief that combat was the appropriate means to the desired end. Although the third chimurenga and the spiritual battles of the Masowe Apostles pointed to the same political dream, rights to land were justified differently. Ancestors were put forward as the reason one supported Mugabe's chimurenga, based on the assumption that Zimbabwean citizens wanted to earn their living as peasant farmers and thus be connected to norms inherited from traditions of the past agrarian lifestyle. On the other hand, many of the stories told by Johane's followers portray him as a messenger through whom God defeated forces of evil, including ancestral spirits. The Masowe Apostles' relationship to ancestors was thus divided between those who would politicize ancestral claims to land and those who wanted land but distanced themselves from their forebears.

Patriarchy and Women of the "Verses"

The Masowe Apostles' zealous battle against Satan and malevolent ancestral spirits also extended to cultural violence against the women in their midst, whom they associated with sin. Masowe preachers often invoked beliefs in God and the "laws of nature" as the reason for keeping women out of leadership roles. An evangelist from one of the groups I visited in Harare asserted, "God created us men with natural gifts to lead in society. We exercise our gifts at home; in church and the wider society . . . women must obey." He went on: "Men are strong. They honor women with proposals for marriage. As men we are stronger and it is our God-given duty to give women 'our seed' so that they bear children and feed us in the home, clean, and obey the rules that we lay down for there to be order in the world. They have no stamina for a real fight with Satan . . . that should be left to us men. We sit apart at prayer meetings because men and women were created different."[23] One of the official documents produced by early followers of Johane Masowe states: "We honor the 'sisters' greatly because they represent the house of God . . . however, they have no power to give rules in the church . . . they must listen to the rules passed by God in whose name they pray to respect men."[24] In other words, women may have gifts of their own for men to honor.

But "the rules passed by God" require women to obey men, who represent "the word of God" on earth.

When it came to instilling in their audiences a sense of morality, Nzira and other male Masowe preachers frequently addressed the problem of sin in terms that focused on women. It was common to hear sermons against adultery, prostitution, and witchcraft, sins for which women were framed as the main perpetrators of evil. Women participated in this narrative by voluntarily stepping forward to have their demons fought by prayers for the cleansing power of the Holy Spirit. Claiming to possess the power of the Spirit, Nzira often subjected women to rhetorical attack during sermons, and expected women to answer his calls for repentance, thus placing himself as a mediator to God for the spiritually inferior women. At one meeting, the prophet Nzira was halfway through a sermon when he suddenly started shouting at women: "Keep quiet! You stupid women! You are all witches or prostitutes always thinking about sex when some of us are trying to pray."[25] He went on to abuse men who doubted his authority, calling them "women" to insult and feminize them, indicating that none could challenge his power. Nzira's dim views of women may have translated into personal violence—in March 2003 he was arrested and imprisoned on charges of rape.[26]

Women's responses to Nzira and the broader culture of sexism within the movement show the complexity of their role among the Apostles. The women came out to pray in large numbers because of a spiritual quest for liberation suited to them. Their substantial presence served to remind the male preachers of an idea that seems to have particular sway among young men in contemporary Africa: that women are more prone to sin than men, and that they need to be controlled for peace and prosperity to be produced. In fact, the concept of Satan has became iconic of the flaws Shona men saw in their women in Zimbabwean society. The men who acted as preachers and official leaders among Masowe Apostles created a language of evil in which images of witchcraft made women simultaneously vulnerable and culpable. Female ancestors were blamed for enticing women to practice witchcraft or act maliciously, thereby disrupting peace and harmony in society. Masowe Apostles talked about witches, especially "Mbuya (Grandma) the Witch," to express their fears of Satan. Women were said to be more susceptible to demonic possession and treated as scapegoats for destroying communal peace. The battle against Satan and evil thus became a struggle against female power, as both were seen as violating God's prescribed order. To complicate matters further, some women followed Border Gezi's teaching and began participating in the political rallies hosted by Mugabe's regime. Their spiritual quest thus combined hopes for freedom from sin with the search for freedom from economic hardships as described by Mugabe and endorsed by the leaders of the Masowe Apostles weChishanu.

A handful of men usually acted as the official leaders of the spiritual wars against Satan waged in front of large numbers of women. I observed a group with fifteen men and eighty women; another had three men and twenty-five women. Opposite the Coca-Cola factory on Seke Road, I often saw thirty or more men sitting before one hundred or more women with their infants.[27] At almost every gathering, one or two men dominated the proceedings after reminding women that there are *mirao* (rules and regulations) stating that they should obey men. Once, a group of twenty women and their children sat in the hot sun for at least an hour before the prayers began. They were unable to proceed with the prayer meeting until the appointed male leader of the community arrived. When two young men turned up an hour late, one was a new member attending only because he wanted counseling and prayers for healing his AIDS. The second, Petros, was in his early twenties. Petros acted as official leader of a community with at least fifteen women elders twice his age who were far more familiar with the teachings of Johane Masowe than their young leader. Because of the rules requiring female obedience, it was essential that Petros act as the official worship leader. He declared the meeting open, preached about God's love for everybody, and made official announcements about future events. His sermon showed an unusual high regard for women. He touched on some of the attractive elements of Masowe teaching, encouraging love and sharing among the children of God. The women gave the young man time to practice expressing what he understood of Masowe theology, and stopped him once they realized he was running out of things to say. Women elders took over the leadership by singing songs they referred to as "verses" to conclude the sermon. Six hours later, when it was time to go home,

Petros was asked to show his authority by declaring the meeting closed and announcing the next meeting.[28] This pattern was repeated at all the prayer meetings that I attended when young men sought to legitimize their leadership status by preaching and trying to articulate Johane Masowe's teachings.

Despite the rampant sexism within the Masowe Apostles, there were resources and precedents within the movement that can be used to promote peace and justice. Johane Masowe recognized the importance of women in his church; he clearly did not expect them merely to attend passively and listen to men imparting their knowledge about God. Indeed, according to Terence Ranger, Johane Masowe aroused the suspicions of Europeans by his radical defiance of patriarchy, and even became notorious for accommodating runaway women.[29] Johane Masowe considered women his companions in matters of faith and created official roles for them to demonstrate that he honored women.[30] To qualify as special members of his prayer team, young women took vows of chastity and led lives of prayer, rather like nuns or sisters in the Catholic Church. Madzimai Meggi was appointed leader of the sisters, whose main responsibilities were to sing the gospel, and give counsel to men by sharing ideas revealed to them through prayer. Because most of the original members were semiliterate, "the word of God" was spread through song, and so those women who were responsible for the singing were in a position of particular esteem. In short, Johane Masowe considered women capable of enlightening men about divine truths.[31]

Women appear in foundational Masowe texts as important members of the spiritual community, and not subjects for men to manipulate and demonize in prayers of exorcism. In the collection of special documents amassed by the anthropologist Clive Dillon-Malone, and known as the "Gospel of Johane Masowe Apostles," men are told to honor their sisters as a necessary part of any meaningful prayer meeting where God's presence is felt. Various titles are used in the text to designate the sacred nature of the singers' responsibility: "the house of God," "the city of Jerusalem," and "guardians of the ark" are some of the phrases expressing the importance of women in the church. The singers who traveled with Johane are referred to as "the wives of Baba Johane." The term *madzimai* (wives) has spiritual significance in the Mwari religion, as anyone who speaks in the name of God is his wife. Indeed, Johane Masowe himself was a "wife" among fellow wives in laying the foundations of this wilderness church.[32]

Moreover, women have assumed a leadership role in church ritual. The majority of the women I met while conducting my research were mothers who brought their children to pray alongside them. Many of the single women were either divorced or widowed, and needed to be careful because of their susceptibility to attack by the male preachers. The girls who came as virgins clearly enjoyed particular status within the group as special channels for the voice of God. Nevertheless, it seemed to matter more that the women sang, regardless of their marital or parental status, and that they sang enough to keep the fighting spirit of the men in check. One woman I interviewed said that she knew about women who followed strict rules and consciously avoided sex in preparation for healing ceremonies, especially if they were healers themselves. She continued, "Johane wanted to be sure we are a recognized part of this church . . . there are so many women. . . . Any time one of us feels inspired by the Holy Spirit, songs fill our hearts and our brothers have to share in our joy." In all the venues of prayer I visited, including many without a special group of singers or "sisters," it was the norm to hear women lead the singing of verses. Women were free to interrupt sermons to sing the gospel, and male preachers had to wait for them to finish the verses. Some women deliberately checked the sexist behavior and speeches of male leaders by interrupting their sermons with proclamations of the gospel in song. The men would stop, sometimes halfway through sentences, until the women finished their pleas for great peace and harmony at prayer.[33]

Prayer songs were widely understood, by Shona and Masowe Apostles alike, as the principal method of conveying divine truths, and women were the primary mediums for this transmission. In Shona culture, the norm is for women to sing. Some women sing to educate their children about morality; others sing at gatherings of male community leaders to ensure that their husbands and fathers understand the burdens of their lives. In an awkward family situation, *vatorwa*—literally outsiders or strangers, as the women who marry into the lineage are known—sing to remind elders of the lineage about the blind spots in family politics.[34] Similarly, women of the Masowe Apostles treated singing as crucial, and this element of ritual is unlikely to be usurped by men. On a few occasions men tried to sing as a way of asserting their authority and, at one meeting, three men stood up to sing gospel songs in front of one hundred women. Predictably, the men failed to evoke a response from the audience and started waving their hands in the direction of the women for someone to assist them.[35]

Women also claimed special access to divine grace during Masowe ceremonies. On a hot Sunday afternoon in July 1997, a group of white-robed Masowe Apostles gathered in a meadow surrounding Lake Chimombe near Harare. Twenty women sat with me facing east. Unlike the six young men who were present, our heads were covered with white linen. Otherwise, we all wore white robes and prayed barefoot. The men, including the official leader, sat facing west about six feet away. When I inquired about the reason for the different directions, my women informants explained that during prayers, ancestral spirits (both male and female) could only run west, toward the sunset, the place of darkness. "Our men see themselves as the leaders of the spiritual battles waged here. . . . *Madzibaba* [male elders] want to make sure that these powerful evil spirits do not come back to possess us after efforts are made to exorcise them." Explaining the position of women, Susan went on: "We face the east because the *zuva* [sun] rises from the east to give light to the world and with it God sends the Mweya Mutsvene [Holy Spirit]." She continued, pointing at both men and women: "We all come here for the blessings of Mweya Mutsvene that blow in the wind from the east, through our hearts, cleansing us, giving us strength, and driving the forces of evil that go west."[36] Facing east was special to women because of the unmediated access it offered to the Holy Spirit. Other women similarly indicated that the Holy Spirit, understood in Shona as Izwi raMwari (voice of God), was heard and felt as a life-giving power and source of knowledge that speaks to humanity from the realm of light (*ruzivo*) in the east.[37] The women followers of the Masowe Apostles prayed in the knowledge that they could receive the gifts of the Holy Spirit that came from the east. While the men faced west to protect the site of prayer against evil spirits, the east-facing women enjoyed the bless-ings of God's spirit blowing in from *mabvazuva*, the place of the ris-ing sun.[38]

During moments when women's voices were heard, especially through the singing of verses taken from the Bible that speak of the love of God, men retreated from their positions of authority. Once the moment to turn east came, they demonstrated their readiness to make peace by bowing down to pray individually alongside their women and children as equals before God. It was also the norm to ask anyone who heard "the voice" or felt they had something inspira-tional to say to do so. The word Masowe Apostles used to describe this stage of the proceedings is *zvakazarurwa,* or revelations, during which time nothing stood between the believer and God. On one oc-casion, a woman prophesied doom to the evangelist. "Ndanzwa ["I heard" or "I feel"] I should tell you that God punishes those who take his name in vain." The woman spoke facing the evangelist and claimed to be doing so in the name of Holy Spirit. The evangelist stepped back into the crowd to let the proceedings end with a healing ceremony, carried out by everyone in song.[39] *Zvakararurwa* thus marked a limi-nal time of transcending hierarchy, as believers were reminded that they were all children of God.

Even in this Zimbabwean religious culture saturated with ideas of fighting and men asserting exclusive leadership prerogatives, the rank-and-file (mostly female) members of the Masowe Apostles were able to assert their direct relationship to God by appealing to and capitalizing on the more universalistic doctrines and rituals of their religion. By singing "verses" until the preachers slowed down or stopped talking, women used the special role given to them in Masowe Apostles churches. In so doing they exercised some control over their own space at prayer meetings, interfering with sermons that clashed with their understanding of God, and arguably increasing egalitarian-ism, and therefore a kind of peaceful harmony, among the believers. Women thus challenged, both subtly and openly, the patriarchal grip on society without rupturing established gender relations. Indeed, the women worked within, rather than against, aspects of the commu-nity's accepted body of religious truth in order to maintain status and dignity.

HEALING CEREMONIES AS SCHOOLS FOR PEACE-BUILDING

Numerous scholars have emphasized the importance of healing in African appropriations of Christianity, even arguing that healing is the main attraction of the African Initiated Churches such as Masowe Apostles.[40] Matthew Schoffeleers invited scholars to look at folk ideas underlying Africans' interpretation of the gospel in terms of the healing ministry of Jesus.[41] He explained that healing ceremonies, rather than simply being opportunities for people to experience or testify to the supernatural, helped believers feel integrated into society.[42] The healing ceremonies that attracted people to the Masowe Apostles would not have been as effective without women helping to create the peaceful environment in which holistic healing takes place. To borrow a phrase of Johane Masowe, the role of women in helping to establish peace begins with "crying in the wilderness," which expresses profound feelings of displacement as well as the cause for a longing for redemption.

Female Masowe Apostles often released tension by allowing one another to share problems of life in the wider society. At one healing ceremony, several women made public their feelings of marginality by announcing the injustices found in the wider society. Women laid hands on the poor and the sick, and treated cases of depression through counseling. Some women sang and danced while others raised their hands in the air, shook themselves about, and fell to the ground in spiritual dramatizations of things gone wrong in their lives. As if responding to the way some of the male preachers behaved like military leaders in the battle against evil, women wept amid songs of prayer, reminding each other of God's promise of deliverance from evil through sharing information and helping one another find solutions to problems. In contrast to the belligerent posturing and force often characterizing the worship style of the male Masowe leadership, women showed a readiness to brush aside the male egoisms of preachers and enjoy a shared ministry of empathy and compassion, especially during healing ceremonies.

When healing ceremonies were underway, the sacred wilderness became a place to uplift one another in faith, with believers transcending the boundaries of sex to lay hands on one another in prayer. Usually this ceremony took place well after the preaching, allowing men the chance to drop their guard, come forward, and behave calmly and humbly as they let women known to be blessed with the gift of healing exercise their ritual power by praying for them. The Masowe Apostles did not necessarily expect miraculous healings that contradict the laws of nature,[43] but emphasized courage and peace of mind. Sick people, including victims of the AIDS pandemic who faced certain death would come and go. The healing ceremonies were similar to group therapy: the sick were allowed to express their longings for good health, they gave others a chance to assist them (sometimes through counseling), and others prayed for their wellbeing. Dillon-Malone refers to similar practices in Zambia as "holistic healing," a way of addressing social, psychological, and physical ailments in one system of therapy.[44]

During their healing ceremonies, Masowe Apostles engendered social relations that are relatively equal and even favor women to some degree. These rituals provided moments when the martial spirit of male preaching was subdued and the ethos of compassion and solidarity, exemplified by the female healers, was highlighted as the community ideal. While the primary purpose of the ceremonies was to provide relief from physical and spiritual ailments, they performed a powerful function in healing social and psychological rifts among the people. Such rituals possess significant potential to work as locally appropriate mechanisms for conflict resolution and reconciliation by providing indigenous models through which people recognized and experienced, if only temporarily, a more just, equitable, and harmonious social order.

CONCLUSION

Gender differences were clearly visible in the language that male and female Masowe Apostles used to articulate their suffering and corresponding religious aspirations. Mugabe's rhetoric about the third chimurenga seemed to have an audience among the male leaders of the Masowe Apostles in Zimbabwe because it resonated with their bellicose spiritual imagery, which was then easily translated into the political sphere. Some male prophets and preachers frequently employed images of themselves struggling in a war with sin and evil that also led them to point fingers at women as if they were the main enemy. Others reached out to women, whose large membership and active involvement in prayer meetings of Masowe Apostles made the movement visible as a church for the marginalized in Zimbabwean society. In their worship, women expressed a longing for greater equity, harmony at prayer, and healing. Women generally shared their suffering as part of healing ceremonies where women were more active ritual participants than the men.

Masowe Apostles weChishanu churches actively backed Mugabe, supported ZANU/PF-led violence, and like many other groups inheriting the teaching of the original Jonane Masowe Apostles, projected their images of evil onto women. This represents a particular appropriation of Christianity combined with indigenous beliefs of ancestors as guardians of African lands. Capitalizing on these widespread beliefs, Mugabe was able to convince many Zimbabweans to participate in the violence of the third chimurenga. It would help the cause for justice and peace to pay attention to the quests for spiritual and temporal fulfillment that explain the long hours that Masowe Apostles spent together at prayer. The creative ways that Masowe women used to confront oppression are significant for peace-building in a country like Zimbabwe. With 90 percent of the total population attending some form of worship service regularly, the example of female worship within the Masowe Apostles provided a model for turning African churches into havens for peace and justice.[45] Sites of prayer could be transformed so that what was taught on a ritual plane about justice, peace, and love fed into ways of solving social problems caused by poverty, disease, unemployment, and the victimization of the weak through political violence. As this study of Masowe Apostles shows, it is time for the few people interested in peace-building in Zimbabwe and other African countries to understand the pervasiveness of male exclusivist, militant, and sexist tendencies in popular religious movements, and make note of their clash with goals of the same religions insofar as some adherents associate worship with hopes for justice, peace, and love for all.

NOTES

1. I. Mukonyora, "Foundations for Democracy among Evangelical Christians in Zimbabwe," in *The Bible and the Ballot Box: Evangelical Faith and Third World Politics*, ed. T. O. Ranger (New York: Oxford University Press, 2008). Parts of this paper are extracts from my book, *Wandering a Gendered Wilderness: Suffering and Healing in an African Initiated Church* (New York: Peter Lang Publishing Group, 2007).

2. M. Engelke, *A Problem of Presence: Beyond Scripture in an African Christian Church* (Berkeley: University of California Press, 2007).

3. Observations made at Prophet Nzira's sacred wilderness in Chitungwiza, Harare, between September and October in 1999; see http://en.wikipedia.org/wiki/Border_Gezi.

4. Fieldwork in Harare between 1999 and 2000.

5. T. Ranger, *Revolt in Southern Rhodesia 1896–1897* (London: Heinemann, 1967).

6. D. Lan, *Guns and Rain: Guerillas and Spirit Mediums in Zimbabwe* (London: James Currey, 1985).

7. M. Bourdillon, *Where Are the Ancestors? Changing Culture in Zimbabwe* (Harare: University of Zimbabwe Publishers, 1993).

8. R. Weiss, *Women and the War in Zimbabwe* (Gweru: Mambo Press, 1980), 31.

9. Zimbabwe Human Rights NGO Forum, "Order out of Chaos, or Chaos out of Order? A Preliminary Report on 'Operation Murambatsvina,'" June 2005, 1–37.

10. Interviews with women showed that their own understanding of God clashed with the triumphalism that many of the male leaders associated with God's power. Yet, women continued to attend prayer meetings in large numbers. Fieldwork in Harare, 1996–2000.

11. African men were required to have "passes," registration certificates showing that they were workers in farms, mines, and towns. Otherwise, they were expected to remain in marginal rural areas. C. M. Dillon-Malone, *The Korsten Basketmakers: A Study of the Masowe Apostles, An Indigenous African Religious Movement* (Manchester: Manchester University Press, 1978), 15.

12. Angela Cheater, *Idioms of Accumulation: Rural Development and Class Formation* (Harare: Mambo Press, 1984), 1–6.

13. Dillon-Malone, *Korsten Basketmakers*, 15.

14. Interview with Nengomasha in National Archives of Zimbabwe FAOH/4, 1–59, 1977, 15.

15. Margaret Kileff suggests that the real date of birth of Johane Masowe was 1915; see C. Kileff and M. Kileff, "The Masowe Vapostori of Seki:

Utopianism and Tradition in an African Church," in *The New Religions of Africa*, ed. B. Jules-Rosette (Norwood, NJ: Ablex Publishing Co., 1979), 151–67.

16. Dillon-Malone, *Korsten Basketmakers*, 9–11.

17. Ranger, *Revolt in Southern Rhodesia*, 380.

18. B. G. M. Sundkler, *Bantu Prophets in South Africa* (Oxford: Oxford University Press, 1961; Cambridge: James Clarke & Co., 2004), 76.

19. Mukonyora, *Gendered Wilderness*, 91–106.

20. I. Mukonyora, "Dramatizations of Life and Death by Johane Masowe Apostles," *Swedish Missiological Themes* 88, no. 3 (2000): 409–30.

21. Mukonyora, *Gendered Wilderness*, 99–100.

22. "Signs" in Evangelist Gore's oral account cited by Dillon-Malone, *Korsten Basketmakers*, 143. In Shona, messengers become those they represent and can be called by the same name. In this case, the Greek concept of *logos* used in John's Gospel and translated as Izwi raMwari (Voice of God) became Johane the preacher standing for its truth.

23. Fieldwork on Marimba Hill, Harare, September 1999.

24. Dillon-Malone, *Korsten Basketmakers*, 35. Today there are many groups of Masowe Apostles, but none brings us as close to the founder as the Gospel of God Church with oral history of the founder's immediate friends and followers.

25. Nzira, sermon delivered in Chitungwiza, September 1999.

26. C. F. Hallencreutz, *Religion and Politics in Harare 1890–1980* (Uppsala: Swedish Institute of Missionary Research, 1998), 185–206.

27. I. Mukonyora, "Marginality and Protest: The Roles of Women in Shaping the Masowe Thought Pattern," *Southern African Feminist Review* 5 (2000–2001): 1–21.

28. Fieldwork in Avondale, near Twin Rivers School, Harare, July 1999.

29. T. Ranger, "Poverty and Prophetism," unpublished paper in the National Archives of Zimbabwe, 1981, 1–44.

30. "Vadzimai vaJohane Masowe," in *The Good News of Johane Masowe for Africa*, ed. C. Dillon-Malone (Lusaka: Teresianum Press, 1987), 47.

31. I. Mukonyora, "The Complementarity of Male and Female Imagery in Theological Language: A Study of the Valentinian and Masowe Theological Systems" (D.Phil. dissertation, University of Oxford, 1997), ch. 8, "Masowe Teaching on Revelation."

32. Dillon-Malone, *Korsten Basketmakers*, 65; cf. M. L. Daneel, *God of the Matopo Hills: An Essay on Mwari* (The Hague: Mouton, 1970) and *Old and New in Southern Shona Independent Churches*, vol. 1 (Leiden: Mouton, 1971), 22; and H. Aschwanden, *Karanga Myths of Creation: An Analysis of the Consciousness of the Karanga in Zimbabwe* (Gweru: Mambo Press, 1989), 28.

33. Engelke, *A Problem of Presence.*

34. This remains a common practice among Shona people today, primarily at funerals.

35. Among Maranke Apostles led by another John the Baptist, Johane Maranke from Makoni District, the men tend to silence women, even singers, and some have groups of men who enjoy singing in deep voices as if staging a show. The women in some of these groups are passive. Fieldwork in Marlborough, Harare, 1996. B. Jules-Rosette, *African Apostles: Ritual and Conversion in the Church of John Maranke* (Ithaca, NY: Cornell University Press, 1975).

36. Conversation with Susan at Lake Chimombe, Harare, 1994.

37. Daneel, *God of the Matopos Hills;* cf. T. O. Ranger, *Voices from the Rocks: Nature, Culture and History in the Matopos Hills of Zimbabwe* (Bloomington: Indiana University Press, 1999).

38. The east is universally recognized by Masowe Apostles as the source of divine truth and light. Johane Masowe frequently referred to Revelation 7:2: "I saw another angel ascending from the east, having the seal of the living God: he cried with a loud voice." Other biblical passages reinforcing the special significance of the east and the favor with which the Apostles view it include Genesis 2:8; Genesis 3:24; Exodus 14:21; Jeremiah 18:12; and Revelation 16:12.

39. Fieldwork at Lake Chimombe, Harare, July 1998.

40. M. L. Daneel, *Zionism and Faith Healing in Rhodesia: Aspects of African Independent Churches* (The Hague: Mouton, 1970).

41. M. Schoffeleers, "Folk Christology in Africa: The Dialectics of a N'anga Paradigm," *Journal of Religion in Africa* 19, no. 2 (1989): 157–83.

42. M. Schoffeleers, "Ritual Healing and Political Acquiescence in Africa," *Journal of the International African Institute* 60, no. 1 (1991): 1–25.

43. The Masowe Apostles do not stigmatize one another about HIV/AIDS or about psychological distress. They recognize that when handling the ailments that arise from difficulties and frustrations with life, healing means different things to different people.

44. C. Dillon-Malone, "The Mutumwa Churches of Zambia: An Indigenous African Religious Healing Movement," *Journal of Religion in Africa* 14, no. 3 (1983): 204–22.

45. I. Phiri, *Proclaiming Political Pluralism: Churches and Political Transition in Africa* (London: Praeger Publishers, 2002), 36–40, 55, 121–22.

Part III

New Religious Public Spheres and the Crisis of Regulation

CHAPTER 6

"Devil Bustin' Satellites"

How Media Liberalization in Africa Generates
Religious Intolerance and Conflict

Rosalind I. J. Hackett

While scholarship on the intersections of religion, media, and culture has improved significantly since the late 1990s (see, for example, Hoover and Lundby 1997; Hoover and Clark 2002; Hoover 2006), there is still a lack of attention paid to the impact of religion and media, taken together, for conflict and peace-building issues. This is especially the case for the African context. This essay aims to enhance our understanding of the increasingly salient role of the media in religiously related conflict and peace-building. Moreover, it constitutes a response to one of the editors of *Religion and Media* (de Vries and Weber 2001) who called for more research on the implications of the intersection of religion and media "for down-to-earth laws and rights, transnational belonging and multicultural citizenship, tolerance and hospitality" (de Vries 2001, 42).

Struggles over agency, access, and representation in media landscapes, or mediascapes (Appadurai 1996), are indeed increasingly integral to public debates about citizenship and participation. However, in the case of Africa, they are heightened, not just by lingering fears of marginalization, but also by dreams of domination in the new democratic and capitalistic dispensations that now characterize many African states. Bruce Lincoln (2003, 6) observes that when a culture's most bruising conflicts assume religious, rather than ethical or aesthetic, character, they can be more destructive than ever (see also Juergensmeyer 2003 [2001]). Building on this, I argue that Africa's new media revolution is replicating, if not intensifying, old, as well as generating new, forms of religious conflict.

This perspective may appear counterintuitive to many, notably to those who espouse more optimistic notions of modernization, globalization, and free markets. However, I argue that the rapid deregulation of the media in most parts of Africa, coupled with a rising Christianization—or rather Pentecostalization and evangelicalization—of the airwaves, is not leading to a happy and equitable marketplace (cf. Bourdieu 2003, 84). In fact, we are witnessing the emergence of an intolerant, and at times, aggressive, religious broadcasting culture.[1] The examples I propose to highlight are not as egregious as the call for genocidal cleansing by Radio-Télévision Libre des Mille Collines in Rwanda in 1994 (Gourevitch 1998), nor the one-sided, inflammatory reporting of Muslim-Christian riots in neighboring towns by Radio Kaduna in 1987, which served to mobilize Muslims and exacerbate the violence in northern Nigeria (Hackett 2003b; Ibrahim 1989). The deleterious effects naturally vary in terms of context and intentionality, but since the 1990s there is more persuasive research on mass media effects (Preiss et al. 2006). Moreover, we know the failure to respect the precarious rights relating to freedom of expression and freedom of religion and belief can provide a warrant for broader discrimination and, potentially, conflict and violence (see Boyle 1992). Many observers are pointing their fingers at the media for generating these new patterns of religious and cultural intolerance. The Radio Netherlands program on counteracting hate media notes in this regard, that "nowadays, more often than ever in the past, the media, particularly the electronic media, are instrumental in setting off and sustaining these wars and conflicts."[2] Some recent publications (notably following the Rwandan genocide) seek to investigate this relationship between media and conflict in Africa, although with scant attention to religious factors (Onadipe and Lord 1999; Article 19 1996; Frohardt and Temin 2003).

To clarify, this study is not another lament about media imperialism and fatalism, now generally perceived as outdated theoretical models that viewed consumers as primarily victims (Nyamnjoh 2004; Sreberny-Mohammadi 1996). Nor is it a rant against globalization. However, it is about how the mass media in Africa represent a significant new interface for negotiating the power relations among and within religious groups, and between religious groups and the state

(Meyer and Moors 2006). It is about the power of imaginations to create a space where ideas are shaped about what constitutes reality and morality, and where social spaces and action are reconfigured (Bayart 2005 [1996], cited in Meyer 2006a 302–3). It concerns new forms of human exclusivity as well as of connectivity, of "closures" as well as "cultural flows" (Nyamnjoh 2004, 64). Stewart Hoover, one of the leading thinkers in the field of religion and media, talks of the "double articulation of the media" in that they are both shapers and products of culture (Hoover 2006, 8).

On that note of paradox, and to summarize the thrust of this essay, I argue that the focus on the intersections of media, religion, and conflict can prove instructive in at least five ways. First, as the work of Birgit Meyer and her associates has so convincingly demonstrated, postcolonial societies have been profoundly transformed by the rise of print, broadcast, and new electronic media with their capacity to constitute new communities and publics, and new senses of self and other.[3] In these changing public spheres, and this is very much the case for Africa with more than its quota of failed states, it is frequently religious publics that emerge to challenge the legitimacy of the nation-state. Thus, examining the nexus of religion, media, and conflict takes us to the heart of what Monroe Price calls the new "market for loyalties" and its attendant conflicts (Price 1994; see also Price 2002). Second, our particular focus enables a clearer picture of identity construction in contemporary Africa to emerge—one that rescues religious identity from the stranglehold of ethnicity in both popular and academic discourses. The fact that religious organizations predominate over ethnic associations in the modern mass-mediated public spheres in Africa, and the fact that modern religious identities may be paraded over ethnicity to legitimate public participation, point to the new sites, symbols, and strategies that must be investigated in seeking to understand inter- and intra-communal conflict.[4] Third, employing the media as a central category of analysis with regard to the relationship between religion and conflict leads to a greater recognition of the sheer complexity of hegemonic and counter-hegemonic forces, and social and discursive processes, which shape religious coexistence.[5] It provides us with what has been termed "clues to conflict" (Frohardt and Temin 2003). Fourth, studying the ways in which

new religious media relate to contemporary conflict settings can illu-
mine both the flashpoints and the processual dynamics at work in
such contexts. This perspective opens new windows onto the ways
in which communities can experience cumulative alienation through
negative and/or under-representation and eventually resort to violence. The recent scholarship on ethnic minority media (Cottle 2000;
Browne 2005), mediatized conflict (Cottle 2006), media framing in relation to political participation (V. Price 1992; Gilboa 2002), and U.S.
foreign policy (Entman 2004), as well as perceptions of terrorism
(Norris, Kern, and Just 2003), is apposite here. So too is the current
phase of "media effects" research, which can identify a significant effect of media violence on aggressive social behavior (Christensen and
Wood 2007). Fifth, given that many perceive the modern media to be
both part of the problem pertaining to cultural anxieties relating to
(religious) difference, as well as part of the solution, this can devolve
into interesting forms of engaged scholarship. Indeed, Robert White
argues that normative claims have always been an inherent part of
communication studies, linking it to the development of democracy,
human rights, and communitarian values (White 2003, 192; see also
Ginsberg, Abu-Lughod, and Larkin 2002; Tomaselli and Young 2001;
Husband 2000).

To argue my case for a more critical examination of media liberalization in present-day Africa and its consequences for religious broadcast cultures, I begin by discussing the nature and extent of the media
revolution currently underway in Africa. I suggest that Africa provides an important regional location for observing and understanding
this type of development since the growth of the media industry has
occurred relatively recently (since the early 1990s), and relatively rapidly, in most countries. It allows us to compare how state and non-
state actors are negotiating this new mediatization of the public
sphere. I concentrate on the electronic media because of their growth
and influence, and, in particular, Christian involvement in this new
sector. In the subsequent section, I contend that there are four main
areas that give rise to discontent and conflict: (1) inequitable access;
(2) encroachment; (3) defamation, and (4) consumerism. I close with
reflections on possible mediations of the paradoxes of the media in
Africa today.

Media Liberalization

Constraints of space do not permit me to offer a history of the broadcast media in Africa, nor can I even, much as it is needed, trace the development of religious broadcasting on the continent.[6] Rather, I intend to focus on the changes that have occurred in the media sector, opening up new possibilities of participation for religious actors and organizations.[7] As Jon Anderson suggests in his important research on media in the Muslim world, the new mediated public sphere opens "the social field to new spokespeople and new discursive practices [that] not only challenge authority long since thought settled to interpret what religion requires, but also blurs boundaries between public and private discourse and fosters new habits of production and consumption" (Anderson 2003, 887).

Clearly, the most significant development has been the liberalization of the media sector (see, for example, Ansah 1994). This has occurred in conjunction with, or as a consequence of, the democratization processes underway in many African states (Nyamnjoh 2004). The dismantling of state monopolies of the broadcast and print media (there were some independent newspapers), and the commercializing of airtime and ownership have radically altered the media landscape (Fardon and Furniss 2000), with significant consequences for religious communication and practice (Meyer 2006a). Now mass media organizations are owned by private entrepreneurs, religious organizations, political parties, existing media houses, development organizations, and local communities.[8] Assessing these trends, Cameroonian communications scholar Francis Nyamnjoh argues that the threats to a "free, open and participatory media system and society" in Africa derive as much from "repressive governments as much as rich nations, international financial institutions and the global corporate media" (Nyamnjoh 2004, 60).[9] In other words, Africans find themselves caught between repression and profit, because of the collusion between state and global capital (ibid., 63). Similarly, Jean Comaroff and John L. Comaroff, writing of the conundrums and predicaments of the current phase of "Millennial Capitalism," observe that "these transformations have expressed themselves increasingly in a spirit of deregulation, with its taunting mix of emancipation and limitation" (2004, 31).

Radio is the most vibrant sector of the African broadcast industry. In fact, Africa is known as the "radio continent" (Mytton 2000).
It is often said that there are more homes with radios than access to
running water in Africa. Radio has become more diversified and com-
mercialized in the post-independence period, moving from the region's capital cities to local neighborhoods, broadcasting predominantly in FM, but sometimes in shortwave and increasingly in a
digitalized format.[10] Uganda is a telling example, with over 150 radio
stations, 69 percent of which cater to audiences in the thirty-eight
different languages of the country.[11] The Malian radio landscape is one
of the most dynamic in Africa, with nearly 400 radio stations having
received authorization to broadcast since 1991, and of those, 250 actually on air (in 2008).[12] Community radio stations have proliferated
in post-apartheid South Africa. There are now more than a hundred
stations, broadcasting in diverse languages.[13] Media liberalization has
allowed religious organizations to exert their influence over the domestic airwaves and command high audiences—particularly among
women.[14] More than one-third of the FM stations in the Democratic
Republic of Congo, for example, are believed to be owned and controlled by religious groups, mainly evangelical Christian churches.[15]
Radio Pulpit, a Christian radio station in South Africa, enjoys national coverage, while in Kenya the leading radio station in the most
populous area (the Rift Valley) is Sayare FM, a Christian-oriented private station.[16] Before 2002, Sierra Leone had no community radio stations; by 2006, it had twenty-four, of which seven were religious.[17]

Television is a very attractive medium, and it is now consider-
ably enhanced by the addition of digital satellite television (DStv),
launched by MultiChoice (with headquarters in South Africa) in Africa in 1995. But television is costly, and most countries have only
added a few private stations to the preexisting state-run broadcasting companies (northern and southern Africa, as well as Uganda, are
the exceptions).[18] Foreign programming tends to dominate television
broadcasts. For example, U.S. televangelist Pat Robertson's Christian Broadcasting Network (CBN) is constantly expanding its broadcast schedule around Africa, with both old (*Turning Point,* the *700
Club*) and new (*One Cubed*—a youth-oriented Christian music program) staples.[19] Some states have tried to limit this reliance on outside

(non-African) sources. The new Africa Magic channel launched by DStv in February 2004 features entertainment and cultural production from Africa. Some film productions from Kenya are currently being shown, although Nollywood (as the Nigerian film industry is known) predominates.[20]

Despite my focus in this essay on the broadcast or electronic media, some reference has to be made to the rise of computer-mediated communications and use of the Internet. It is not just the larger religious organizations, notably of the evangelical and Pentecostal variety, that are developing web presence and community,[21] but also smaller ministries that can cater in a personal way to prayer requests from members and nonmembers alike.[22] Similarly, we are observing increasing interconnectivity and interactivity with improved media technologies. Radio 786, a Muslim community radio station in Cape Town, South Africa, has successfully exploited the symbiotic relationship between print, broadcast, and web-based communications technologies (Haron 2004, 153–54).[23] With the blurring and convergence of media boundaries comes a de-differentiation of "on air" and "online" worship. Churches and other religious organizations can now stream their broadcasts through their websites, claiming enhanced healing and proselytizing capabilities.[24] In addition, multimedia combinations create informational and communicative possibilities at the humblest levels, as in the case of UNESCO's "suitcase radio."[25]

NEW RELIGIOUS ECONOMIES AND MEDIA UNIVERSES

The deregulation of both the media and religion in this new phase of democracy and liberalization in Africa has generated new forms of competitiveness for public attention, resources, and legal status. Synergies have emerged linking contemporary technology and theology. Religious groups that privilege proselytism and trans-denominational networking thrive on the sacred canopies, or more appropriately, sacred webs that are woven in and around the globe.

In this connection, media outlets love to vaunt their technical statistics and outreach power. For example, Spirit FM declares that it has 15 million listeners in Africa through its Spirit Network and its

5 full-powered, state-of-the-art FM stations. They also proudly advertise that they broadcast in English and local languages, offering programs of music and teaching 24 hours a day to Ghana, Togo, Ivory Coast, Uganda, Tanzania, Sudan, Congo, and Kenya.[26] FEBA Radio states on its website: "Don't be fooled by the short in shortwave,"[27] and World Wide Christian Radio enthuses about the 4 state-of-the-art 100-kilowatt transmitters that serve the world on 10 different broadcasting channels to nothing less than "a global audience."[28] Trinity Broadcasting Network (TBN), operating out of Irving, Texas, is the world's largest Christian television network, and claims to produce more original Christian programs than any other religious network.[29] Three Angels Broadcasting Network (3ABN) announced in mid-2007 that it had a "thrilling new device" allowing one to "plug and play" 3ABN TV when traveling using Internet Protocol TV.[30] Reinhard Bonnke's religious organization announced with great excitement on their website that "for the first time ever, a CfaN Crusade was broadcast LIVE, by satellite, direct from the Oshogbo crusade site, via studios and rebroadcast stations in Jerusalem, Washington and England, to countless millions of homes in over 200 nations. In a partnership with Rory and Wendy Alec of GOD TV, a live studio and satellite base station was flown in from South Africa and set up to make such an up-link possible."[31] EWTN, or Eternal Word Television Network, described as the world's largest media organization, signed an agreement with PANAMSAT in 2002 to reach 75 million homes in 100 countries on cable systems, wireless cable, DS low-power TV, and individual satellite users. They claim that with this agreement they now transmit to more than 98 percent of the world's population.[32] These types of business arrangements between churches, para-church agencies, production companies, and service providers are increasingly common.

Winning souls and reaching the unreached are the primary markers of some Christian networks. "Have you ever dreamed of broadcasting to the spiritually impoverished souls of some distant land?" asks Pan American Broadcasting.[33] HCJB World Radio has been "touching lives around the globe" since 1931.[34] With local partners it now has ministries in more than 100 countries and broadcasts the gospel in nearly 120 languages and dialects. *Atmosphere for Miracles,* claims Pastor Chris Oyakhilome, the founder of Christ Embassy Church in Lagos, "transmits God's healing power to viewers around the world wherever the programme is televised."[35] The GOD Channel's free-to-air signal is available via satellite throughout Africa, enabling television viewers to now experience "anointed Christian programming" completely free of charge.[36] It is noteworthy that the trope of "family" is commonly used by several of these stations and production companies to denote the relationships that they are building in order to Christianize the continent, indeed the world. Top Radio in Uganda claims it is "strategically placed" around the nation to "help the people of Uganda live fulfilled lives in Jesus Christ."[37]

It is tempting to view the burgeoning popular religious marketplace in many parts of Africa through the theoretical lens of the "religious economy." Several authors have argued that this is the optimal perspective to comprehend the "free market in faith" (Chesnut 2003, 149), whether in Latin America (Gill 1998) or the United States (Finke and Stark 2003). This theory still has to be tested in the African context (although, see Ukah 2003, especially 206–7), but once again, the new mass-mediated public spheres appear to underscore the need for theoretical optics that can make sense of pluralism and competition, as well as intersecting discourses of faith, values, consumption, and power (see, for example, Meyer 2004; M. de Witte 2003; Schulz 2003; Ukah 2003).[38]

FRICTIONS AND FRAGMENTATIONS

Audience research, notably in Africa, lags behind institutionally oriented research on media policy and ownership, or on program content (Myers 2008, 6). This is not surprising given the more demanding nature of such social inquiry (see Ginsberg, Abu-Lughod, and Larkin 2002; Anderson 2003, 891–92). One of the saving graces of the rise of commercial media, however, is the market research they conduct to evaluate the choices of their viewing and listening publics. This does not treat in any depth audience reception, or the type of "thick description" called for by Jon Anderson (2003, after Clifford Geertz), but at least it may provide us with some profiles of

audiences.[39] The current reorientation in media studies toward ethnographic research on audience diversity and people's active use of mass
media (Spitulnik 2000; Hoover and Lundby 1997; Cruz and Lewis
1994; Askew and Wilk 2002, 237–393; Livingstone 1996) may generate more Africa-related studies.[40]

My findings on some of the problematic intersections of religion
and media in Africa are rather more piecemeal and cumulative. They
derive from direct observation, interviews, conversations, anecdotal
evidence, reports of public complaints in either the media or the (electronic) publications of human rights and watchdog groups, speeches
and comments by government officials, and the stated goals and deliberations of professional media and nongovernmental organizations.
Most of the conflicts surrounding religion and the media can be explained through the following four issues: inequities, encroachment
and displacement, defamation, and entertainment. We will look at
each one in turn.

Inequities

It is primarily in the area of ownership, as well as production and
transmission, that one encounters complaints about inequity. Muslims, in particular, have been very vocal, along with traditional practitioners such as Nokuzola Mndende in South Africa (1999), in accusing
the media in Africa of being in the hands of Western, Christian, or
Zionist gatekeepers.[41] It is one of the reasons that Muslims have been
reluctant to develop a media presence. While this is gradually changing with privatization and youth-oriented initiatives, as well as the
quest for parity and equal access to national resources in this new
phase of democratization, there is still a noticeable imbalance in terms
of religious use of the mass media. Muhammed Haron writes of the
way that the various Muslim communities in South Africa have embraced the new opportunities offered by community radio for ownership and control (Haron 2004), but this still represents the exception
to the norm.

One cannot assume that, with liberalization, state control of the
airwaves has lessened. There is still enormous power in granting licenses, capacity, and frequencies. For example, two Muslim commu-

nity radio stations in South Africa (Al-Ansaar in Durban and An-Nur in Port Elizabeth) were given restricted licenses to go on air only during the month of Ramadan (Haron 2004, 150). Governments can pull the strings of the media commissions and other regulatory bodies in order to reward political allies and fend off political enemies.[42] Nyamnjoh underscores the need to pay attention to this level of "rigid regulation of national media and local cultural production," rather than laying all the blame at the feet of global capitalism (Nyamnjoh 2004, 63).

Examples of such state manipulation and collusion abound. After Jerry John Rawlings took power for the second time in Ghana in 1981, only a neo-traditional religious group, the Afrikania Mission, was granted airtime on state radio (M. de Witte 2003). In the Democratic Republic of the Congo (DRC), at the height of armed conflict in 2000, the majority of radio and television networks were shut down, except for religious radio stations (as long as they steered clear of politics).[43] Leo Slingerland, managing director of the newly opened (in 1999) Family TV and FM in Kenya, revealed to me that he had only managed to obtain a broadcasting license for his Christian media organization because of his Christian and family connections. In fact, at the time President Daniel arap Moi was much criticized for his government's less than transparent and inequitable issuing of broadcasting licenses—giving preferential access to conservative churches, as they did not contest his authority unlike other mainstream religious organizations.[44] Issuing licenses to religious bodies rather than secular ones has provided the Kenyan and some other African governments a "risk-free means for the authorities to prove their democratic credentials."[45] Such a move, coupled with the fact that religious organizations were among the few groups in Africa that could afford to invest in such expensive enterprises as radio stations, resulted in considerable growth of religious (mainly Christian) radio stations. Even if they did not have strong financial backing, Christian organizations had the experience and expertise to turn shipping containers into radio stations (TransWorld Radio), produce wind-up radios, and organize radio churches.

Even where governments held back on issuing licenses to religious stations, they might still favor particular religious groups by turning a blind eye to bias in program content.[46] This is well evidenced in Ghana, where private FM stations stack their primetime early morning programming in favor of their predominantly (Pentecostal) Christian audiences with gospel music, Christian perspectives on social issues, and pastors as presenters (M. de Witte 2003, 177; Hackett 1998). The managing director of JOY FM, the oldest of the private stations, informed me in May 2000 he would never invite members of other religions onto his station. The reasoning is usually based on consumer demands or religious proclivities. In some states in northern Nigeria, Christians have no access to airtime, whether public or commercial.[47]

Media commissions can also be part of the problem. In 2004, the Nigerian National Broadcasting Commission (NBC) imposed a controversial ban on miracles. The edict stated that Nigerian broadcasters were no longer allowed to show miracles on television in a way that was not "provable and believable." Television stations that failed to abide by the ruling would be fined, and their equipment could be confiscated. News of this ban spread far and wide, but the NBC was not forthcoming when asked what would constitute verification of a miracle.[48] Reactions to this ban were mixed—some welcomed the cutback in faith-healing programming,[49] others protested the ban and claimed their religious rights.[50] Christ Embassy, one of Nigeria's largest Pentecostal churches whose mainstay is a highly popular television program, *Atmosphere for Miracles*,[51] went to court to challenge the ban.[52] Others, such as T. B. Joshua's Synagogue Church for All Nations, also renowned for its "miracle" healing activities, ignored the restriction. Rumors even circulated that the ban was part of a Muslim conspiracy to prevent Christians from stealing their members.[53] Lagos-based Media Rights Agenda expressed concern about the ban, stating, "we believe that the NBC Director General should not with executive fiat ban them. Miracles and belief in them are essential characteristics of Christianity and banning miracles in religious broadcast will therefore tamper with the totality of the Christian faith as presented in such broadcasts."[54] They further added that "religion is a very sensitive matter in Nigeria and any decision affecting the broadcast of any aspect of it must be taken with caution so it does not create room for further crisis in a nation already overwhelmed by a state of insecurity." They went on to recommend a high-level consultation with all parties involved, with input from other countries on how they handle the broadcasting of "miracle healing" services.

Mass media, with their history as an instrument of propaganda, are recognized as having inbuilt inequities. After all, the history of the global media is closely tied to the history of the twentieth century, namely, wars, decolonization, and science and technology (Ady 1999). Studies conducted on the role of the media in central Africa in promoting peace and democracy reveal that journalists more frequently toe the party line rather than favoring independent, investigative reporting (Institut Panos 2002). Nyamnjoh singles out the private media in particular for serving as mouthpieces for divisive opposition as well as religious, ethnic, and regional groups, and for failing to curb extremism and intolerance (Nyamnjoh 2005, 56). In a most interesting article exploring the "transnational paths of delivery of electronic communications," broadcasting law expert Monroe Price finds that such paths are far from neutral (Price 1999; cf. also Parks 2005). In fact, he compares them to trade routes in their efforts to gain power or sovereignty. Hent de Vries reminds us that the media are more than means of communication—they mediate and construct sensibilities regarding citizenship, for example (de Vries 2001). The power of the media, along with their inequities and biases, has made many religious groups increasingly aware of the need to ensure they are not left behind in the new power struggle over the airwaves.

Encroachment and Displacement

In the past, boundary maintenance was more feasible between religious communities. Now non-Christians fear not just the penetrating preaching of high-tech crusades, such as that of the popular German Pentecostal preacher Reinhard Bonnke and his Christ for All Nations campaign, but also the aggressive marketing techniques and seductive technologies of healing and counseling to which they are increasingly exposed. As objectified and commodified spiritual power, the ubiquitous video and cassette tapes are perhaps even more subversive in terms of providing alternative religious options (Coleman 2000, 172).[55] The Mombasa (Christian) radio station, Radio Baraka, is popular with Muslims as it broadcasts in Swahili in the mornings. Muslim women feel comfortable visiting the station to talk about their problems.[56] Islamic-led governments may ban Christian radio stations in their territories, as in many northern Nigerian states, but they can rarely stop the messages being broadcast from just over the border in neighboring countries.[57] A survey that I conducted with graduate students of Central University College in Ghana in 2001 found that several Muslims admitted to secretly listening to the tapes and broadcasts of the popular charismatic preacher, Rev. Dr. Mensa Otabil. There are reports, which I have not yet been able to confirm, that Christian motivational and biblical text messages are being sent (unsolicited—although they can be solicited) to MTN cell phone subscribers in South Africa.

Reinhard Bonnke used to speak of his goal to cover the African continent—from Cape to Cairo—with the blood of Jesus by the year 2000. Today his website opens up with a more global focus in terms of links and images.[58] But the crusades page reveals his special focus on Africa with news and reports, accompanied by the most impressive photos of huge crowds. (Interestingly, many crusades occur in Nigeria despite Bonnke's having been airlifted/evicted from there in 1991 and being told by northern Muslim leaders not to return. However, after being invited back by President Olusegun Obasanjo in 1999, he has been organizing his mega-events in the north again.[59]) The crusade narratives testify to the empire-building designs of the Christ for All Nations enterprise. For instance, in Ikirun, Nigeria, in November 2003, we read that "soon the words of life were pouring out over the vast crusade site, as 60,000 people were encouraged to *turn from dark-ness* into the light of Calvary. The multitude of hands that eagerly shot up accepting Jesus as Lord and Savior was proof enough that *Ikirun land was being favored* by the presence of the Holy Spirit."[60]

Bonnke likes to speak of how, in some locations, the land has to be prepared, both physically and spiritually, for the crusades. Trees and shrines were leveled, and the land reclaimed from the "jungle" for the Ayangba crusade in March 2005. Speaking of this crusade and a neighboring one in Jalingo, he intoned: "The Gospel hit that area like lightning! It crushed and destroyed heathen religion and set the people free from a million fears. I never before felt in my spirit that an ancient satanic infrastructure had been destroyed, and the Kingdom of God established with [such] power."[61] He has also claimed at other Nigerian crusades that "Jesus is the Savior of Nigeria" (Jos crusade, 2000) and that "the blood of Jesus is the best cure for a sick land" (Jos crusade, 2005). All of these discourses of displacement from one of Africa's most influential evangelists are rendered even more threatening to Muslim and traditional religious leaders by their magnification through modern media technologies. Flooding the print and broadcast media with announcements of impending crusades—in a range of local and national languages—may be an effective marketing technique, but it is also an effective tool of alienation.

Saturation of an area with targeted programming is a strategy employed by the Christian Broadcasting Network (CBN) through its global outreach and international programming division— WorldReach. The goal of CBN WorldReach is to take the gospel message to 3 billion people and to see 500 million people brought to faith in Jesus Christ.[62] This "media blitz," as it is termed, saturates a selected region over a concentrated period of time, using all forms of media: television programming, radio shows, videotapes, and literature. One of their key strategies has been to partner with other Christian ministries worldwide and in-country to maximize the impact. There are also follow-up strategies encouraging feedback for viewers and association with local church leaders and organizations.

Another Christian missionary organization—Trinity Broadcasting Network (TBN)—talks about the "new angel's footprint" that now covers several African countries due to the "technological 'angels' in mid-heaven, beaming Jesus into homes and hearts around the world."[63] In terms reminiscent of the colonialist era, GOD TV informs its viewers that it is "Broadcasting from Jerusalem to the Ends of the Earth."[64] After the network was launched in South Africa in 2002, South Africans were told by the new director of GOD TV Africa, Oliver Raper, that they would find the programming relevant, since "[it] is truly a *global village type* channel."[65] He highlights the instrumentality of the media in the global evangelistic enterprise: "Reinhard Bonnke's cry, 'From Cape Town to Cairo, Africa will be saved!' still resounds today. . . . I believe it wholeheartedly and I know that through GOD TV we will see this happen in my lifetime."[66]

178 Rosalind I. J. Hackett

Viewers are reassured that despite the global outreach of this ministry to more than two hundred nations, they will always get "front row seats." This is because GOD TV beams directly into believers' homes daily, and usually live, coverage of revival and apostolic conferences from "revival hotspots" around the world. Analysts of televangelism have demonstrated how this creative balancing of intimacy and great scope, personal needs and broader project, account for its success (Hadden and Swann 1981; Peck 1993; Hoover 1988; Coleman 2000, 177–79). Given the obvious preference for live broadcasts or webcasts, broadcasters often have to disguise the fact that the program is recorded in advance.[67] So to the power of the message is added the power of the medium. Just as promoters hope that it will inject faith into the unsaved, detractors fear its magical powers (Lyons and Lyons 1987; see also Coleman 2000, 179).

At the local level, communication in the form of posters, banners, and flyers can trigger protest, especially in educational institutions as has occurred in Nigeria. Wording of flyers and banners—such as "Welcome to Jesus Campus" or "God's All-Consuming Fire is Sweeping Nigeria," which connotes a takeover or transformation of a shared space—was at the root of the Kafanchan and Kano riots (1987 and 1991 respectively; Hock 1996; on Nigeria more generally, see, Ukah 2008).

The Christianization of space involves countering one's enemies. Sound is considered by some to be a very effective form of spiritual warfare. For example, the Spirit FM Network, an American organization that develops Christian radio stations in Africa (Ghana and Uganda to date) declares one of its primary goals as "*to counter the rapid growth of Islam* through sound Christian programming and great inspirational music."[68] Power evangelism may also be utilized as a way of purifying the territory (see, for example, DeBernardi 1999). Numerous incidents reported on Human Rights Without Frontiers' electronic news service regarding religious intolerance and persecution involve violent attempts to suppress the Pentecostal practice of loud worship.[69] In fact, the refusal by several Ghanaian Pentecostal churches to desist from noise-making during traditional festival periods in the capital, Accra, has resulted in several years of conflict, necessitating intervention by senior religious leaders and government officials (van Dijk 2001; Hackett 1999). This serves to illustrate that, in Africa's congested urban spaces, it is often difficult to escape the sounds of one's neighbors, especially when those sounds are electronically reproduced, and often "retransmitted" by individual and religious communities to gain maximal proselytizing effect.

Cornering the market may prove in the long run to be the most effective weapon against one's religious competitors. As noted above, Christian organizations in Ghana, predominantly of the Pentecostal and charismatic variety, have come to dominate the radio airwaves in the Accra region. Kwabena Asamoah-Gyadu tellingly situates this in a wider context: "The main agenda of Pentecostal/Charismatic churches therefore, is to bring their influence to bear on all aspects of national life including discouraging any official recognition of other faiths, and the media have proved a very powerful means of achieving this end" (Asamoah-Gyadu 2005).[70] In Nigeria, the displacement of the opposition is even more overt. Walter Iherijika reports that commercial airtime, now dominated by Pentecostal televangelists, and a lucrative source of revenue for financially strapped stations (notably at the state level), has edged out public service religious programming in some areas (Ihejirika 2005).[71] He also notes that the previous pattern of Christian programming on Sundays and Muslim programming on Fridays has gone by the wayside, with Pentecostal programs now being aired at any time and any day of the week. He notes that this violates the 10 percent allocation of airtime for religious programming as stipulated in the National Broadcasting Code (section 3.4, article 8).

Defamation

In seeking to control this new competitive and discursive space, and to build their own communities, many religious groups in Africa are adopting new discourses of power and demonization (Smith, this volume; Ellis and ter Haar 2004; Westerlund 2003; Comaroff and Comaroff 1999). These discursive strategies reflect and generate cleavages, as well as (perceived) inequalities between groups. Often, it is the aggressive language that offends, whether the use of "crusade," "harvesting souls," "darkness," and so forth. TBN publicizes widely their "Devil Bustin' Satellite."[72] In other contexts, the language may be more metaphorical and the demonizing messages more coded so as to avoid the scrutiny of regulatory bodies and codes of ethics, yet they can be transparent to many.[73] Ugandan Muslims (who are not an insignificant minority at 12 percent) complain about Christian evangelists using the airwaves—they purportedly own at least seven FM stations and two television stations—to perpetrate "lies against Islam."[74] In May 2006, gunmen attacked a Pentecostal radio station (Hope FM) in Nairobi, Kenya, following a program that compared teachings of the Bible and the Qur'an, and that urged Kenyans to convert to Christianity. One person died and the building was set on fire.[75] On stage in Africa, mega-evangelist Reinhard Bonnke is perhaps more guarded, paying courtesy calls on Muslim heads of state (Gifford 1994, 16), while the newsletters that circulate to donors outside Africa are more direct in naming the enemy—whether Islam or traditional religion. For example, in a 2001 letter to prayer partners, Bonnke linked the lack of development in the city of Ibadan in Nigeria and the "hold of darkness over this town" to its traditional religious heritage.[76]

Even before the first Coptic Christian satellite TV channel, Aghapy TV, was launched in Egypt in November 2005, fears were being expressed that it might follow the pattern of other Christian satellite channels based outside the country (for example, a Cyprus-based Christian satellite channel called Al-Hayat) and allow programming critical of Islam. The station's objective was defended by the supervisor, Bishop Boutros: "All we want to do is to promote our religion in the proper manner, to counter foreign channels that promote Christianity in strange ways."[77] Citing the station's striking motto, "If we are not on air, we are not on earth," the head of Coptic youth affairs, Bishop Moussa, said that the station was intended primarily to service and unify the Coptic community, in Egypt as well as in Europe and North America.[78] Referring to the Coptic community's beleaguered minority status in Egypt, Aghapy executive director Father Bishoy al-Antony explained: "We first proposed to have our own radio in 1951. It was rejected and since then it has been our dream to have this TV. . . . It is not easy to build churches in Egypt, so this is like home delivery, church on air," he added.[79] However, even Copts themselves—who make up about 10 percent of the Egyptian population—were divided as to whether the new channel would deliver on its promises and not be a source of offending Muslims and fueling religious tensions with new forms of proselytization, notably through the medium of a U.S.-operated satellite network.

Generally it is the Pentecostals at the deliverance end of the spectrum who deploy more demonizing rhetoric (van Dijk 2004; Hackett 2003a; Meyer 1999) and images (Ukah, this volume),[80] although the advocates of the prosperity gospel seem to have turned up the volume on their dualistic theology. For example, during a January 2004 visit to the Winners' Chapel in Jos, we heard the preacher announce that we had just left hell to enter heaven by coming into their beautiful church. Evangelicals, with their emphasis on personal salvation and the protective community of the "saved," may sensationalize the "before" and celebrate the "after" existences. This dualistic orientation characterizes many of the Christian morality tales, which are a popular feature of the Nigerian video film industry. It is noteworthy that these films circulate widely in many parts of Africa (McCall 2004, [2004]; Daniel [2004]). Dualism and demonism naturally accentuate awareness of religious "Others." As Asonzeh F.-K. Ukah states, in his study of Nigerian Christian (predominantly Pentecostal) video films, "the fight against an opposite gives Pentecostalism its relevance, its texture, and defines its impact on society" (Ukah 2003, 221). Birgit Meyer contends that these negative "imaginations of tradition are to a large extent trapped in the discursive frame of 'traditional Christianity versus traditional religion,' which has its roots in nineteenth-century encounters between missionaries and Africans" (Meyer 2005, 303). In the case of Tanzania, Bernadin Mfumbosa notes a rise in antagonism between Muslims and Christians using media outlets (especially newspapers) in the current phase of deregulation. He attributes this to the erosion of traditional modes of communication and reconciliation, due to attacks by radical Christian as well as Muslim groups on local forms of indigenous cultural and religious practice.[81] Such demonization of "pagan ignorance" is evidenced in the new genre of video films produced in northern Nigeria since 2000 that treat the superiority of Islam. These films reflect wider political and legal attempts to revitalize and expand Sharia in the North, amid fears of southern Christian hegemony and general social degradation (Krings 2005).

A prime example of the new mass-mediated discourses of demonization is Nigeria's (perhaps West Africa's) largest and most influential deliverance ministry, Mountain of Fire and Miracles.[82] The essential teaching of the general overseer and founder, Dr. O. Olukoya, is "absolute holiness within and without, as the greatest spiritual insecticide, and a condition for heaven." The worldwide deliverance ministry (with branches in China, India, Europe, and North America) is a "do-it-yourself gospel ministry where your hands are trained to wage war and your fingers to fight." When Olukoya, a published microbiologist and molecular geneticist, attacks his enemies as "satanic dogs" or "wicked rods," he is targeting primarily moral deviants (such as, according to him, homosexuals, adulterers, thieves, etc.), backsliders, evil acts (for example, loose tongues, sexy dressing, idolatry— "the curse of the black race"), and nefarious powers ("ancestral curses") primarily found in traditional religious culture (Hackett 2011). He appears to skirt critical social issues and political corruption; nor does he include any direct references to Islam in his writings, as far as I can tell.

Olukoya is not alone in expending his homiletic energies on the bondages and blockages created by any form of association with traditional religious culture, but he is arguably the most militant and well publicized (through the website and his numerous publications). His style and message serve as a model for other aspiring deliverance workers. The same could be said for the late South African Muslim preacher, Ahmed Deedat, whose polemics against Christianity were widely publicized and circulated in many parts of Africa (Westerlund 2003). While not denying the popular appeal of such leaders and the positive transformations that they may effect in people's lives, insecurities and dehumanizing discourses arguably help foster a climate of fear, intolerance, and incivility, especially when they enjoy multimedia dissemination (Hackett 2007).[83] Knut Lundby and Daniel Dayan refer to this type of fragmented and fractured public space as a "discontinuous credoscape" (Lundby and Dayan 1999, 406). It may explain in part why there are several references to the heightened role of the media in inciting acts of violence and discrimination on religious grounds in the United Nations Commission on Human Rights' revised resolution on "Combating Defamation of Religions."[84] Along similar lines, the International Media Council, established by the World Economic Forum in 2006, held its 2007 meeting in Davos under the rubric of "Fanning the Flames: Is the Media Fueling the Clash of Civilizations?"[85]

Entertainment

Despite the role played by radio stations in laying the roots of democratic culture in Africa (Senghor 2001), the majority of the new radio stations are commercial. This has given rise to fears about the loss of public interest programming and its capacity to promote civil society values. In order to appeal to the widest possible audiences and retain government approval, programming is oriented to entertain, as well as to inform and educate. The Family TV (Kenya) statement of purpose is a case in point: "As a Christian broadcast house, Family Media was formed for the purpose of advancing the message of Jesus Christ by providing quality wholesome Christian entertainment in conformity with God's word."[86] Family-oriented programming not only favors those religious actors and groups who can generate high audience ratings, but also those who can successfully appeal to a broad public base in the most inoffensive way possible.[87] For example, research surveys suggest that an estimated 6.5 million viewers watched a week-long media blitz of family-oriented Christian programming staged by *Turning Point*, CBN's flagship program to Africa in Zambia and Zimbabwe in 2000.[88]

The undermining of public service broadcasting by more popular independent stations is seen by many as a regrettable aspect of social and cultural fragmentation more generally. Such critics bemoan the lack of serious information and current affairs coverage (Herman and McChesney 1997). As rightly noted on an earlier version of the Panos website, "[African] governments often threw open the gates without wondering what sort of broadcasting mix they were letting in, and without asking themselves whether any controls were still necessary."[89] The commercialism and predominance of entertainment, chiefly music and soap operas, is further challenged on the grounds that it appeals primarily to the monied urban classes. Nyamnjoh accuses both the Anglophone South African subscription television service Digital Satellite Television (DStv) and its French counterpart, Canal Horizon, of having "virtually colonized the palates of elite Africans along linguistic and cultural lines" and their "routinized, standardized or McDonaldized international sport and entertainment" (2004, 71; see also 2005, 51). Michael Budde, in his critical study of the power of the global culture industries in industrial countries, suggests that even parents and religious leaders are "not insulated from the deleterious effects of media monopolization of attention" (Budde 1997, 83).

The consumerist model drives not only the entertainment of mass audiences but also the servicing of religious publics.[90] Writing of the changing, post-liberal landscape in the United States, Jeffrey Stout observes with extreme concern the ways in which "talk radio, cable television, and the Internet have significantly increased the proportion of information that the average individual receives from sources entirely within his or her particular enclave" (Stout 2003, 114).[91] He sees this as seriously undermining the possibilities of shared public discourse.[92] Outlets that do provide public news and opinion are attacked by the "enclave-oriented providers" who would profit from manipulating and serving the needs of differentiated consumerist constituencies. Concurring with his analysis, I would add that this type of separatism and loss of religious cross-talk is highly problematic, and unfortunately paralleled in the increasingly privatized school system.[93]

Paradoxes and Prospects: Empire-Building or Flow Reversal?

The questions and concerns that I have raised in this essay regarding the rise of new religious media must be seen against the broader global debates about the *paradoxes* of new media developments (McChesney, Newman, and Scott 2005; McChesney 2000). As Nigerian journalist and communications specialist Akin Fatoyinbo rightly suggests, the old debates of the 1970s and early 1980s on the New World Information and Communication Order (NWICO) have been reopened "due to the newly enforced domination of developing countries by the industrial nations as a result of the new information technologies, particularly in radio and television broadcasting." Indeed, there exist various regional and international bodies that seek "to enable a truly global and equitable information suprasystem" (Ady 1999, 213).[94] The Panos Institute (London), for example, in collaboration with other partners, is now working to see how existing and potential broadcasting policies can include the poor and marginalized.[95] However, there is general agreement that this new world information and communication order has only enjoyed limited success to date. Many doubt that the Habermasian (Habermas 1991 [1962]) unfettered intermediate space for rational-critical communication has been realized (see Anderson 2003; cf. also Hendy 2000). There are also concerns that the market approach to the broadcasting industries has not always yielded the desired outcomes in terms of balanced growth and reliable revenue.[96] Writing of Latin America, Jesus Martin Barbero contends that thinking about communication from the perspective of culture "unsettles" the "technological optimism" of the field of communication studies (Barbero 2006, 44).

It is not hard to find proponents, however, of the potential for new media technologies to challenge state and corporate hegemonies. Akin Fatoyinbo laments the dominance of radio and TV channels by foreign broadcasters, yet views optimistically the potential of new technologies not only to democratize the media but also to reverse the information and communication technologies (ICT) flows (Fatoyinbo 1999; van Binsbergen 2004). He gives the example of WorldSpace, a digital satellite radio corporation based in Washington, D.C., and founded by Noah Samara, an African of Ethiopian/Sudanese ancestry.[97] In fact, WorldSpace is the pioneer of direct satellite delivery of digital audio radio services around the world. Samara wanted "to provide direct satellite delivery of digital audio broadcasting services to the emerging and under-served countries of the world" (ibid.). There are now two satellites over Africa and Asia, each with three beams. The technology also allows either local community radio stations or large international broadcasters to rent channels on the

WorldSpace satellites to transmit programming directly to hand-held radio sets on the FM channels or digital audio receivers. The not-for-profit arm of the corporation, known as First Voice International, broadcasts "first voice" developed from content produced locally by African community broadcasters, nongovernmental organizations, media agencies, and other community-based organizations.[98] In Fatoyinbo's words, "Now that is going global from the local" (ibid.).

For some, the future of broadcasting in Africa lies with low-power radio broadcasting. LPFM stations operate against the trend of commercial media monopolies. Owned by religious groups, charities, environmental groups, schools, and governmental agencies, the stations use as few as 100 watts, in contrast to the 50,000 wattage of commercial stations. Whereas LPFM stations beam programs to their communities (typically within a radius of three or four miles), the signals of commercial stations can be heard for one hundred miles. In 2003, the South African Community Media Policy Research Unit, together with the Freedom of Expression Institute (FXI), lobbied the communications regulator, the Independent Communications Authority of South Africa (ICASA), to broaden access to the airwaves, thus allowing these micro-radio stations to operate and their communities to enjoy freedom of expression and information.[99] They do, however, note the dangers of creating ghettoized communities with this class of broadcasting.[100]

In contrast, political scientist John Keane has a more positive reading of the role of the media in the various global public spheres in reducing the parochialism, and heightening the self-reflexivity, of global civil society (Keane 2003, 170–72). Local cultural production, such as cartoons, music, and video films can provide outlets for social and political critique (Nyamnjoh 2004; Mbembe 2001), but there is less evidence of religious leaders being subject to the same satirical attack as politicians and heads of state. In his work on television and moral discourse in Belize, Richard Wilk emphasizes the importance of examining social discourse about television in order to understand it as a medium (Wilk 2002). While less direct than analyzing cultural content or social effects, how people talk about television illumines the ways in which they are now objectifying new concepts of culture, subjectivity, and otherness (ibid., 295). Clearly such an approach lends itself to any consideration of religious media, and is highly relevant in the African context, where communal listening and viewing practices are common.

In the introduction to their important volume on the anthropology of media, the editors rightly argue that it is inappropriate to predicate research in this area on "oppositional logics" because of the "simultaneity of hegemonic and anti-hegemonic effects of 'technologies of power'" (Ginsberg, Abu-Lughod, and Larkin 2002, 23). Similarly, Goran Hyden and Michael Leslie, writing of the rise of informal media of communication in Africa in the last decade, in response to the shortcomings of the formal media, argue that it may well be that neither the radical conception of the media as a top-down agency nor its antithesis of the media as a bottom-up agency of empowerment is adequate to help us understand the role of media as agents of transmission of cultural and political values (Hyden and Leslie 2002, 23). So the jury is still out on these key developments, and much will depend on local media, religious, and political environments, as well as the influence of international organizations.[101] As a seasoned and critical analyst of media trends in southern Africa, Keyan Tomaselli opines that "much of what is going to be said and written about Africa's new media will reflect their economic masters" (Tomaselli 2002, 152).

These ambivalent discourses on the new media feed into current debates concerning appropriate or inappropriate imbrications of the media and religious expression, as well as the place of religion in, and which type of religion is best for, the changing public sphere (Soares 2004). As stated earlier, the secularist paradigm of many civil society and international nongovernmental organizations results in little serious analysis of the intersections of media and religion. It is as if religious organizations did not feature on the map of contemporary Africa. But clearly one cannot ignore the power of the media in whatever form. A young Muslim activist from Ibadan told me that he did not have to switch on his television to know that the media in his traditionally pluralistic city were now dominated by Christian evangelists. Similarly, who can avoid, let alone not be drawn to Reinhard Bonnke's Christ for All Nations juggernaut when it rolls into town, with its capacity to stage crusades for hundreds of thousands of people? Many a non-Christian has gone with the flow, seeking miracles amid the catharsis and anonymity of a mega-spectacle. This may be about greater religious choice, but it is also about the rise of more exclusivist forms of religion, better equipped than ever before to effect changes in the social and moral landscapes of African societies.

This inattention to religion means that the otherwise valuable study of the media in central Africa by the Panos Institute, referred to above, only addresses the ways in which media institutions treat the promotion of traditional culture, as well as peace and conflict issues. A document as influential as UNESCO's "Communication Training in Africa: Model Curricula" discusses ethnicity but not religion as a source of community segregation and integration.[102] Similarly, UNESCO's programs on "Media in Conflict and Post-Conflict Situations," notably the one on "Partnership for Media and Conflict Prevention in West Africa," do not address religion.[103] Organizations that seek to empower local communities, such as OneWorld Africa— a global community of producers and broadcasters sharing audio for and ideas on radio for development in Africa[104]—do not seem to address religious communities or religious issues.[105] Consequently, might it not be surprising that many religious organizations take inspiration from transnational corporations or their family partners, instead of more enlightened professional associations and progressive nongovernmental organizations?

Concluding Remarks

In this closing section I would like to reiterate the major themes of this chapter, and consider what future changes might or should occur to counter the regressive trends adumbrated above. I have sought to demonstrate some of the negative outcomes of media deregulation for questions of religious tolerance and pluralism in Africa's rapidly changing public spheres. I have not tried to argue that this focus on the problematic aspects of the rise of new religious media represents the whole picture, only that I wanted to shed more light on what I consider to be neglected developments. Nor have I proposed that there are always explicit connections between media use and religious conflict, let alone violence. I do believe—in keeping with new research on minority media and media framing—that it is possible to argue that even though the media are not deterministic, they are increasingly influential in shaping perceptions of cultural and religious difference or sameness, and in facilitating or impeding the enjoyment of individual and/or collective rights. These are all integral to any consideration of peace and conflict issues in Africa today (see Frère 2007; Mbaine 2006).

African political leaders are clearly more concerned about political opposition—as evidenced by the continued existence of problematic "insult laws"[106]—than they are about inequitable or uncivil religious use of burgeoning media environments. And yet, as the recent BBC report on media development in Africa indicates (*African Media Development Initiative* 2006, 31), religious media are far from insignificant in the political economy of broadcasting. South Africa is one of the few places in Africa today where there have been distinct efforts to harness the media for the promotion of harmonious religious coexistence through public debate and participation (Hackett 2006b). It is an ongoing project that could usefully be replicated in other locations. There needs to be public dialogue about how production and transmission are sensitive to the needs of the various religious communities, for more and more minority groups want to enjoy at least some programming consonant with their own lifestyles (cf. Browne 2005, 197).[107] Along with more effective, independent media commissions, and media watchdog organizations attentive to the saliency of religion in democratizing, if precarious, political arenas,[108] scholars of religion and media could play their part in promoting research and dialogue in these areas. Africa's multiethnic, multireligious, and multimedia environments need befitting research at the levels of ownership, production, transmission, and reception.[109] Religious leaders, too, need to think more critically about the short- and long-term consequences of promoting their organizations at the expense of others, and adopt less unilateral, self-centered notions of human and constitutional rights.

Other factors may serve to mitigate the new patterns of marginalization and exclusion described in this essay. More stable political and economic conditions, more respect for the rule of law, and improved professionalism in the media sector could serve to heighten healthy competition, even nurture new forms of cooperation, between religious groups.[110] With the increase in computer-mediated communications, religious practice may become more customized and privatized, lessening the impact of broadcast media. In other contexts, such as Ghana, the saturation of the media by Pentecostal and charismatic organizations may have a nulling, overkill effect.[111] What has been described as Africa's "communitarian praxis" could serve to override corporate media culture to provide accessible and responsible media (Fackler 2003), or new media entrepreneurs could decide to actively counter religious extremism through the development of modern, moderate programming as in the case of the new Islamic satellite channel, Al Risala in Egypt.[112] However, with continuing debates about the paradoxical nature of global trends, and anxieties about the rise of more militant and media-savvy strains of conservative religion worldwide, Africa will surely constitute a strategic location in the foreseeable future for observing and managing these developments.

NOTES

Earlier versions of this chapter were aired at the Joan B. Kroc Institute for International Peace Studies, where I was a Visiting Rockefeller Fellow from 2003 to 2004, at the European Association for the Study of Religion conference in August 2005, and at the African Studies Center, Leiden, in March 2007. Portions of the text appear in Hackett 2006c.

1. Meyer and Moors (2006, 12) emphasize the contestations and politics of difference that accompany the emergence of new, mass-mediated religious publics.

2. http://www.rnw.nl (accessed March 1, 2004). A clear example is the role of Radio Biafra in sustaining Nigeria's civil war from 1966 to 1970 (Offor 2002).

3. See the website of the Pionier research program, *Modern Mass Media, Religion and the Imagination of Communities,* http://www2.fmg.uva.nl/media-religion (accessed June 27, 2007). On Egypt, see Hirschkind 2006.

4. In fact, in the BBC World Service 2005 survey "Who Runs Your World?" a majority of Africans put religion above any other factor, and surprisingly few identified ethnicity as the most significant factor (6 percent); http://news.bbc.co.uk/2/hi/africa/4246754.stm (accessed September 16, 2005).

5. I am here drawing on the insightful work of Simon Cottle on race and ethnic minorities and the media (Cottle 2000).

6. Studies of African media, few as they are at present, pay scant attention to religious broadcasting. They are generally more interested in the history of media institutions and the links between the media, development, and democratization. See, for example, Bourgault 1995; Fardon and Furniss 2000; Holmes 1999; Maduka 1989; Minnie 2000; Mytton 2000; Opoku-Mensah 1998; Walsh 1996; Tomaselli and Dunn 2001; Tomaselli, Tomaselli, and Muller 1990; Hyden, Leslie, and Ogundimu 2002; Noam 1999. However, there is an encouraging body of ethnographic research on the smaller, informal and popular media. See Larkin 1997; Schulz 1997; Hackett 1998; Ukah 2003; M. de Witte 2003; Soares 2004.

7. For a general, up-to-date analysis of the field, see Hoover 2006.

8. The *African Media Development Initiative: Research Summary Report* notes that in some countries, such as the Democratic Republic of Congo, Tanzania, and Zambia, "religious media may be the primary or sole area of non-state sector development since 2000" (2006, 31).

9. See also *African Media Development Initiative* (2006, 31).

10. For an excellent overview of the radio scene in Africa, see Myers 2008, http://www.amarc.org/documents/manuals/12481943581Radio_and_Development_in_Africa,_a_concept_paper.pdf (accessed May 22, 2011).

11. See the 2008 report by Balancing Act, http://www.balancingact-africa.com/news/broadcast/issue-no24/top-story/rapid-increase-in-th/bc (accessed May 22, 2011).

12. See the report by Panos West Africa, "Radio and ICT in West Africa: Connectivity and Use" (2008), http://www.cipaco.org/sources/Radio%20and%20ICT%20in%20West%20Africa_light_couv.pdf (accessed May 22, 2011).

13. http://www.southafrica.info/about/media/radio.htm (accessed May 22, 2011).

14. See Myers 2008, 14.

15. Radio France Internationale, 2008, cited by Myers 2008, 14.

16. See *African Media Development Initiative* (2006) cited by Myers 2008, 14.

17. *African Media Development Initiative* (2006, 30).

18. Commercial regional television in Uganda has grown from one channel in 2000 to eight by 2005 (*Africa Media Development Initiative* 2006, 34). A third of them are owned by religious entities (ibid., 31). Operators such as Next Generation Broadcasting Africa (NGB Africa) are now working with state-run TV in Uganda, Ghana, and Kenya to offer commercial pay TV, http://www.ngbroadcasting.com/in_the_world.php (accessed May 23, 2011).

19. http://www.cbnafrica.com/ (accessed May 23, 2011).

20. http://www.nationmalawi.com/articles.asp?articleID=7457 (accessed March 11, 2004).

21. A pertinent example here would be www.christembassy.org.

22. In conducting research for this paper and its presentation in Jinja, I was surprised to find that several local ministries in the area had websites, for example, http://www.busogachurchesofchrist.com/, http://www.christultd .org/churches.htm (accessed February 4, 2005).

23. See also Radio Pulpit, South Africa's leading religious broadcaster, http://www.radiopulpit.co.za/ (accessed September 5, 2007).

24. See, for example, Spirit FM and Trinity Broadcasting Network, www.tbn.org.

25. http://www.unesco.org/webworld/news/2001/010914_mali.shtml (accessed May 26, 2004). Four of these were donated to radio stations in Timbuktu, Mali, in 2001, to enable radio staff to produce "radio-browsing" programs. In such programs, the presenter browses the Internet in response to listeners' questions, describes in local languages the websites selected, and discusses their contents with a local expert.

26. http://www.spirit.fm/africa.html (accessed March 8, 2004).

27. http://www.feba.org.uk/cgweb03/_sto/shortwavestory.htm (accessed February 29, 2004).

28. http://www.wwcr.com.

29. http://www.tbn.org/index/php/3.html (accessed October 23, 2003).

30. http://www.3abn.org/announcements.cfm (accessed June 25, 2007).

31. http://sa.cfan.org/CrusadeReport.aspx?id=5088 (accessed September 3, 2007).

32. www.panamsat.com.news/pressview.asp?article=1282 (accessed February 4, 2005).

33. http://www.radiopanam.com/ (accessed February 4, 2005).

34. http://www.hcjb.org/ (accessed May 30, 2004).

35. http://www.christembassy.org (accessed February 4, 2005).

36. As stated on their website, "the GOD Channel's dedicated Africa feed is broadcast twenty-four hours a day on two major satellites—Thaicom 3 across the continent of Africa and PAS 7 in southern Africa—which means that every TV owner in Africa, who has a dish and decoder, is able to watch the channel. It also means that the GOD Channel signal can be easily pulled down and redistributed via terrestrial transmitters to viewers in the most remote areas, who can pick up the channel without a satellite decoder." http:// www.god.tv/node/47?region=41 (accessed May 29, 2011).

37. http://www.christianlifeministries.org/home/radio.html (accessed September 6, 2007).

38. As an instance of how religious programming gets "marketed" in Ghana and around Africa, see Marleen de Witte's account of the International Central Gospel Church (M. de Witte 2003, 188–90).

39. See, for example, the audience research conducted on Ghana's International Central Gospel Church, which revealed a broader and more diverse media audience than the church's membership (M. de Witte 2003, 193).

40. The work of Lila Abu-Lughod on the way rural Egyptians appropriate or contest visions of modernity via national and imported soap operas (Abu-Lughod 1995), and Purnima Mankekar's ethnography of television viewing by women in India, demonstrating the critical role television has played in the realignment of class, caste, consumption, religion, and politics (Mankekar 1999), would be exemplary here. While focused on the Internet, Lorne Dawson's and Doug Cowan's excellent collection of studies on the effects on religion online and the effects of online religion on offline religion might also yield fruits (Dawson and Cowan 2004). Meyer and Moors caution, however, against "overemphasizing the agency of audiences in processes of appropriation" more generally (2006, 15). For an example of audience research on religion from Nigeria, see Ihejirika 2004.

41. For a radical Nigerian perspective, see Ado-Kurawa 2000.

42. The *African Media Development Initiative Report* (2006, 32) also claims that in the countries that they surveyed, "the ultimate power still lies with the state."

43. http://unesco.org/courier/2001_04/uk/medias.htm (accessed September 9, 2003).

44. Robert O'Doul, "The People's Voice," *G21 The World's Magazine* (2000); http://www.g21.net/africa7.html (accessed September 30, 2003).

45. Ibid.

46. The Nigerian government has continually resisted granting licenses to religious broadcasters in order to protect the delicate balance between Muslims and Christians in the country.

47. Most of the irregularities occur with the state, rather than the federal, broadcasting stations. Ogbu Kalu, personal communication, March 20, 2007.

48. For some of the feedback, see "The NBC Ban of Unverified TV Miracles," http://www.nairaland.com/nigeria/topic-40.0.html (accessed May 29, 2011). For a more theoretical perspective, see Hent de Vries' reflections on the similarities and differences between "miracles" and "special effects" (de Vries 2001, 23–29).

49. Rev. Fr. Gabriel Osu, "Halting Advertising of Miracles: A Stitch in Time," *The Guardian on Sunday,* May 30, 2004, 24.

50. "Miracle Broadcast: Court Asked to Stop NBC's Directive," *This Day,* May 18, 2004, 7.

51. http://loveworldchristiannetwork.org/Webtv/.

52. Sam Olukoya, "Nigerians Divided by TV Miracle Ban," *BBC News*, June 8, 2004, http://news.bbc.co.uk/1/hi/world/africa/3784659.stm (accessed June 26, 2007). In February 2011, the Advertising Standards Authority of South Africa (ASASA) banned all television programs about "miracles" by the Believers LoveWorld Incorporated, (aka Christ Embassy) headed by pastor Chris Oyakhilome. David Ajikobi, "South Africa bans Christ Embassy 'miracle' slots" *Next,* February 5, 2011. http://234next.com/csp/cms/sites/Next/Home/5673158-146/story.csp (accessed May 29, 2011).

53. Anna Borzello, "Crackdown on Nigeria TV Miracles," *BBC News*, April 30, 2004, http://news.bbc.co.uk/1/hi/world/africa/3672805.stm (accessed June 26, 2007).

54. "On The World Press Freedom Day 2004," April 30, 2004, http://www.mediarightsagenda.org/pressapril_04.html (accessed June 26, 2007).

55. The thousands of tapes of the controversial Lagos-based Prophet T. B. Joshua are openly marketed in this way.

56. Information from Bob Fortner, Words of Hope, Grand Rapids, Michigan, March 2, 2004.

57. See, in the case of Sudan, http://woh.gospelcom.net/news/news .php?id=86 (accessed February 4, 2005) and IBRA Radio, a Scandinavian Pentecostal Christian radio ministry that broadcasts from Uganda (www .ibra.org) (accessed June 25, 2007).

58. www.cfan.org. His vision of the continent of Africa, washed in the precious Blood of Jesus is discussed in his autobiography, *Living a Life of Fire: An Autobiography* (E-R Productions, 2009). The U.K. website flashes messages about how CfAN has been evangelizing Africa for more than twenty-five years, and how they have seen "over 55 million documented decisions for Christ" and "millions healed and set free from oppression." While "towns, cities and nations [have been] transformed by the Gospel," the "fields of Africa are still white unto harvest." http://www.cfan.org.uk/donate/ (accessed May 24, 2011). See also Gifford 1987.

59. That Nigeria represents Bonnke's most productive mission site is evidenced by a 2007 interview with Pat Robertson on CBN's *700 Club*, where he claimed that CfAN had more than 9 million people complete "decision cards" in 5 months with 5 crusades and that they planned to increase the number of crusades to 10 per year. http://www.cbn.com/700club/features/bonnke_raisedpastor.aspx (accessed September 3, 2007).

60. http://www.cfan.org/{English-Intl}/[SouthAfrica_Site]/index -crusade_report.asp (accessed March 12, 2004) (my emphasis).

61. http://www.cfan.org/%7BEnglish-Intl%7D/%5Bsouthafrica _site%5D/content.asp?id=0000630&page=01 (accessed February 11, 2005).

62. www.cbn.org (accessed September 3, 2007).

63. http://www.tbn.org/about/newsletter/index/php/art:244 (accessed February 29, 2004).

64. http://www.godnetwork.com (accessed March 13, 2004). Now available at http://www.god.tv/homepage?region=42 (accessed May 29, 2011).

65. http://www.godnetwork.com/watchUs/africa/newsarticle.aspx (accessed March 13, 2004) (my emphasis).

66. See also "Covering Africa with Christian Radio," http://www.petersfoundation.com/charity.htm (accessed March 8, 2004).

67. Rev. Dr. Mensa Otabil, personal communication, Accra, July 6, 2001.

68. http://www.spirit.fm/africa.html (accessed March 8, 2004).

69. http://hrwf.net.

70. Available at http://www.waccglobal.org/en/20052-christian-fundamentalism-and-the-media/526-Reshaping-Sub-Saharan-African-Christianity.html (accessed May 29, 2011).

71. This is in violation of the National Broadcasting Code, section 3, 4, articles 1 and 3, which stipulates the provision of equitable air-time and appropriate opportunity for all religious groups. National Broadcasting Commission, *National Broadcasting Code* (Lagos, 1993).

72. http://www.tbn.org/about/newsletter/index.php/244.html (accessed June 29, 2007).

73. Barbara Cooper has an excellent example of this from her research on evangelical and Pentecostal Christians in Niger (2006, 74).

74. Shashank Bengali, "Uganda at the Forefront of Africa's Boom in Evangelical Christianity," Knight Ridder Newspapers, March 22, 2006 (available at http://wwrn.org/articles/20928/) (accessed May 23, 2011).

75. Rodrique Ngowi, "1 Dead in Kenya Religious Station Attack." AP, May 13, 2006. The attack received much international coverage, including a condemnation from the UNESCO director-general, May 18, 2006, http://portal.unesco.org/ci/en/ev.php-URL_ID=22163&URL_DO=DO_TOPIC&URL_SECTION=201.html (accessed June 24, 2007).

76. "Ibadan 2001," *Countdown Letter 2*. Christ for All Nations (n.d. [2001], 3). Note: this "town" is one of Africa's largest metropoles with a population of around more than 3 million people.

77. Reem Nafie, "Many Wary of Faith-Based TV," November 17–23, 2005, Issue No. 769, http://weekly.ahram.org.eg/2005/769/eg11.htm (accessed June 27, 2007).

78. Vivian Salama, "Aghapy TV Brings Teachings of Coptic Church into Homes of Followers," *The Daily Star,* November 23, 2005, http://freecopts.blogspot.com/2005/11/aghapy-tv.html (accessed June 27, 2007).

79. "Coptic Christians Get Own Satellite Television Station amid Egypt Tension," Agence France Presse, November 2, 2005, http://www.comeandsee.com/modules.php?name=News&file=article&sid=693 (accessed November 27, 2007).

80. Although Pentecostals found themselves on the receiving end in July 2007 in Uganda after a pastor was caught trying to bring an electric shock machine into the country. For several weeks the press was alive with critical op-eds, mocking cartoons, and a range of sympathetic to scathing letters from the public over the so-called wired pastors. By July 23, the government was announcing new measures for regulating the newer churches. Chris Ahimbisibwe, "Govt to Eliminate Fake Churches, says Buturo," *New Vision*, July 23, 2007, http://wwrn.org/articles/25743/?&place=eastern-africa&section=church-state (accessed May 23, 2011).

81. Personal communication, July 15, 2006. Similar observations were also made by Katharina K. Wilkens and Franz Wijsen about the increasingly aggressive styles of religious broadcasting and street preaching in Tanzania. Personal communication, July 8, 2007.

82. http://www.mountain-of-fire.com (accessed March 14, 2004).

83. In a survey conducted in Tanzania, respondents answered that videos exerted a more negative influence on tensions between Muslims and Christians, and more than half thought that it would be good to ban videos for this reason (Wijsen and Mfumbusa 2004, 36).

84. E/CN.4/2004/L.5, April 13, 2004. The European Union has been developing a new lexicon for public communication on terrorism and Islam, to avoid alienation and confrontation, notably in light of the Danish cartoon controversy. "EU Lexicon to Shun Term 'Islamic Terrorism,'" Reuters, April 11, 2006, http://www.wwrn.org/article.php?idd=21129&sec=33&con=47 (accessed April 14, 2006). Archbishop Desmond Tutu called on the media to be more careful in their choice of words when reporting on religious conflict. "Tutu Calls for Better Media Reporting of Religion," Reuters, June 27, 2007, http://wwrn.org/article.php?idd=25523 (accessed June 29, 2007). See also studies by Richardson 2007, 1996; McCloud 2004; Beckford 1999 on the deviant labeling of nonmainstream religious groups.

85. For an analysis of the crucial role played by the media in generating moral panic and countermovements with regard to new religious movements (NRMs), see Richardson and Introvigne 2007.

86. http://www.familykenya.com/Statement.htm (accessed March 11, 2004).

87. Cf. Neil Postman's *Amusing Ourselves to Death*. Jeremy Carrette and Richard King lament and critique the ideological affinity between contemporary spirituality and contemporary capitalism (Carrette and King 2004).

88. For data on such media blitzes, see http://www.go-tell.org/page3 .HTM (accessed September 3, 2007).

89. http://www.panos.org.uk/global/Rprojectdetails.asp? ProjectID=1026&ID=1002 (accessed September 9, 2003).

90. In Kenya, Muslims wanting to avoid Christian-dominated programming on Sundays on both public and private stations, or international (CNN) news coverage of controversial topics, such as Iraq, often resort to Lebanese or Egyptian satellite channels, such as soap operas—if they can afford it.

91. Cf. Geschiere and Meyer's observation that cultural closure frequently accompanies global flows (Geschiere and Meyer 1998).

92. Cf. the work of Markus Prior (2007), which demonstrates that in a high choice media environment (cable and Internet) preferences for entertainment over information result in people more readily removing themselves from political knowledge and action than they did in the broadcast age.

93. Although, in his excellent comparative study of changing patterns of community radio use and ownership by South African Muslim communities, Muhammed Haron notes that phone-in discussion programs on topics of international concern (with follow-up international website links), or what he terms "localized 'international' programmes," have proved to be highly successful in developing audience participation (Haron 2004, 153–54).

94. See, for example, the "World Summit on the Information Society," http://www.geneva2003.org/wsis/index_c01_3_18.htm, which includes guidelines from many civil society organizations. See also the African Charter on Broadcasting 2001 (Windhoek Declaration), http://portal.unesco.org/ci/en/ ev.php-URL_ID=1595&URL_DO=DO_TOPIC&URL_SECTION=201 .html (accessed September 3, 2007).

95. http://www.panos.org.uk/global/Rprojectdetails.asp?ProjectID =1026&ID=1002&RProjectID=1060 (accessed March 10, 2004).

96. See, for example, "FM Radios Wobble in Fiery Airwaves," *The Monitor* (Kampala), April 20, 2004, http://allafrica.com/stories/200404200199 .html (accessed April 21, 2004). The demise of TV Africa in October 2003, for financial reasons, after five years of operations was also a blow to those who saw free-to-air commercial television as the future of African media. E. Abiorh-Odidja, "TV Africa's Demise Ends Free-to-Air Television in Africa?" *ProficeAfrica,* July 18, 2004, http://www.profileafrica.com/ commentary.ablorh.011004.htm (accessed June 5, 2005).

97. www.worldspace.com.

98. www.firstvoiceint.org.

99. Suzanne Charlé, "(Low) Power to the People: FM Mini-stations put Neighborhoods on the Air," Ford Foundation Report, Summer 2003, http://

www.comminit.com/ctrends2003/sld-8326.html (accessed March 11, 2004); "South African Government Urged to Allow Community Radio." Afrol News, June 23, 2003, http://www.afrol.com/News2003/sa018_comradio.htm (accessed September 30, 2003).

100. See Myers 2008, 5 on the risks of "hate radio" in the community radio sector.

101. The public disagreements over the launching in November 2005 of satellite television for the Coptic Christian minority in Egypt are an excellent case in point, http://www.copts.net/detail.asp?id=813 (accessed December 20, 2005).

102. http://www.unesco.org/webworld/publications/com_training _en.pdf (accessed March 11, 2004).

103. http://portal.unesco.org/ci/en/ev.php-URL_ID=22225& URL_DO=DO_TOPIC&URL_SECTION=-465.html (accessed June 27, 2007).

104. http://radioafrica.oneworld.net (accessed March 11, 2004).

105. But see the initiative of some Nigerian journalists in April 2011: James Ngahy "Reporting on religious coloured conflict," http://www .africafiles.org/article.asp?ID=25242 (accessed May 29, 2011).

106. Peter Feuilherade, "Africa 'Must Scrap Insult Laws,'" June 4, 2007, BBC News 24, http://news.bbc.co.uk/1/hi/world/africa/6719535.stm.

107. For a fine example of how the media can take a balanced perspective on a volatile issue, see "This Is Not about Freedom of Speech," *Mail & Guardian* (South Africa), February 10, 2006, http://www.misa.org/cgi-bin/ archives.cgi?category=1&view=2-06 (accessed September 3, 2007).

108. A pertinent example would be the Muslim Media Watch Group founded in 2001 by a group of Muslims in Kwara State, and led by Dr. Lateef Oladimeji, who teaches at the University of Ilorin and has his own weekly Muslim TV talk show on Nigerian Television Authority, Ilorin.

109. An international conference on "New Media and Religious Transformations in Africa" took place in Abuja, Nigeria in July 2008 and a volume of the same title, edited by Rosalind I. J. Hackett and Benjamin Soares is in progress.

110. On the significance of media professionalism, ethics, and training, see Nyamnjoh 2005, chapter 2. The *African Media Development Initiative* (2006, 79) notes that professional and ethical standards remain low in Africa's media sector.

111. Personal communication, Birgit Meyer, July 11, 2006.

112. Ursula Lindsey, "The New Muslim TV: Media-savvy, Modern, and Moderate," *Christian Science Monitor,* May 2, 2006.

REFERENCES

Abu-Lughod, Lila. 1995. "The Objects of Soap Opera: Egyptian Television and the Cultural Politics of Modernity." In *Worlds Apart: Modernity Through the Prism of the Local,* edited by A. Miller. New York: Routledge.

Ado-Kurawa, Ibrahiim. 2000. *Shari'ah and the Press in Nigeria: Islam versus Western Civilization.* Kano: Kurawa Holdings Limited.

Ady, Jeffrey C. 1999. "Transcending the Dialectic of Culture." In *Towards Equity in Global Communication,* edited by R. C. Vincent, K. Nordenstreng, and M. Traber. Cresskill, NJ: Hampton Press.

African Media Development Initiative: Research Summary Report. 2006. London: BBC World Service Trust.

Anderson, Jon W. 2003. "New Media, New Publics: Reconfiguring the Public Sphere of Islam." *Social Research* 70(3):887–906.

Ansah, P. A. V. 1994. "Privatization of Radio: Implications and Challenges." In *Independent Broadcasting in Ghana: Implications and Challenges,* edited by K. Karikari. Legon: Ghanaian Universities Press.

Appadurai, Arjun. 1996. *Modernity at Large: Cultural Dimensions of Globalization.* Minneapolis: University of Minnesota Press.

Article 19. 1996. *Broadcasting Genocide: Censorship, Propaganda & State-Sponsored Violence in Rwanda 1990–1994.* London: Article 19.

Asamoah-Gyadu, J. Kwabena. 2005a. "Anointing Through the Screen: Neo-Pentecostalism and Televised Christianity in Ghana." *Studies in World Christianity* 11(1):9–28.

———. 2005b. "Reshaping Sub-Saharan African Christianity." *Media Development* 42(2).

Askew, Kelly M., and Richard R. Wilk, eds. 2002. *The Anthropology of Media: A Reader.* Oxford: Blackwell.

Barbero, Jesus Martin. 2006. "Between Technology and Culture: Communication and Modernity in Latin America." In *Cultural Agency in the Americas,* edited by D. Sommer, 27–51. Durham, NC: Duke University Press.

Bayart, Jean-François. 2005 [1996]. *The Illusion of Cultural Identity.* Trans. J. R. Steven Rendall, Cynthia Schoch, and Jonathan Derrick. Chicago: University of Chicago Press.

Beckford, James A. 1999. "The Mass Media and New Religious Movements." In *New Religious Movements: Challenge and Response,* edited by B. Wilson and J. Cresswell. New York: Routledge.

Beyer, Peter. 2003. "Constitutional Privilege and Constituting Pluralism: Religious Freedom in National, Global, and Legal Context." *Journal for the Scientific Study of Religion* 42(3):333–39.

Bourdieu, Pierre. 2003. *Firing Back: Against the Tyranny of the Market.* Trans. L. Wacquant. New York: New Press.

Bourgault, Louise M. 1995. *Mass Media in Sub-Saharan Africa.* Philadelphia: University of Pennsylvania Press.

Boyle, Kevin. 1992. "Religious Intolerance and Incitement to Religious Hatred." In *Striking a Balance: Freedom of Expression, Hate Speech and Non-Discrimination,* edited by S. Coliver. London: Article XIX and University of Essex.

Browne, Donald R. 2005. *Ethnic Minorities, Electronic Media and the Public Sphere: A Comparative Approach.* Cresskill, NJ: Hampton Press.

Budde, Michael. 1997. *The (Magic) Kingdom of God: Christianity and Global Culture Industries.* Boulder, CO: Westview Press.

Carrette, Jeremy, and Richard King. 2004. *Selling Spirituality: The Silent Takeover of Religion.* New York: Routledge.

Castells, Manuel. 1997. *The Information Age: Economy, Society and Culture.* Oxford: Blackwell.

Chesnut, R. Andrew. 2003. *Competitive Spirits: Latin America's New Religious Economy.* New York: Oxford University Press.

Christensen, P. Niels, and Wendy Wood. 2007. "Effects of Media Violence on Viewers' Aggression in Unconstrained Social Interaction." In *Mass Media Effects Research: Advances Through Meta-analysis,* edited by R. G. Preiss, B. Mae, N. B. Gayle, and M. Allen, 145–68. Mahwah, NJ: Lawrence Erlbaum Associates.

Clark, Lynn Schofield. 2003. *From Angels to Aliens: Teenagers, the Media, and the Supernatural.* New York: Oxford University Press.

Coleman, Simon. 2000. *The Globalization of Charismatic Christianity.* Cambridge: Cambridge University Press.

Comaroff, Jean, and John Comaroff. 1999. "Occult Economies and the Violence of Abstraction: Notes from the South African Postcolony." *American Ethnologist* 26(2):279–303.

———. 2004. "Privatizing the Millennium: New Protestant Ethics and the Spirits of Capitalism in Africa, and Elsewhere." In *Religion, Politics, and Identity in a Changing South Africa,* edited by D. Chidester, A. Tayob, and W. Weisse. New York: Waxmann Munster.

Cooper, Barbara. 2006. *Evangelical Christians in the Sahel.* Bloomington: Indiana University Press.

Cottle, Simon. 2006. *Mediatized Conflict: Developments in Cultural and Media Studies, Issues in Cultural and Media Studies.* Maidenhead: Open University Press.

Cottle, Simon, ed. 2000. *Ethnic Minorities and the Media: Changing Cultural Boundaries.* Buckingham and Philadelphia: Open University Press.

Cruz, Jon, and Justin Lewis. 1994. *Viewing, Reading, Listening: Audiences and Cultural Reception.* Boulder, CO: Westview Press.

Dahlgren, Peter. 1997. "Cultural Studies as a Research Perspective: Themes and Tensions." In *International Media Research,* edited by J. Corner, P. Schlesinger, and R. Silverstone. New York: Routledge.

Daniel, Trenton. [2004]. "Nollywood Confidential, Part 2." *Transition* 13(95):110–28.

Dawson, Lorne L., and Douglas E. Cowan, eds. 2004. *Religion Online: Finding Faith on the Internet.* New York: Routledge.

DeBernardi, Jean. 1999. "Spiritual Warfare and Territorial Spirits: The Globalization and Localization of a Practical Theology." *Religious Studies and Theology* 18(2):66–96.

Ellis, Stephen, and Gerrie ter Haar. 2004. *Worlds of Power: Religious Thought and Political Practice in Africa.* New York: Oxford University Press.

Entman, Robert M. 2004. *Projections of Power: Framing News, Public Opinion, and U.S. Foreign Policy.* Chicago: University of Chicago Press.

Fackler, Mark. 2003. "Communitarian Media Theory with an African Flexion." In *Mediating Religion: Conversations in Media, Religion and Culture,* edited by J. Mitchell and S. Marriage. London: T & T Clark.

Fardon, Richard, and Graham Furniss, eds. 2000. *African Broadcast Cultures: Radio in Transition.* Oxford: James Currey.

Fatoyinbo, Akin. 1999. "Africa and the Information Revolution: A Chance to Leapfrog into the Future." *D+C Development and Cooperation* 2:17–19.

Finke, Roger, and Rodney Stark. 2003. "The Dynamics of Religious Economies." In *Handbook for the Sociology of Religion,* edited by M. Dillon. New York: Cambridge University Press.

Frère, Marie-Soleil, ed. 2007. *The Media and Conflicts in Central Africa.* Boulder, CO: Lynne Rienner.

Frohardt, Mark, and Jon Temin. 2003. *Use and Abuse of Media in Vulnerable Societies.* Vol. 110, *Special Report.* Washington, DC: United States Institute of Peace.

Geschiere, Peter, and Birgit Meyer, eds. 1998. *Globalization and Identity: Dialectics of Flow and Closure.* Oxford: Blackwell.

Gifford, Paul. 1987. "'Africa Shall Be Saved': An Appraisal of Reinhard Bonnke's Pan-African Crusade." *Journal of Religion in Africa* 17:63–92.

———. 1994. "Reinhard Bonnke's Mission to Africa, and His 1991 Nairobi Crusade." *Wajibu* 9(1):13–19.

———. 2004. *Ghana's New Christianity: Pentecostalism in a Globalising African Economy.* Bloomington: Indiana University Press.

Gilboa, Eytan, ed. 2002. *Media and Conflict: Framing Issues, Making Policy, Shaping Opinions.* Ardsley, NY: Transnational Publishers.

Gill, Anthony. 1998. *Rendering Unto Caesar: The Catholic Church and the State in Latin America*. Chicago: University of Chicago Press.

Ginsberg, Faye, Lila Abu-Lughod, and Brian Larkin, eds. 2002. *Media Worlds: Anthropology on New Terrain*. Los Angeles and Berkeley: University of California Press.

Gourevitch, Philip. 1998. *We Wish to Inform You that Tomorrow We Will be Killed with Our Families*. New York: Picador.

Habermas, Jurgen. 1991 [1962]. *The Structural Transformation of the Public Sphere: An Inquiry into a Category of Bourgeois Society*. Reprint ed. Cambridge, MA: MIT Press.

Hackett, Rosalind I. J. 1998. "Charismatic/Pentecostal Appropriation of Media Technologies in Nigeria and Ghana." *Journal of Religion in Africa* 26(4):1–19.

———. 1999. "Radical Christian Revivalism in Nigeria and Ghana: Recent Patterns of Conflict and Intolerance." In *Proselytization and Communal Self-Determination in Africa*, edited by A. A. An-Na'im. Maryknoll, NY: Orbis Books.

———. 2003a. "Discourses of Demonisation in Africa." *Diogenes* 50(3):61–75.

———. 2003b. "Managing or Manipulating Religious Conflict in the Nigerian Media." In *Studies in Media, Religion and Culture*, edited by J. Mitchell and S. Marriage. Edinburgh: T & T Clark.

———. 2006a. "Mediated Religion in South Africa: Balancing Air-time and Rights Claims." In *Media, Religion and the Public Sphere*, edited by B. Meyer and A. Moors. Bloomington: Indiana University Press.

———. 2006b. "A New Axial Moment for the Study of Religion?" *Temenos* 42(2):93–111.

———. 2007. "Competing Universalisms: New Discourses of Emancipation in the African Context." In *La rationalité, une ou plurielle?* edited by Paulin Houtondji, 163–71. Dakar: CODESRIA; Paris: UNESCO.

———. 2011. "Is Satan Local or Global? Deliverance Lagos-Style." In *Pentecostalism and Globalisation*, edited by A. Adogame and U. Berner. Bayreuth: Bayreuth University.

Hadden, Jeffrey K., and Charles E. Swann. 1981. *Prime Time Preachers: The Rising Power of Televangelism*. Reading, MA: Addison-Wesley.

Haron, Muhammed. 2004. "The South African Muslims Making (Air)Waves during the Period of Transformation." In *Religion, Politics, and Identity in a Changing South Africa*, edited by D. Chidester, A. Tayob, and W. Weisse. New York: Waxmann Munster.

Hendy, David. 2000. *Radio in the Global Age*. Cambridge: Polity Press.

Herman, Edward S., and Robert W. McChesney. 1997. *The Global Media: The New Missionaries of Corporate Capitalism*. London: Cassell.

Hirschkind, Charles. 2006. *The Ethical Soundscape: Cassette Sermons and Islamic Counterpublics.* New York: Columbia University Press.

Hock, Klaus. 1996. *Der Islam-Komplex.* Hamburg: Lit Verlag.

Holmes, Patricia A. 1999. *Broadcasting in Sierra Leone.* Lanham, MD: University Press of America.

Hoover, Stewart M. 1988. *Mass Media Religion: The Social Sources of the Mass Media Church.* Newbury Park, CA: Sage.

———. 2006. *Religion in the Media Age: Religion, Media and Culture.* New York: Routledge.

Hoover, Stewart M., and Lynn Schofield Clark, eds. 2002. *Practicing Religion in the Age of the Media.* New York: Columbia University Press.

Hoover, Stewart M., and Knut Lundby, eds. 1997. *Rethinking Media, Religion, and Culture.* Thousand Oaks, CA: Sage.

Husband, Charles. 2000. "Media and the Public Sphere in Multi-Ethnic Societies." In *Ethnic Minorities and the Media,* edited by S. Cottle. Buckingham: Open University Press.

Hyden, Goran, and Michael Leslie. 2002. "Communications and Democratization in Africa." In *Media and Democracy in Africa,* edited by G. Hyden, M. Leslie, and F. F. Ogundimu. New Brunswick, NJ: Transaction Publishers.

Hyden, Goran, Michael Leslie, and Folu F. Ogundimu, eds. 2002. *Media and Democracy in Africa.* New Brunswick, NJ: Transaction Publishers.

Ibrahim, Jibrin. 1989. "The Politics of Religion in Nigeria: The Parameters of the 1987 Crisis in Kaduna State." *Review of African Political Economy* 45(6):65–82.

Ihejirika, Walter. 2004. *An Audience Ethnography on the Role of the Mass Media in the Process of Conversion of Catholics to the Pentecostal Churches in Nigeria.* Rome: Gregorian University.

———. 2005. "Media and Fundamentalism in Nigeria." *Media Development* 42(2).

Institut Panos. 2002. *Afrique Centrale, des médias pour la démocratie.* Paris: Karthala.

Juergensmeyer, Mark. 2003 [2001]. *Terror in the Mind of God: The Global Rise of Religious Violence.* Berkeley and Los Angeles: University of California Press.

Keane, John. 2003. *Global Civil Society.* New York: Cambridge University Press.

Krings, Matthias. 2005. "Muslim Martyrs and Pagan Vampires: Popular Video Films and the Propagation of Religion in Northern Nigeria." *Postscripts* 1(2–3):183–205.

Larkin, Brian. 1997. "Hausa Dramas and the Rise of Video Culture in Nigeria." In *Nigerian Video Films,* edited by J. Haynes. Jos: Nigerian Film Corporation.

Liebes, Tamara, and Elihu Katz. 1994. *The Export of Meaning: Cross-Cultural Readings of Dallas.* Cambridge: Polity Press.

Lincoln, Bruce. 2003. *Holy Terrors: Thinking About Religion after September 11.* Chicago: University of Chicago Press.

Livingstone, Sonia. 1996. "On the Continuing Problem of Media Effects." In *Mass Media and Society,* edited by J. Curran and Michael Gurevitch. London: Hodder.

Lundby, Knut, and Daniel Dayan. 1999. "Mediascape Missionaries? Notes on Religion as Identity in a Local African Setting." *International Journal of Cultural Studies* 2(3):398–417.

Lyons, A. P., and H. D. Lyons. 1987. "Magical Medicine on Television: Benin City, Nigeria." *Journal of Ritual Studies* 1.

Maduka, V. I. 1989. "The Development of Nigerian Television (1959–1985)." In *Nigeria Since Independence: The First Twenty-Five Years,* edited by P. Ekeh and G. Ashiwaju. Ibadan: Heinemann.

Mankekar, Purnima. 1999. *Screening Culture, Viewing Politics: An Ethnography of Television, Womanhood, and Nation in Postcolonial India.* Durham, NC: Duke University Press.

Mbaine, Adolf E., ed. 2006. *Media in Situations of Conflict: Roles, Challenges and Responsibility.* Kampala: Fountain Publishers.

Mbembe, Achille. 2001. *On the Postcolony (Studies on the History of Society and Culture).* Berkeley and Los Angeles: University of California Press.

McCall, John C. 2004. "Juju and Justice at the Movies: Vigilantes in Nigerian Popular Videos." *African Studies Review* 47(3):51–67.

———. [2004]. "Nollywood Confidential: The Unlikely Rise of Nigerian Video Film." *Transition* 13/1(95):98–109.

McChesney, Robert W. 2000. *Rich Media, Poor Democracy: Communication Politics in Dubious Times.* New York: New Press.

McChesney, Robert W., Russell Newman, and Ben Scott, eds. 2005. *The Future of Media: Resistance and Reform in the 21st Century.* New York: Seven Stories Press.

McCloud, Sean. 2004. *Making the American Religious Fringe: Exotics, Subversives, and Journalists, 1955–1993.* Durham: University of North Carolina Press.

Merry, Sally Engle. 2003. "Human Rights Law and the Demonization of Culture (And Anthropology Along the Way)." *PoLAR: Political and Legal Anthropology Review* 26(1):55–76.

Meyer, Birgit. 1999. *Translating the Devil: Religion and Modernity among the Ewe in Ghana.* Edinburgh: Edinburgh University Press.

———. 2004. "'Praise the Lord': Popular Cinema and Pentecostalite Style in Ghana's New Public Sphere." *American Ethnologist* 31(1):92–110.

———. 2005. "Mediating Tradition: Pentecostal Pastors, African Priests, and Chiefs in Ghanaian Popular Films." In *Christianity and Social Change in Africa: Essays in Honor of J.D.Y. Peel,* edited by T. Falola. Durham, NC: Carolina Academic Press.

———. 2006a. "Impossible Representations: Pentecostalism, Vision, and Video Technology in Ghana." In *Religion, Media, and the Public Sphere,* edited by B. Meyer and A. Moors. Bloomington: Indiana University Press.

———. 2006b. *Religious Sensations. Why Media, Aesthetics and Power Matter in the Study of Contemporary Religion. Inaugural Lecture, 6 October 2006.* Amsterdam: Vrije Universiteit.

Meyer, Birgit, and Annelies Moors, eds. 2006. *Religion, Media, and the Public Sphere*. Bloomington: Indiana University Press.

Minnie, Jeanette. 2000. "The Growth of Independent Broadcasting in South Africa." In *African Broadcast Cultures: Radio in Transition,* edited by R. Fardon and G. Furniss. Oxford: James Currey.

Mndende, Nokuzola. 1999. "From Racial Oppression to Religious Oppression: African Religion in the New South Africa." In *Religion and Social Transformation in Southern Africa,* edited by T. G. Walsh and F. Kaufmann. St. Paul, MN: Paragon House.

Musa, Bala. 2000. "Pluralism and Prior Restraint on Religious Communication in Nigeria: Policy versus Praxis." In *Religion, Law, and Freedom: A Global Perspective,* edited by J. Thierstein and Y. R. Kamalipour. Westport, CT: Praeger.

Myers, Mary. 2008. "Radio and Development in Africa: A Concept Paper." Prepared for the International Development Research Centre (IDRC) of Canada (2008). http://www.amarc.org/documents/manuals/ 12481943581Radio_and_Development_in_Africa,_a_concept_paper .pdf. Mytton, Graham. 2000. "From Saucepan to Dish: Radio and TV in Africa." In *African Broadcast Cultures: Radio in Transition,* edited by R. Fardon and G. Furniss. Oxford: James Currey.

Noam, Eli M., ed. 1999. *Telecommunications in Africa*. New York: Oxford University Press.

Norris, Pippa, Montague Kern, and Marion Just, eds. 2003. *Framing Terrorism: The News Media, the Government, and the Public*. New York: Routledge.

Nyamnjoh, Francis B. 2004. "Global and Local Trends in Media Ownership and Control: Implications for Cultural Creativity in Africa." In *Situating Globality: African Agency in the Appropriation of Global Culture,* edited by W. van Binsbergen. Leiden: Brill.

————. 2005. *Africa's Media: Democracy and the Politics of Belonging.* London: Zed Books.

Nye, David E. 2006. "Technology and the Production of Difference." *American Quarterly* 58(3):597–618.

Offor, Joseph Okechukwu. 2002. *Community Radio and Its Influence in the Society: The Case of Enugu State—Nigeria.* Frankfurt: IKO.

Onadipe, Abiodun, and David Lord, eds. 1999. *African Media and Conflict.* Rev. ed. London: Conciliation Resources.

Opoku-Mensah, Aida, ed. 1998. *Up in the Air: The State of Broadcasting in Southern Africa.* London: Panos Institute.

Parks, Lisa. 2005. *Cultures in Orbit: Satellites and the Televisual.* Durham, NC: Duke University Press.

Peck, Janice. 1993. *The Gods of Televangelism/the Crisis of Meaning and the Appeal of Religious Television.* Cresskill, NJ: Hampton Press.

Preiss, Raymond G., Barbara Mae Gayle, Nancy Burrell, and Mike Allen, eds. 2006. *Mass Media Effects Research: Advances Through Meta-analysis.* Mahwah, NJ: Lawrence Erlbaum Associates.

Price, Monroe E. 1994. "The Market for Loyalties: Electronic Media and the Global Competition for Allegiances." *Yale Law Journal* 104(3):667–705.

————. 1999. "Satellite Broadcasting as Trade Routes in the Sky." *Public Culture* 11(2).

————. 2002. *Media and Sovereignty: The Global Information Revolution and Its Challenge to State Power.* Boston: MIT Press.

Price, Vincent. 1992. *Public Opinion.* Thousand Oaks, CA: Sage Publications.

Prior, Markus. 2007. *Post-Broadcast Democracy: How Media Choice Increases Inequality in Political Involvement and Polarizes Elections.* New York: Cambridge University Press.

Rabinow, Paul. 2002. "Midst Anthropology's Problems." *Cultural Anthropology* 17(2):135–49.

Radio France Internationale, 2008. *Appui à la structuration du secteur radiophonique en Afrique francophone: Rapport d'expertise République Démocratique du Congo.* Version finalemars 08 Internal document, French Foreign Ministry: Paris (cited in Myers 2008, 14).

Richardson, James T. 1996. "Journalistic Bias Toward New Religious Movements in Australia." *Journal of Contemporary Religion* 11(3):289–302.

Richardson, James T., and Massimo Introvigne. 2007. "New Religious Movements, Countermovements, Moral Panics, and the Media." In *Teaching New Religious Movements,* edited by D. G. Bromley, 91–111. New York: Oxford University Press.

Schulz, Dorothea. 1997. "Praise Without Enchantment: *Griots,* Broadcast Media, and the Politics of Tradition in Mali." *Africa Today* 44(4):443–64.

————. 2003. "'Charisma and Brotherhood' Revisited: Mass-Mediated Forms of Spirituality and Urban Mali." *Journal of Religion in Africa* 33(2):146–71.

Sen, Amartya. 1992. *Inequality Examined*. Delhi: Oxford University Press.

Senghor, Diana. 2001. *The Panos Institute in the Face of New Challenges: Radio Pluralism and ICTs in West Africa* 2001 (accessed March 10, 2004). Available from www.fao.org/docrep/003/x6721e/x6721e36.htm.

Soares, Benjamin F. 2004. "Islam and Public Piety in Mali." In *Public Islam and the Common Good*, edited by A. Salvatore and D. F. Eickelman, 205–26. Leiden: Brill.

Spitulnik, Debra. 2000. "Documenting Radio Culture as Lived Experience: Reception Studies and the Mobile Machine in Zambia." In *African Broadcast Cultures: Radio in Transition*, edited by R. Fardon and G. Furniss. London: James Currey.

Sreberny-Mohammadi, Annabelle. 1996. "The Global and the Local in International Communications." In *Mass Media and Society*, edited by J. Curran and Michael Gurevitch. London: Arnold.

Stout, Jeffrey. 2003. *Democracy and Tradition*. Princeton: Princeton University Press.

Tomaselli, Keyan. 2002. "Media Ownership and Democratization." In *Media and Democracy in Africa*, edited by G. Hyden, M. Leslie, and F. F. Ogundimu. New Brunswick, NJ: Transaction Publishers.

Tomaselli, Keyan, and Hopeton S. Dunn, eds. 2001. *Media, Democracy and Renewal in Southern Africa*. Critical Studies in African Media. Colorado Springs, CO: International Academic Publishers.

Tomaselli, Keyan, and Miranda Young, 2001. "Introductions: Revisiting Media and Human Rights." *Critical Arts* 15(1).

Tomaselli, Ruth, Keyan Tomaselli, and Johan Muller, eds. 1990. *Broadcasting in South Africa*. Chicago: Lake View Press.

Ukah, Asonzeh F.-K. 2003. "Advertising God: Nigerian Christian Video-Films and the Power of Consumer Culture." *Journal of Religion in Africa* 33(2):203–31.

————. 2008. "Seeing is More Than Believing: Posters and Proselytization in Nigeria." In *Proselytization Revisited: Rights Talk, Free Markets, and Culture Wars*, edited by R. I. J. Hackett. London: Equinox Publishing.

van Binsbergen, Wim. 2004. "Can ICT Belong in Africa, or Is ICT Owned by the North Atlantic Region?" In *Situating Globality: African Agency in the Appropriation of Global Culture*, edited by W. van Binsbergen and R. A. van Dijk. Leiden: Brill.

van Binsbergen, Wim M. J., and Rijk van Dijk, eds. 2004. *Situating Globality: African Agency in the Appropriation of Global Culture*. Leiden: Brill.

van Dijk, Rijk. 2001. "Contesting Silence: The Ban on Drumming and the Musical Politics of Pentecostalism in Ghana." *Ghana Studies* 4:31–64.

———. 2004. "'Beyond the Rivers of Ethiopia': Pentecostal Pan-Africanism and Ghanaian Identities in the Transnational Domain." In *Situating Globality: African Agency in the Appropriation of Global Culture,* edited by W. van Binsbergen and R. van Dijk. Leiden: Brill.

Vries, Hent de. 2001. "In Media Res: Global Religion, Public Spheres, and the Task of Contemporary Religious Studies." In *Religion and Media,* edited by H. de Vries and S. Weber. Stanford, CA: Stanford University Press.

Vries, Hent de, and Samuel Weber, eds. 2001. *Religion and Media.* Stanford CA: Stanford University Press.

Walsh, Gretchen. 1996. *The Media in Africa and Africa in the Media: An Annotated Bibliography.* London: Hans Zell.

Weiss, Brad, ed. 2004. *Producing African Futures: Ritual and Reproduction in a Neoliberal Age.* Boston: Brill.

Westerlund, David. 2003. "Ahmed Deedat's Theology of Religion: Apologetics Through Polemics." *Journal of Religion in Africa* 33(3):263–78.

White, Robert A. 2003. "The Emerging 'Communitarian' Ethics of Public Communication." In *Mediating Religion: Conversations in Media, Religion and Culture,* edited by J. Mitchell and S. Marriage. London: T & T Clark.

Wijsen, Frans, and Bernardin Mfumbusa. 2004. "The Role of the Media." In *Seeds of Conflict: Religious Tensions in Tanzania,* edited by F. Wijsen and B. Mfumbusa. Nairobi: Paulines Publications Africa.

Wilk, Richard R. 2002. "'It's Destroying a Whole Generation': Television and Moral Discourse in Belize." In *The Anthropology of Media: A Reader,* edited by K. M. Askew and R. R. Wilk. New York: Blackwell.

Witte, John. 2001. "A Dickensian Era of Religious Rights: An Update on *Religious Human Rights in Global Perspective." William and Mary Law Review* 42:707–99.

Witte, Marleen de. 2003. "Televised Charismatic Christianity in Ghana." *Journal of Religion in Africa* 33(2):171–202.

CHAPTER 7

Mediating Armageddon
Popular Christian Video Films as a Source
of Conflict in Nigeria

Asonzeh F.-K. Ukah

A growing literature on the global rise of fundamentalisms has
sought to determine the relationship between religious extremism and violence (Marty and Appleby 1991, 1993a, 1993b, 1994,
1995; Bruce 2000; Almond, Appleby, and Sivan 2003). David Zeidan
(2003, 16) lists exclusivism, militancy, extremism, and radicalism as
core attributes of fundamentalism, and Bruce (2000, 5) argues that
every religion "is capable of producing people who put the promotion of religiously inspired goals above their society's norms." Obvi-
ously, exclusivism implies intolerance of others, as well as the potential
for violence against those with different beliefs or opinions (Wellman
and Tokuno 2004; Nepstad 2004). While Pentecostalism, the subject
of this essay, is a multifaceted religious movement that does not possess all of the characteristics of the ideal-typical fundamentalism discussed by these scholars (cf. Spittler 1994; Varga 1999, Anderson 2004,
258–60; Kimball 2002), some Nigerian manifestations of this rapidly
growing religious movement are so intolerant that they risk becoming
violent or provoking violence from others.[1] Hence Kekong Bisong
seems correct in observing that some of these strands are sources of
"great danger for interreligious [and intra-religious] dialogue in Africa" (2003, 144). New religious movements have transformed the
landscape of religious conflict, as the old tensions between Christianity and Islam are eclipsed, if not replaced, by conflicts within
Christianity (what some scholars refer to as "intra-religious" conflict). As Oshita (2007b, 10) convincingly contends, "there are far

more vibrant exchanges within the intra religious markets in Nigeria than in the larger sphere of perceived Christian-Muslim competition," presenting a situation in which intra-religious conflicts are more likely than so-called inter-religious discord (see also Oshita 2007a).

Nigeria is home to multiple strands of Pentecostalism, each one attempting to appropriate Christianity and make it locally relevant. They are part of a tightly competitive religious economy in which a proliferation of new religious suppliers competes for followers and funds. There is a clear entrepreneurial dimension to this religious growth, given that it has taken place within a context of economic and political collapse: church owner-founders generate new religious products and seek to carve out a niche for their spiritual wares, often in the hopes of generating revenue through tithes. The way in which these religious messages are disseminated transforms not only the religious consumers but also the messages themselves and their producers; thus, to paraphrase Marshall McLuhan in a somewhat different context, the medium is the message. Resembling the mid-twentieth-century American religious marketplace described by R. Laurence Moore (1994, 119–45), the new style of religiosity in Nigeria increasingly tries to shock the public in order to attract attention and create controversy as a branding and marketing strategy. In the quest for public attention and differentiation from other groups, this quest for shock and what could be labeled, at the risk of sounding cynically dismissive, "product uniqueness," has often culminated in intolerance and insensitivity to differing shades of beliefs and religious practice.

In Nigeria, Pentecostalism and media growth emerged out of the traumatic structural transformations taking place in economy and politics in the 1980s and 1990s. In this period of rapid social and economic turbulence, a new form of Pentecostalism emerged, which functioned as a personal problem-solving device positioned to handle, among other things, the pains and contradictions of social change. New media were also emerging simultaneously, and this serendipitous dovetailing energized the new visual imageries of urban religiosity. One such medium is the video film, an industry which, in Nigeria, arose from the ashes of the economic collapse of the mid-1980s. As it became economically unrealistic to produce celluloid films because of the high cost of importing film stocks, filmmakers resorted to video production as a way of remaining in business. Emerging under the same circumstances, Pentecostalism and video films have enjoyed a reciprocally beneficial relationship. With filmmakers and pastors functioning as producers and marketers of Hollywood-style religion, they have reinforced their mutual popularity and profitability.

The economic consequences of the rise of video film have been substantial. By the first decade of the twenty-first century, video film production had emerged as the most popular art form in Nigeria, with an average of forty titles released each week.[2] Video films are feature-length narratives shot and marketed in video format, usually running about ninety minutes. Films commonly run in parts (up to six), a strategy that is designed to maximize profit on serial stories that captivate a large audience. The Nigerian home video industry, sometimes called "Nollywood,"[3] generates more than 300,000 jobs each year and has an estimated annual turnover of more than 25 billion naira and an annual growth rate of 6 percent.[4]

From the beginning of the contemporary video culture in Nigeria, religion has played a prominent role in popularizing and cultivating the medium as a form of education and entertainment (Ukah 2003a; see also Bergesen and Greeley 2000). Many of these films are saturated with religious icons, images, and motifs. Moreover, popular religion, particularly the new Pentecostalism, has entrenched itself through this medium, using it to carry religious messages, images, and propaganda. In this respect, the videos represent an expression of contemporary Nigerian urban culture where religion, especially the new Pentecostalism, demonstrates its formidable power for social mobilization and individual as well as group self-definition. Pentecostal video films function alongside other religious institutions and media as purveyors of religious ideas, preferences, images, and meanings.

Pentecostal churches represent an important clearinghouse for religious video films, and Pentecostal professionals (pastors, church owner-founders, and leaders of large congregations) have become film actors, video producers, and marketers. Through this burgeoning medium, new spiritual entrepreneurs and suppliers have emerged, discovering fresh avenues for creating and sustaining a religious market. Both Christian and secular video producers make use of Christian images, ideas, and motifs in their work, so contemporary Nigerian popular culture and the new Pentecostalism have largely intermingled in locally produced movies. These videos tell religious stories and offer solutions to everyday frustrations or alternatives to traditional social practices; indeed, their content is created with the expectation that viewers have practical problems that need to be resolved. The ideas, images, and stories in the videos represent a powerful way of reaching the religious believer, touching the unbeliever, and addressing the common issues they face. In the hands of some Pentecostal pastors, however, the video medium has also been used for purposes other than simple preaching and proselytizing; it has become an instrument of "Othering" certain elements within society according to particular religious convictions and stereotypes. Videos are used to create as well as reinforce differences between the producers and their target audience on the one hand and the non-Pentecostal public on the other.

Liberty Films and *Rapture*

The most controversial producer of Pentecostal video films in Nigeria is evangelist Helen Esi Ukpai Ukpabio; she embodies the fusion of media and religion that Nigerian Pentecostalism has pioneered. Ukpabio is the founder and director of Liberty Foundation Gospel Ministries (LFGM), which includes Liberty Gospel Church (LGC) and a number of other ventures; its headquarters are in Calabar, Cross River State.[5] In 1998, she went into video film production with the establishment of Liberty Films and Music Plaza (LFMP). As of 2010, Liberty Films had released twenty movies and four musicals since its inception. These movies are marketed by commercial video distributors and the LGC, which has close to seventy branches in four African countries (Nigeria, Ghana, Cameroon, and South Africa). Each branch of LGC is designed to be a movie distribution outlet that circumvents the official marketing channels of video films in Nigeria. Church pastors are expected to preach the gospel of liberty on the one hand and to sell Liberty Films on the other.

Of all Liberty Films' releases, *Rapture* (2002), written and produced by Helen Ukpabio, directed by Fred Amata, and dedicated to "the Body of Christ," sparked the most controversy in Nigeria.[6] *Rapture* dramatizes the events that many Pentecostals and other millennialist Christians believe will take place in the end times, adopted from their interpretation of the biblical passage of 1 Thessalonians 4:16–17 and selected passages from the book of Revelation, and interpreted through the lens of contemporary events. According to the scriptwriter, the movie is about "the greatest event in human history,"[7] the apocalypse. As if to demonstrate its monumental significance, *Rapture* is the only Liberty Film production that has been divided into 2 parts, with a combined running time of 178 minutes. The film's narrative focuses on two thinly fictionalized religious communities, The Restored Church of Christ (RCC),[8] which is Pentecostal in orientation, and The Institute of Infant Jesus (IIJ), clearly representing the Roman Catholic Church. It is worth going into some detail about the film's highly stylized and dualistic presentation of these two religious communities, because it fomented such a storm of intra-religious Christian rancor within Nigeria.

The movie opens with a sincere but misguided priest, Reverend Father Francis (Richard Mofe-Damijo), leading a procession of worshipers into a church building for the celebration of the Eucharist. The opening rites of the Mass are sung in both English and Latin, and the incensing of the altar is executed perfectly by the chief celebrant. The next, lengthy scene shows His Lordship, Bishop Cornelius (Olu Jacobs), hugging, kissing, and finally indulging in sexual intercourse with Reverend Sister Veronica (Gloria Obong). As the bishop's secret lover, Sister Veronica consistently sneaks out of her convent at night to the bishop's waiting car in order to rendezvous with His Lordship. She later confronts the bishop with news that she is pregnant, and is told to "do as usual" and have an abortion. The nun refuses, saying that this would be her seventh abortion for His Lordship; she intends to keep the baby this time. At that moment another nun walks into the bishop's bedroom and shows herself as a favored replacement for the pregnant and now-estranged Sister Veronica. Indeed, throughout the movie, "Reverend Fathers" keep "Reverend Sisters" as concubines in order to "warm themselves for the night."

This fact comes as a surprise to Father Francis, who is stunned when he discovers that His Lordship, the bishop, leads all in this practice.[9]

In the film, the immoral activities of IIJ leaders are contrasted with events taking place in the RCC. The founder and leader of the RCC is the devout Pastor Goodnews (Ashley Nwosu). He is plagued by a bad-tempered wife, Felicity (Anne Uya), who disrupts church programs for superficial reasons such as obtaining the house keys from her husband or getting "shopping money" for the week. Dressed in flamboyant attire with conspicuous face makeup to match, Felicity is shown filing her fingernails while her husband leads a worship service in church. Meanwhile, as Pastor Goodnews holds spirit-filled services, the IIJ is holding a bazaar featuring cultural troupes and masquerades, representing traditional cultural practices regarded as unchristian by many Nigerian Pentecostals. Shortly after this, His Holiness, the pope (Avinaash Bhavinaavi), visits the country to conduct canonization services for a local saint. At the ceremony, the nuns in attendance are shown in shoddy attire, all clutching their rosaries as a casket containing the bones of the saint is carried in procession around the city.[10]

A climactic scene depicts a doctrinal confrontation between a disenchanted Reverend Father Gerald (Eyo Nkute) and Bishop Cornelius. Gerald tells the bishop that he is leaving the priesthood because "I cannot continue to worship God in error." The bishop asks what errors his priest has discovered, and he is given a litany of "false" doctrines: (1) "the celebration of the Mass is an error; it is against the scriptures which state that Jesus is the only and last sacrifice acceptable to God"; (2) the worship of Mary detracts from the worship of Jesus as God and Savior of the world; (3) the central role of the pope and his putative infallibility cause him to appear to "rub shoulders with God"; (4) infant baptism is unbiblical; (5) the office of priesthood is unbiblical as, "in the New Testament dispensation, there is no office of priests, for every 'born-again' Christian is a priest"; and (6) it is wrong to privately "work out our own salvation through penance rather than accepting the truth of salvation by grace of God."

Father Francis, who is present during this doctrinal disputation, is disturbed but unwilling to voice his anxieties. He soon meets with Sister Gold, played by Helen Ukpabio herself, a popular televangelist who agrees to discuss some "doctrinal clarifications" with the priest. During the meeting, Sister Gold "explains" that the Virgin Mary is not in heaven, as only the Trinity and the angels reside there, and further takes issue with the Catholic doctrine of the bodily assumption of the Virgin into heaven. As a result of this conversation, Francis becomes increasingly agitated about his priestly life. However, he is urged by a fellow Reverend Father to calm his anxiety about doctrines and engage in what every priest does: committing fornication with Reverend Sisters.

Father Francis returns to Sister Gold to inform her of his determination to reform the IIJ from within rather than quit, as Father Gerald has done. But, during the discussion, something unexpected and amazing happens: the rapture occurs, with Sister Gold ascending bodily into the clouds while Francis gazes on in utter bewilderment. Significantly, during the rapture, all the members of the RCC are taken up to heaven with the exception of the pastor, his wife, and five others. (A moment of anger and swearing when his wife serves him "cockroaches" for dinner prevents Pastor Goodnews from rapturing.) Predictably, not a single member of the IIJ experiences the rapture. The pews are as full during Mass the following day as they were during the pre-rapture days; the camera executes a visual judgment by juxtaposing an empty RCC hall and a full IIJ church.

In the post-rapture events that unfold, some members and clergy of the IIJ transform into military and paramilitary officials. In full military camouflage and gear they enforce the rule of the Beast, institutionalized in a new world government called the Universal Unity Government (UUG). The Beast and his minions persecute the former Father Francis, who has now aligned himself with the Pentecostal church and has become a pastor of the RCC, and the remnants of the "born-again" community who have not taken "the mark of the Beast."[11] Francis soon becomes the intellectual and biblical leader of the Born-Again group, authoritatively expounding the scriptures in their forest hideout and vividly prophesying the events of the rapture and things to follow. Within three years of the rapture, the pope has become the human head of the world government (UUG) by manipulating and controlling the United Nations, and he receives political and economic allegiance from other state governments. He soon reveals himself to be the Antichrist, closes all churches and confiscates church buildings, bans the Bible and its possession by anyone, proscribes all public gatherings, and floats a new world currency, called 666. He kills leaders of nations who oppose his power, and then displays miraculous power to resuscitate those whom he had previously stricken dead.

The remnant of born-again Christians becomes the only resistance to the rule of the Beast and the new world (dis)order. The group's resistance is not framed in terms of confronting or sabotaging the infrastructure of rule of the UUG but in refusing to take the new mark of identity, the 666 that is inscribed on the foreheads of followers of the Beast as a public sign of allegiance. This refusal of the mark forces the group to go into hiding in caves, groves, and forests. They are later hunted down and captured through information given by Pastor Goodnews's wife, and tortured by former Bishop Cornelius, who is now an army general in the service of the Beast. The captured Christians are beaten, strangled, and executed for refusing to denounce Christ as an impostor. In the final scenes, the severely beaten and battered bodies of Francis and Goodnews are transported in a canoe to a remote island, where they are bound to a pole and abandoned, left to be devoured by wild animals. As the triumphant army of the Beast rows away from the island, a passage from Revelation flashes on the screen: "And He causeth all, both small and great, rich and poor, free and bond, to receive a mark in their right hand or in their forehead. And that no man might buy or sell, save he that hath the mark or the name of the Beast, or the number of his name" (Revelation 13:16–17, NKJV). As this verse slowly fades away, the dedication and exhortation that opened the movie is repeated: "Dedicated to the Body of Christ, the Pentecostal Fellowship of Nigeria (PFN): Remain Rapturable."

THE BAN AND THE LITIGATIONS

The National Film and Video Censors Board (NVFCB) withheld approval for *Rapture,* objecting to its release because, according to the regulatory body, it stereotyped and "denigrated another Christian re-

ligious faith." The NVFCB insisted the film was offensive to a particular (unnamed) religion and the practices and beliefs of its adherents,
and thus violated "public taste."[12] Most significant, the movie was
"deemed [capable of] caus[ing] a breach [of] public law and order."[13]
According to Rosalind Odeh, then executive director of NFVCB,
Rapture portrayed "another religious sect as anti-Christ, as immoral,
insulting another religious sect. You can differ from another religious
sect but don't mock them, don't create room for quarrel. . . . No film-
maker has a right to insult or be disrespectful to any other religious
sect because religion is a very sensitive thing, especially where the
Bible or the Koran is used inappropriately."[14] Helen Ukpabio was
asked by the board to rework certain sections of the movie, particularly the scenes depicting the bishop having sex with nuns, the scenes
of unbridled violence and horror, and the scenes with explicit doctrinal attacks on the thinly veiled Catholic Church. Ukpabio refused,
claiming that *Rapture* was a revelation from God for the present age,
and as such, no secular government agency had the authority "to dictate what goes into or out of her movies."[15] The face-off that ensued
became a media war between Ukpabio and the NFVCB. As a result of
the evangelist's recalcitrance, the NFVCB banned *Rapture,* claiming
that the movie was capable of disrupting the fragile social-religious
peace in Nigeria.

If one considers the November 2002 mayhem that resulted from
an unfortunate publication in a national daily newspaper found offensive by a section of the Muslim community of northern Nigeria, the
fears of NVFCB appear to have been real. In the ensuing feud, between 150 and 200 people were killed, another 320 were hospitalized,
more than 4500 were displaced from their homes, and property worth
more than 10 billion naira ($2.2 billion) was destroyed (Obadare 2004,
192; Paden 2006, 173–75). The Miss World Beauty Pageant, originally
scheduled for Abuja, was moved to London as a result.[16] Apart from
this event, but further reinforcing the country's long history of religious rivalries and tensions (Paden 2006, 30–31, 188–92), a religious
group, the Brotherhood of the Cross and Star (BCS), razed Ukpabio's
church headquarters in Calabar because of the latter's depiction of the
BCS as "satanic," occultist, and unchristian.

Ukpabio went to court to challenge the banning of *Rapture*, resulting in a series of accusations and counteraccusations. She charged
that officials of NVFCB demanded a bribe in order to "sell" approval
of the film to her.[17] Further, she claimed that the banning of *Rapture*
was not simply an act of a government body performing its statutory
responsibilities of regulating the content and quality of films and videos, but rather constituted an attack on her artistic and religious freedom to disseminate her religious views through the video medium.
Ukpabio further claimed the NVFCB and its Catholic director, Rosalind Odeh, were implementing a Catholic agenda against less powerful religious groups, thus giving the controversy a distinctive cast of
religious partisanship.

The NVFCB, using national radio and television networks, appealed to the leaders of the perceived "offended religious group" not
to take the law into their hands. They asserted that the government
was capable of handling the issue through legal apparatuses. The
board hoped that the "offended" group would remain calm and trust
in the legal process to address such blatant insensitivity as portrayed
in *Rapture* and Ukpabio's subsequent public comments. While the
legal showdown surrounding the release of *Rapture* lingered, the
NFVCB insisted that "Helen Ukpabio is really a dangerous signal to
the [Nigerian movie] industry . . . who take[s] delight in disrespecting
our culture . . . destroying it by way of insulting it in [her] films."[18]
The aspect of Nigerian culture that it accused Ukpabio of "disrespecting" was the longstanding atmosphere of religious tolerance and coexistence that makes Nigeria home to a dizzying array of religious
traditions and groups. "Insulting" this cherished norm was deemed
"dangerous" because Nigerian experience and history reveal that such
practice is a recipe for social conflagration (Onuoha 2005, 13).

Ukpabio remained defiant. On December 6, 2002, without approval from NVFCB, she released *Rapture* through her sixty-four
church branches in and outside the country. Numerous copies of the
movie were sent out uncensored, ignoring the NFVCB and circum-
venting official channels of distribution and marketing. With a formal
proscription from the board in place, Ukpabio's exhibition and sale of
the film were illegal.[19] Consequently, in late December 2002, the police issued an arrest warrant for Ukpabio, who was then in Calabar.

The arrest attempt was thwarted, however, because members of her church prevented the police from gaining access to Ukpabio when the police stormed her residence. Instead, they had to be content with searching her Lagos office and seizing *Rapture* videos. In addition, a number of video marketers who were found to have stocked the banned movie were arrested and brought to court.[20] The NFVCB also employed different federal government media, particularly the Nigerian Television Authority (NTA) and the Federal Radio Corporation of Nigeria (FRCN), to announce the banning of the movie, to warn the public against its consumption, and to continually appeal for the denigrated religious group to remain calm.

In Nigeria, however, the mere legal proscription of a film does little to mitigate its impact, in part because of the institutional power of Pentecostal churches and the relative incapacity of the state to regulate media. Four separate sets of litigation followed the release of *Rapture:* two in the federal high court in Lagos, one in Abuja, and one in Calabar, the headquarters of Liberty Films.[21] These cases were all decided in favor of the NFVCB, which of course expressed satisfaction with the judgments.[22] However, *Rapture* has continued to enjoy a widespread audience, and has been sold freely all over Nigeria, Cameroon, Ghana, and South Africa through the branches of LGC.[23] The infrastructure provided by LGC branches is a significant factor in the success of Liberty Films. Since the *Rapture* imbroglio started in 2002, Ukpabio has produced eight other movies (*Child Rescue, Coven 1, I Was Wrong, Hell Fire, Painful Gain [1 & 2]*, and *Light Afflictions [1 & 2]*), which were also distributed and exhibited uncensored, unapproved, and unclassified. In mid-2004, the NFVCB sought and obtained an Order of Interim Injunction from the federal high court in Lagos, restraining Ukpabio from selling all her movies that did not secure the approval and classification of the board.[24] Armed with this legal tool, the board once more raided Ukpabio's Lagos office, carting away several copies of the movies. Three other film sellers at the Nigerian Film Market in Lagos also had their stocks of the movies confiscated and their shops sealed up by the police.[25]

The conflict over the film suggests the incompatibility of a state secularist position that expects all religions to espouse values of civility and pluralism and a unilateral religious perspective that claims sole access to truth. According to Louisa Inyang, the public relations officer and secretary of LFMP, *"Rapture* is a film of judgment and condemnation."[26] Specifically, she noted, it is a movie that passes judgment on certain social, political, religious, and economic developments in contemporary global society. Ukpabio seemed to confirm this when she said: "I am judge who judges anyone who is involved in false religion. . . . The word I speak, the word I preach is judgment enough for the word you hear, the word you see [that is, the movies], the word you read and you don't believe or you despise is what will be used against you."[27]

Nigerian Pentecostals, Ukpabio included, in their attempt to re-make history with themselves at the center, revise the history of entrenched mainline churches so that they appear trapped in a satanic past whose power the Pentecostals strive to vanquish. For example, at the time *Rapture* was in production,[28] Ukpabio, in a one-page news-magazine article entitled "Demonic Origin of the Cross," attacked the practice of infant baptism and making of the sign of the cross on the foreheads of infants. According to Ukpabio, Jesus

> teaches the word and not how to use the chaplet, rosary, crucifix or engraven images. . . . He never preached wood or copper or anything that has such a resemblance. Refrain from emphasizing the cross, its signs, usage and fakeness. . . . The origin of the cross is in paganism, occultism, mysticism and Satanism and never a Christian symbol. . . . From ancient Rome, Babylon, Spain, Egypt, even in Africa, the cross was a very important factor in idol and pagan worship.[29]

In her book *The Seat of Satan Exposed* (1999), which is primarily a vitriolic attack on the Brotherhood of the Cross and Star, her former religious affiliation, as well as all other non-Pentecostal religious organizations, Ukpabio wrote: "The making of the signs of the cross and the use of holy water are as old as paganism and occultism and not an exclusive prerogative of the so-called Christian organisations" (61). She stated also that "Roman [Catholic] nuns who wear crosses on the neck with rosary on the hands" borrowed the practice from "pagan

Rome," where "virgins that were dedicated to the temple of vestal had cross[es] on their neck[s], with beads on their waist bands."[30]

Rapture thus appears to be a visual extension of a long-running trend in the LGC, since Catholic-bashing is a constant feature of the church's rhetoric. Ukpabio, who attended a Catholic school as a teenager, is acquainted with Catholic religious practices but not their doctrinal bases.[31] Testimonies from members who claim to be former Catholics are printed and circulated in the church's newsmagazine. For example, Mary Arop from the LGC headquarters in Calabar recounts: "I was a Catholic of high standing; a chorister majoring in alto and good enough to touch sacred things; little did I know that I was empty and knew nothing about the word of God. I was deep in sin delighting in Bacchus demons. My brands were stout or star beer."[32] A boundary is drawn here between Catholics who consume alcoholic beverages and LGC members who, as born-again Christians, at least publicly refrain from such conduct even when they may indulge in it privately or secretly. Members of LGC have been taught to regard the Catholic Church as "the kingdom of darkness, a realm of ancestral bondages and enslavement."[33] In the same edition of the magazine, another testimony by Roseline Ntui Egbe begins: "I was in the Catholic Church but a great sinner. I come from a Catholic family that has a priest, a knight, sextons, etc. But there was a growing dissatisfaction in me with the preaching, though I did not know my left from right as far as God was concerned. I felt that too much honour and praise were directed to the Virgin Mary than to God."[34] In *Rapture,* one of IIJ members who did not experience rapture lamented, "I was a staunch Catholic but my brothers and sisters and mother were born-again Christians who have all raptured."[35]

In extending the circulation of aggressive anti-Catholic denigration far beyond the walls and publications of LGC churches, the public release of *Rapture* introduced a new element in anti-Catholic stereotyping.[36] Printed materials usually circulate among LGC members, with few copies finding their way outside the circle of LGC membership. However, movies intentionally have a wider audience and greater potential impact, thus requiring the approval of the NVFCB for release.

The Relevance of the *Rapture* Film

Rapture is an important movie in Nigeria for many reasons. While the religious content clearly captured the NVFCB's, as well as the public's, imagination, the movie also touches on a number of other major issues in contemporary Nigerian society, such as the increasing importance of global political and economic orders over local life and culture. New information and communication technologies have also made it possible for world events and global personalities to acquire local relevance. The movie captures these transformations and tensions within contemporary Nigerian society through eschatological language and end-time narratives, thus giving a Pentecostal and apocalyptic slant to social and political criticism. Specifically, Pentecostalism passes judgment on the international political order exemplified by the power of the North and West (the European Union and the United States, and the United Nations). It critiques globalizing economic trends, including dangerous imported commodities, the move toward a common currency, and the power of lending institutions such as the International Monetary Fund (IMF) and World Bank, whose structural adjustment programs (SAPs), imposed in 1986 on Nigeria, are widely blamed for impoverishing and disempowering ordinary Nigerians. *Rapture* thus advocates a religious (Pentecostal) alternative to the official state discourse prevalent in postcolonial societies such as Nigeria. Part of *Rapture*'s appeal to the Nigerian public is thus its aggressive and polemical engagement with contemporary issues, and its portrayal of outsiders as the source of contemporary turmoil in the nation. It offers a religious explanation for the current unfolding of events both locally and globally. Like other visual meaning-making instruments, *Rapture* operates in the space between "spiritual counsel and psychotherapy, as a visual system of references to human fears, desires, pleasures and pains" (Morgan and Promey 2001, 12).

Moreover, the film *Rapture* demonstrates that religious growth cannot be separated from the media, which has become essential to the creation of affect. The massive advertisement and media hype, which the litigations and counter-litigations generated, whetted the public's appetite and stimulated curiosity even before the movie was released. Ukpabio anticipated this interest by spending 12 million naira on *Rapture,* making it her most expensive movie at the time.[37] Such an investment indicates the significance the movie had for her and her religious constituency in promoting their particular beliefs. Of course, the parallels between Ukpabio's *Rapture* and Mel Gibson's *The Passion of the Christ* (2004), which dramatized the death of Christ and raised anti-Semitic sentiments, are clear. The public outcry that followed upon its release, particularly from the Catholic population, which makes up more than 15 percent of the Christian population of Nigeria, had the potential to degenerate into sectarian violence due to religious intolerance in a country increasingly notorious for its many religious conflicts. *Rapture* thus underscores the potent power of images in influencing ideological positions; Nigerian Pentecostal groups have recognized that the audiovisual medium is a powerful instrument of persuasion. Indeed, with the advent of prosperity religion in the country, the power of images to entice a suffering public seeking positive transformation has become overwhelming (Ukah 2004b, 2005).

The depiction of global Catholicism as Satan's instrument of ultimate terror and global insecurity is an acknowledgment of the power and position of the Catholic Church in contemporary religious globalization processes. The attempt to demonize and stereotype Catholicism ironically admits the hegemonic power and nearly irresistible influence of the Roman Catholic Church. Recognizing the Othering, oppositional nature of their rhetoric is important in analyzing Pentecostal self-understanding and self-portrayal, particularly in their use of media. As one aspect of the politics of identity formation, *Rapture* functions as a visual technology that helps create solidarity among a disparate (under)class of Pentecostal, neo-Pentecostal, and other fringe religious groups. Above all, *Rapture* suggests the tragic possibility—or certainty, in prophetic calculations—of the persecution and destruction of smaller religious groups by a large, intolerant, and evil global religion that is in alliance with global governments and their transnational economic organs.

In significant ways, *Rapture* is also an example of the politicization of religion, as well as the use of religion for economic leverage among Pentecostal pastors in Nigeria (Ukah 2004). The politics of solidarity that followed the (s)election of Olusegun Obasanjo as president of the country in 1999 caused many Pentecostal groups to align themselves with a propaganda that proclaimed Obasanjo as "the first born-again president in Nigeria" (T. Ojo 2001, 32). The media propaganda, first by Obasanjo and then by his circle of friends in the Redeemed Christian Church of God (RCCG) and the Pentecostal Fellowship of Nigeria (PFN), created the environment and expectation in some circles that the president would favor his newfound religious constituency.[38] Many Pentecostal pastors and churches were emboldened to produce politically induced, pro-government "prophecies" that likened Obasanjo to a "messiah" sent by God to save Nigeria from imminent collapse. This new messiah was envisaged to be God's instrument who would launch Nigeria into an apocalyptic limelight as a source of salvation for many all over the world. For many prominent Nigerian Pentecostal Christians, Obasanjo's regime was envisaged to be a "pentecostal presidency" (Obadare 2006), espousing a pentecostalite agenda of aggressive expansion as well as political and economic entrenchment. *Rapture* was designed to attract the attention of "a Pentecostal president," and tap into this social frenzy to achieve national acclaim and economic fortune. In a similar way, Ukpabio's *Child Rescue* (2003) was aimed at gaining the patronage of Stella Obasanjo, the wife of the president whose pet project, Child Care Trust, was devoted to eradicating child labor in Nigeria. These efforts at currying favor with a Baptist-turned-Pentecostal president and the Catholic Mrs. Obasanjo were stymied by the NFCVB's ban of Ukpabio's movies, which the board saw as igniting sectarianism via their negative portrayals of Catholicism.

While the depiction of Catholicism in *Rapture* is easily construed as religious intolerance and the failure to respect religious pluralism, Mary Arop, a barrister and an Ukpabio follower, argues that Ukpabio has a right to freedom of religious expression as guaranteed by section 39(1) of the Nigerian constitution.[39] This line of reasoning contends that the movie is an extension of the church, and as such, "the law does not recognize any injury from the pulpit."[40] However, this position fails to recognize the legal framework within which the demonized religious group operates and is protected by the law. Both parties in the dispute appeal to different sections of the law of the land to justify their respective positions. John and Jean Comaroff (2004, 192) suggest that contradictory rights of citizens and the resultant contestations are marks of "the heterogeneous social infrastructure of postcolonies." By resorting to litigations, the differing parties worked under the assumption that "legal instruments have the wherewithal to manufacture something that was not there before, to yield social value, to achieve political ends, even to orchestrate social harmony." It was hoped that the law courts would create an environment of mutual respect for and open-mindedness toward differences in religious beliefs and practices even when lack of accommodation or tolerance is a defining feature of militant religions such as Ukpabio's.

Historical antecedents show, however, that the Nigerian legal infrastructure has not been able to deal with issues of social disorder, particularly religious disorder, especially when rich, famous, or powerfully connected persons are involved. Perpetrators of religious conflict in Nigeria have never been prosecuted and sentenced through the legal system. This is so because, as Comaroff and Comaroff point out, "in the ordinary course of things, power produces right, not rights power . . . law alone is not what separates order from chaos or an equitable society from a state of savagery" (Comaroff and Comaroff 2004, 192; see also Oshita 2007a). Ultimately, tolerance and nonviolence cannot be mediated through the courts. While the NFVCB was successful in mitigating a potentially violent situation through its actions, it did not create a situation in which Ukpabio would recognize the social value of mutual respect and coexistence of diverse groups with differing religious ideologies. It is unlikely that Ukpabio will make more movies like *Rapture,* but she has yet to demonstrate a moderation of her religious bigotry or Pentecostalist xenophobia. She may only fear the potential consequences of a repeat attempt, as she confessed later that "the movie set us back several millions of naira because we really invested so much [in its production]. It was a big loss and really slowed down our ministry."[41]

With Tracy McVeigh's publication in December 2007 in the London *Observer* of a short article titled "Children are Targets of Nigerian Witch-Hunts,"[42] which in part dealt with Ukpabio's culpability—through her movies, books, and teaching—in the upsurge of attacks on children believed to be witches, Ukpabio has been embroiled in unending controversies with media houses, child rights campaigners, and Internet bloggers who accuse her of explicit and implicit support for a rash of attacks on children in Akwa Ibom State of Nigeria. McVeigh's article was followed up with the broadcast of a documentary, *Saving Africa's Witch Children,* by UK's Channel 4 television station in November 2008, a program that generated massive outcry against Ukpabio when it was sliced up and posted on YouTube and also rebroadcast by HBO and other global media outlets such as the Australian Broadcasting Corporation. Evidently, enmeshed in accusations and counter-accusations with global media houses, litigations against human rights campaigners, humanist organizations, and bloggers has preoccupied the moviemaker's attention, further vitiating her energy and draining her financial resources.

Rapture reinforces popular Pentecostal self-representation as a righteous community and denigration of the Catholic community as worshipers of the devil and persecutors of the righteous followers of God. Employing the "seductive power of images," such a portrayal is directed at modifying opinion and public perception of a section of society (De Concini 1998). The movie reassures the Pentecostal public of its righteousness, that whatever pain it experiences on earth is a sign of its intimate relationship with Christ. It fails to challenge the Pentecostal viewer to consider alternative views about the world as it is; instead, it directs blame toward Catholics, who are portrayed as haters of God and his righteous people. The ridiculing of another religious community works to enhance Pentecostals' own self-image as lovers of God working to bring about an eschatological resolution of contemporary world history. *Rapture* points to a different (re)configuration of time and history, according to a specific interpretation of Christian scripture.

The release of *Rapture* illustrates the importance that leaders of the new Pentecostalism attach to appealing to a particular constituency and supplying pleasing fantasies rather than a more constructive reevaluation of social problems. In fact, it may be argued that the denigration of non-Pentecostal religious groups in movies produced by Pentecostal groups and leaders is an aspect of the emergence of a new religious class, a form of local Pentecostal elitism. Importantly, it functions to create a space and framework within which to critique large-scale social transformation and restructuring. In the case of *Rapture,* this critique is framed in the rhetoric of the apocalypse, a Christian concept that has been appropriated afresh by Pentecostal entrepreneurs not only to critique and agitate members of society but to redefine group self-image by negatively stereotyping other groups.

Clearly, the movie provides the language and symbols, as well as the motives and a possible trigger, for intra-Christian conflict. Moreover, the manner in which the officials of NVFCB appealed to the Catholic community for calm is an indication of the film's destabilizing potential. On a positive note, it created an environment for the Christian Association of Nigeria to emphasize the importance of tolerance in a religiously plural society, thus bringing to the fore the need for caution and discipline by religious leaders of all persuasions. For example, the Catholic Bishops' Conference of Nigeria, through its director of communications, Reverend Father Emmanuel Badejo, decried the "abusive, destructive and irresponsible exercise of freedom in the name of artistic creativity in our country where mutual tolerance runs on a short fuse."[43] Although *Rapture* is in the market, the Catholic community has insisted that if it had received the official approval of the government, nothing "could have stopped the adherents of the offended religion from reacting in the same way as the Kaduna gladiators," referring to the Muslim ringleaders who engineered the anti-blasphemy mayhem of November 2002.[44] The public furor generated by *Rapture* illuminated the fact that religious conflicts are not necessarily fought by trained soldiers but often by a civilian population, which then constitutes the majority of aggressors and victims.

Abuses of religious freedom often degenerate into violent crises, as the Sharia experience in northern Nigeria has shown. This is all the more so where and when there is obvious religionization of the already tense patterns within social, economic, and political life (Kukah 1993; Enwerem 1995, Ostien, Nasir, and Kogelmann 2005; Danfulani 2005). Furthermore, the frequency of religiously based conflagration in Nigeria, as well as the inability of the state to control the activities of groups that portend trouble for the wider society, is indicative of the weakness of central political authority. As sociologist Rodney Stark (2001, 115; 2003) points out, political disorder often yields a

high degree of religious disorder. There has been a progressive weakening of the Nigerian state since the mid-1980s, with attendant ethnic
and religious conflicts (Kukah 1992; Enwerem 1995). In a deregulated
religious market, the pressure to maintain a high level of religious
activity can exacerbate religious differentiation and consequent religious intolerance, which often lead to religious conflicts (see Hackett,
this volume).[45] High levels of official corruption,[46] the manipulation
of religion for financial and social gains, and the conflation of religious and political identities have all contributed to this process of
recurring religious violence in Nigeria. In sum, the controversy surrounding the making and marketing of *Rapture* reveals the confusion
in which the Nigerian state is embroiled as it struggles to control cultural and religious polyphony and prevent conflict; all of this is made
worse by the fact that the state's own powers have been simultaneously stripped by structural adjustment and globalization, and the
power of nongovernmental and religious institutions has grown cor-
respondingly.

CONCLUSION

The crisis sparked by *Rapture* points to the growing power of the
media in inculcating religious difference and discord. *Rapture* emerged
from a culture in which violence and horror have become a daily aspect of urban life. It is also indicative of the state of religion within the
culture, where competition for a market niche is an important aspect
of recruitment strategies adopted by different Pentecostal groups in
search of quality membership (Ukah 2003b, 258–60; 2004b; Hackett
2003). In this context, conflict becomes a function of competition for
resources. *Rapture* is not just a Christian film designed to proselytize
or warn believers of a dangerous Other; to many people, including
some filmmakers, it is an abuse and misuse of the right to freedom of
religious expression and artistic creativity. In dramatizing the events
of the biblical *eschaton,* or end time, *Rapture* narrates the apocalypse
as the radical transformation of both individuals and social relationships. The movie paints a picture of social and metaphysical dualism,
a Manichaean encounter between ultimate good and ultimate evil.

And yet it is noteworthy that no physical violence resulted from the release of the movie. As Appleby (2001, 822) rightly points out, "peace-building" includes "conflict prevention and management." The efforts of the Catholic authorities, together with those of the NFVCB and other social commentators, who counseled and cautioned youth in particular not to respond violently to the alleged insults and provocations of Ukpabio as crystallized in *Rapture,* can be seen as a crucial peace-building precedent in Nigeria. Considering that a perceived insult to a religious group in Nigeria not too long before the release of *Rapture* caused the death of more than two hundred people and the destruction of property worth several billions of naira, the nonviolent response of the Catholic Church was generally commended as demonstrative of the peace-building potential of certain religions (Nepstad 2004). Religion is an ambivalent phenomenon that "is a source not only of intolerance, human rights violations, and extreme violence, but also of nonviolent conflict transformation, the defense of human rights . . . and reconciliation and stability in divided societies" (Appleby 2001, 821). The restraint demonstrated by the adherents of the "offended religion" shows the willingness of some religious groups to seek peace, social respect, and redress within the social and legal framework of the rule of law. By not responding in kind, the Catholic Church provided an alternative approach and perspective to the one espoused by Ukpabio.

Furthermore, the disruption caused by *Rapture* demonstrated that moviemakers who engage in the negative stereotyping of other groups in the country know that there will be a price to be paid for flagrant disrespect of other people's religious and cultural sensibilities. In order to forestall the irresponsible use of this medium in the pursuit of religious agendas, the different stakeholders in the Nigerian video industry (such as the Directors Guild of Nigeria, the Film Producers Association of Nigeria, and the NVFCB) need to develop an acceptable ethical code for members of the industry that will make peace-building, or at least the inculcation of social respect and mutual tolerance, an important value and objective of artistic creativity.[47]

Rapture illustrates the explosive potential of biblical and media manipulation. Intended to secure the attention of a supposed born-again president, the movie went unnoticed by a distracted president and then was banned.⁴⁸ Helen Ukpabio, an adept lobbyist and media mogul,⁴⁹ prolonged the crisis by instituting legal actions against the NFVCB at the cost of more than 1 million naira, which reduced her profit margin but enhanced her media visibility. The *Rapture* controversy revealed the role of media, ideology, and money in fanning the embers of sectarian conflict on an intra-religious level, while also reflecting the power of media to construct and market religious identity and difference.

Catholic leaders and laity in Nigeria made conscious decisions not to react violently to the provocative and prejudicial images in *Rapture*, and their verbal protests and physical restraint are models of a nonviolent response by an offended community. However, the group that most effectively worked to keep the peace in this case was not a particular religious organization or leader, but rather the government censorship body, the NVFCB. The board's decision to ban Ukpabio's film reflected a normative priority of preserving (inter- and intra-) religious harmony and avoiding potential conflict over absolute protection of freedom of expression. This case thus also reflects the enduring validity and viability of the African state, even in the wake of exogenous and endogenous threats to its hegemony. The controversy over the film *Rapture* also demonstrates the central importance of leadership, whether religious or secular, in defusing tense situations in which the conditions are ripe for violence and seem to be escalating.

NOTES

The author thanks Professor Rosalind I. J Hackett for her encouragement and inspiration in preparing this paper, which was first presented at the conference on Religion in African Conflicts and Peacebuilding Initiatives, held at Jinja Nile Resort, Uganda, April 1–3, 2004. Patti Esohe Ukah and Dr. Oshita O. Oshita read an early draft of the paper; the author is grateful for their comments and observations. Also, I am grateful to Patrick Mason and the editors of this volume for their various comments and suggestions toward improving this essay. Whatever shortcomings left in it are the author's responsibility.

1. For example, the pastor-owner of Christian Prayer Assembly in Lagos, Nigeria, Reverend Emeka Ezeugo, recently set two members of his

church ablaze with gasoline for "committing fornication." One of the victims later died in hospital from third-degree burns and the pastor was subsequently tried in court and sentenced to death. The death sentence is yet to be carried out. There are similar Pentecostal churches that thrive on intolerance, some even physically demolished other churches located in the same vicinity, accusing them of "stealing" its members.

2. With a minimum of two thousand titles released each year since the beginning of this decade, Nigeria is the highest producer of home videos in the world. See *Tell* magazine (Lagos). October 20, 2003. Some of these releases are not registered with the National Film and Video Censors Board (NFVCB) (set up by decree No. 85 of 1993), the government agency with the statutory responsibility of vetting and regulating the film industry.

3. The designation "Nollywood" is coined by Western media perplexed by the phenomenal popularity of locally made movies in Nigeria. It is sometimes used to represent Nigeria as a country where low-budget movies, costing on the average of $10,000, are made in five days. Nollywood expresses "the emergence of some of the most imaginative experiments in low cost filmmaking on the globe" (Tunde Kelani, a Nigerian filmmaker, in *The Guardian* [Lagos], June 6, 2004, 64).

4. See *SuccessDigest* (Lagos), June 2004, 14.

5. LFGM is an organization that is both vertically and horizontally integrated, with subsidiaries such as Liberty Gospel Church (LGC), Liberty Films, Liberty Press, Treasure Bible Place, and Liberty Music. In early 2004, Ukpabio started constructing a state-of-the-art hotel in Uyo, Akwa Ibom State, to add to the flourishing economic empire that LFGM represents. Liberty Press not only publishes books and magazines from LGC, but also produces students' exercise books that are marketed widely in southeastern Nigeria through LGC parishes and church members.

6. This dedication is all the more interesting considering that at the time of the release of *Rapture,* LGC was not, and still is not, officially registered with the PFN. The dedication of *Rapture* to the PFN therefore appears to be a ploy to garner the support of the Pentecostal community in Nigeria in the controversy that the movie was anticipated to cause in the country. The producer described this as "associating with the PFN for the business [that accrues from such relationship] and not for the spirit [of the organization]." Aside from seeking public support of the association in her battles with the government and other non-Pentecostal groups, Ukpabio targets PFN officials and their churches as possible outlets and markets for her products, particularly films and books (personal communication from Helen Ukpabio, Calabar, May 17, 2004).

7. Information on jacket of the film.

232 Asonzeh F.-K. Ukah

8. Ironically, "RCC" could also stand for the Roman Catholic Church.

9. All citations from the movie are transcriptions by the author.

10. On March 22, 1998, Pope John Paul II visited Nigeria to beatify Reverend Father Cyprian Michael Iwene Tansi (1903–64) who was ordained a priest for Onitsha Archdiocese, but in 1951 became a monk of Mount Saint Bernard Abbey, near Nottingham, England, where he lived and worked until his death in 1964. A few weeks before this event, the remains of Tansi were exhumed and flown to Nigeria, where they were reburied at Onitsha Ecclesiastical Province. It is this event that the movie caricatures. The historical aspects of the film indicate that it is intending to offer a social commentary, albeit from a religious perspective.

11. Revelation 13:16–18: "[The Beast] forced all men . . . the number of the beast . . . stands for a certain man. The man's number is six hundred sixty-six." This verse is repeated several times in the movie.

12. *Nollywood* (Lagos), August 27–September 10, 2004, xi.

13. See "Erring Home Video Dealer Docked in Abuja," *Daily Trust* (Abuja), January 7, 2003.

14. "Film Board Cautions against Provocative Films," *This Day* (Lagos), January 1, 2003.

15. *Nollywood* (Lagos), August 27–September 10, 2004, xi.

16. *This Day* newspaper had, on November 16, 2002, published a piece in reaction to the controversy then raging in the country about the hosting of the Miss World Beauty Pageant in Nigeria. The article, written by Isioma Daniel, questioned the sincerity of Muslim groups who had attacked the pageant as indecent. "The Muslims thought it was immoral to bring 92 women to Nigeria and ask them to revel in vanity," the piece said. "What would Muhammad think? In all honesty, he would probably have chosen a wife from one of them." The violent unrest that followed these short statements was enough to cause the organizers of the event to move it to London.

17. The author was present during a press briefing in Calabar by Ukpabio in October 2002 at the end of which a fat brown envelope stuffed with naira bills was handed to the journalists as unsolicited inducement to present her own side of the story adequately.

18. *Nollywood* (Lagos), August 27–September 10, 2004, xi.

19. According to Decree 85 of 1993, which set up the NFVCB, (part III, section 34[1], "no person shall exhibit, cause or allow to be exhibited a film without a censorship certificate issued by the board for such exhibition."

20. In January 2003, John Ani was arrested for selling and distributing copies of *Rapture I* and *II* and arraigned before an Abuja High Court. See *Daily Trust* (Abuja), January 7, 2003.

21. Personal interview with Helen Ukpabio, Calabar.

22. In a statement posted on its official website, the NFVCB states, "The celebrated case between Helen Ukpabio (a known religious film producer) and the Censors Board with the IG [inspector general] of police as codefendant has been decided in favour of the board. The case which was determined by the Federal High Court Calabar, has lingered for the past four years in an intensive legal gymnastics. The legal unit of the Board, in a report expressed satisfaction with the manner justice was meted out." http://www.nfvcb.gov.ng/mediacenter.php?pagesectionid=3 (accessed June 21, 2007).

23. *The Coven 1* was also released through Ukpabio's churches without the approval of NVFCB. A visit to the branch church in Johannesburg in March 2007 revealed stacks of different home videos in VCD format on sale in the church.

24. The injunction was issued by Honorable Justice M. L. Shuaibu.

25. *Nollywood* (Lagos), August 27–September 10, 2004, xi.

26. Personal interview with Louisa Inyang, LFMP Office, Surulere, Lagos, September 13, 2002.

27. Personal interview with Helen Ukpabio, LFMP Office, Surulere, Lagos, October 15, 2002.

28. The shooting of *Rapture* was already in progress in September 2001, as is evident from an interview granted by Richard Mofe-Damijo on his role as Reverend Father Francis in *Rapture* and published in *GEL Magazine* (Lagos) 1, no. 7 (September 2001): 4. Evangelist Ukpabio was the publisher of *GEL*, a newsmagazine that is now defunct.

29. Helen Ukpabio, "Demonic Origin of the 'Cross,'" *GEL Magazine* (Lagos) 1, no. 4 (May 2001): 9.

30. Ibid.

31. On a CV posted on her website, Ukpabio stated she attended St. George's Catholic School, Falomo-Ikoyi, Lagos.

32. *Liberty Magazine* 5, no. 3 (December 2003): 25.

33. Ibid., 26.

34. Ibid., 27.

35. While Ukpabio states in the media that her movie was not against Catholics, statements like the one cited clearly indicate her position.

36. In several press interviews Ukpabio denied having Catholics in mind in the making of *Rapture,* but a noncritical viewer will reach a different conclusion. The movie opens with the beginning of the Mass sung in Latin, and in the credits at the end there is the character, "Pope," who is identified as Avinaash Bhavinaav. There is also the singing of the Angelus as well as the recognition of the pope as a political and religious leader during his visit as he inspects a Guard of Honor, an event that makes national news in the movie.

37. At the time *Rapture* was made, it was the most expensive movie made in Nigeria.

38. For the politics of identity reconstruction for Olusegun Obasanjo within the Pentecostal circle, see Ukah (2003b, 197–201). For a Pentecostal portrayal of Obasanjo as a "born-again" Christian, see Ayuk (2002, 194–95); for a more nuanced examination of the remaking of Obasanjo as a "pentecostal president," see Obadare (2006).

39. Romanus Arop, "Dissemination of Religious Information: The Legal Implications," *Liberty Magazine* 2, no. 1 (May 2000): 16.

40. Ibid.

41. Ukpabio, *The Vanguard* (Lagos), February 7, 2004, http://www .vanguardngr.com/articles/2002/features/fe407022004.html (accessed July 4, 2007).

42. http://www.guardian.co.uk/world/2007/dec/09/tracymcveigh .theobserver (accessed April 13, 2010).

43. Emmanuel Adetoyese Badejo, "Sustaining Responsible Communication," http://www.thisdayonline.com/archive/2003/02/13/20030213art01 .html (accessed July 4, 2007).

44. Ibid.

45. According to Wellman and Tokuno (2004, 293), "As the awareness and reality of cultural and religious diversity increases in the modern period, the need to defend and articulate one's religious symbol systems increases."

46. That the NFVCB could not enforce the ban on *Rapture* was because of corruption in the system that allowed the movie to be marketed freely and the producer to reap huge financial benefits from the ensuing legal tussle that fueled media publicity for the movie.

47. The producer of *Rapture* agrees that the banning of the film produced international awareness for her work and generated a market for the movie that has exceeded original market projections. Also, as a result of the controversies, the movie was classified by West Africa International Magazine as "the Best Gospel Film in Nigeria, and for which . . . Ukpabio got nominated for Nobles International Award 2003" (*Liberty* Magazine 5, no. 3 [December 2003]: 34).

48. The Pentecostal euphoria that marked the [s]election of Obasanjo as president in 1999 gradually faded as the president demonstrated that he had little regard for Christian leaders whom he abuses publicly, calling the Plateau State chairman of PFN "an idiot" (*Midweek Scoop* [Lagos] 5, no. 20 [August 17, 2004]: 5 and 8). In the face of increasing anti-Christian posturing from the president, according to Kukah, there are still some Christian "seers and dreamers marketing the blood of Jesus" who scramble for state patronage (see Matthew Hassan Kukah, "Plateau: State of Emergency as Metaphor," *The Guardian* [Lagos], May 30, 2004, 10–12).

49. Ukpabio paid huge sums of money to several journalists whom she frequently invited to her office in Lagos and to her residence in Calabar for

"press releases" (drafted by a [paid] journalist who works with *Newswatch* magazine in Lagos) and interviews in order to get her versions of the story in public. It is common knowledge in Nigeria that politicians and church owner-founders dole out bribes to journalists in order to receive favorable media coverage or suppress critical media perspectives about their activities.

REFERENCES

Almond, Gabriel A., R. Scott Appleby, and Emmanuel Sivan. 2003. *Strong Religion: The Rise of Fundamentalisms around the World.* Chicago: University of Chicago Press.

Anderson, Allan. 2004. *An Introduction to Pentecostalism.* Cambridge: Cambridge University Press.

Appleby, R. Scott. 2001. "Religion as an Agent of Conflict Transformation and Peacebuilding." In *Turbulent Peace: The Challenges of Managing International Conflict,* edited by Chester A. Crocker, Fen Osler Hampson, and Pamela Aall, 821–40. Washington, DC: United States Institute of Peace.

Ayuk, Ayuk Ausaji. 2002. "The Pentecostal Transformation of Nigerian Church Life." *Asian Journal of Pentecostal Studies* 5(2):189–204.

Beavis, Mary Ann. 2002. "'Angels Carrying Savage Weapons': Uses of the Bible in Contemporary Horror Films." *Journal of Religion and Film* 7(2) (http://www.unomaha.edu/~wwwjrf/Vol7No2/angels.htm) (accessed October 1, 2003).

Bergesen, Albert J., and Andrew M. Greeley. 2000. *God in the Movies.* New Brunswick, NJ: Transaction Publishers.

Birman, Patricia, and David Lehmann. 1999. "Religion and the Media in a Battle for Ideological Hegemony: The Universal Church of the Kingdom of God and TV Globo in Brazil." *Bulletin of Latin American Research* 18(2):145–64.

Bisong, Kekong. 2003. "Human Right and Religious Freedom in Nigeria." *The Oracle: International Journal of Culture, Religion and Society* 1(3):138–46.

Brouwer, Steve, Paul Gifford, and Susan D. Rose. 1996. *Exporting the American Gospel: Global Christian Fundamentalism.* New York: Routledge.

Bruce, Steve. 2000. *Fundamentalism.* Cambridge: Polity Press.

Comaroff, John L., and Jean Comaroff. 2004. "Criminal Justice, Cultural Justice: The Limits of Liberalism and the Pragmatics of Difference in the New South Africa." *American Ethnologist* 31(2):188–204.

Danfulani, Umar H. 2005. *The Shari'a Issue and Christian-Muslim Relations in Contemporary Nigeria*. Stockholm: Almqvist & Wiksell International.

De Concini, Barbara. 1998. "Seduction by Visual Image." *Journal of Religion and Film* 2(3).

Enwerem, Iheanyi M. 1995. *A Dangerous Awakening: The Politicization of Religion in Nigeria*, Ibadan: IFRA.

Frykholm, Amy Johnson. 2004. *Rapture Culture: Left Behind in Evangelical America*. New York: Oxford University Press.

Gifford, Paul. 1998. *African Christianity: Its Public Roles*. London: Hurst.

Hackett, Rosalind I. J. 2003. "Discourses of Demonization in Africa and Beyond." *Diogenes* 50(3):61–75.

Haynes, Jonathan, ed. 2000. *Nigerian Video Films*. Rev. ed. Athens: Ohio University Center for International Studies.

Kimball, Charles. 2002. *When Religion Becomes Evil*. New York: Harper-Collins Books.

Kramer, Eric W. 2001a. "Law and the Image of a Nation: Religious Conflict and Religious Freedom in a Brazilian Criminal Case." *Law & Social Inquiry* 26:35–62.

———. 2001b. "Possessing Faith: Commodification, Religious Subjectivity, and Collectivity in a Brazilian Neo-Pentecostal Church." Ph.D. dissertation, University of Chicago.

Kukah, Matthew Hassan. 1992. "The Politicization of Fundamentalism in Nigeria." In *New Dimensions in African Christianity*, edited by Paul Gifford, 183–206. Ibadan: Safer Books.

———. 1993. *Religion, Politics and Power in Northern Nigeria*. Ibadan: Spectrum Books Limited.

LaHaye, Tim, and Jerry Jenkins. 1995. *Left Behind: A Novel of the Earth's Last Days*. Wheaton, IL: Tyndale House Publishers.

———. 1996. *Tribulation Force: The Continuing Drama of Those Left Behind*. Wheaton, IL: Tyndale House Publishers.

———. 1997. *Nicolae: The Rise of the Antichrist*. Wheaton, IL: Tyndale House Publishers.

———. 1998a. *Apollyon: The Destroyer is Unleashed*. Wheaton, IL: Tyndale House Publishers.

———. 1998b. *Soul Harvest: The World Takes Sides*. Wheaton, IL: Tyndale House Publishers.

———. 1999. *Assassins: Assignment: Jerusalem, Target: Antichrist*. Wheaton, IL: Tyndale House Publishers.

———. 2000a. *Indwelling: The Beast Takes Possession*. Wheaton, IL: Tyndale House Publishers.

———. 2000b. *The Mark: The Beast Rules the World*. Wheaton, IL: Tyndale House Publishers.

———. 2001. *Desecration: The Antichrist Takes the Throne*. Wheaton, IL: Tyndale House Publishers.

———. 2002. *The Remnant: On the Brink of Armageddon*. Wheaton, IL: Tyndale House Publishers.

———. 2003. *Armageddon: The Cosmic Battle of Ages*. Wheaton, IL: Tyndale House Publishers.

———. 2004. *Glorious Appearing: End of Days*. Wheaton, IL: Tyndale House Publishers.

Marshall, Ruth. 1993. "'Power in the Name of Jesus': Social Transformation and Pentecostalism in Western Nigeria 'Revisited.'" In *Legitimacy and the State in Twentieth-Century Africa: Essays in Honour of A.H.M. Greene,* edited by Terence Ranger and Olufemi Vaughan, 213–46. London: Macmillan Press.

———. 1995. "'God is not a Democrat': Pentecostalism and Democratisation in Nigeria." In *Christianity and Africa's Democratisation,* edited by Paul Gifford, 239–60. Leiden: Brill.

Marty, Martin E., and R. Scott Appleby, eds. 1991. *Fundamentalisms Observed*. Chicago: University of Chicago Press.

———. 1993a. *Fundamentalisms and Society*. Chicago: University of Chicago Press.

———. 1993b. *Fundamentalisms and the State*. Chicago: University of Chicago Press.

———. 1995. *Fundamentalisms Comprehended*. Chicago: University of Chicago Press.

———. 2004 *Accounting for Fundamentalisms*. Chicago: University of Chicago Press.

Mbon, Friday M. 1992. *Brother of the Cross and Star: A New Religious Movement in Nigeria*. Frankfurt am Main: Peter Lang.

McAlister, Maleni. 2003. "Prophecy, Politics and the Popular: The *Left Behind* Series and Christian Fundamentalism's New World Order." *South Atlantic Quarterly* 102:773–98.

Moore, R. Laurence. 1994. *Selling God: American Religion in the Marketplace of Culture*. New York: Oxford University Press.

Morgan, David, and Sally M. Promey. 2001. "Introduction." In *The Visual Culture of American Religion,* edited by David Morgan and Sally M. Promey, 1–24. Berkeley: University of California Press.

Nepstad, Sharon Erikson. 2004. "Religion, Violence and Peacemaking." *Journal for the Scientific Study of Religion* 43(3):297–301.

Obadare, Ebenezer. 2004. "In Search of a Public Sphere: The Fundamentalist Challenge to Civil Society in Nigeria." *Patterns of Prejudice* 38(2): 177–98.

————. 2006. "Pentecostal Presidency? The Lagos-Ibadan 'Theocratic' Class and the Muslim 'Other.'" *Review of African Political Economy* 110:665–78.

Oha, Obododimma. 1999. "Myth-making and the Legitimization of Leadership." In *Perspectives on Mythology*, edited by Esi Sutherland-Addy, 33–47. Accra: Goethe-Institut.

Ojo, Matthews A. 2006. *The End-Time Army: Charismatic Movements in Modern Nigeria*. Trenton, NJ: Africa World Press.

————. 2007. "Pentecostal Movements, Islam and the Contest of Public Space in Nigeria." *Islam and Christian-Muslim Relations* 18(2):175–88.

Ojo, Tony. 2001. *Let Somebody Shout Hallelujah! The Life and Ministry of Pastor Enoch Adejare Adeboye*. Lagos: Honeycombs Cards and Prints.

Onuoha, Enyeribe. 2005. "Religion and State in Nigeria." *International Humanist News*, August:12–13.

Oshita, O. Oshita. 2007a. *Conflict Management in Nigeria: Issues and Challenges*. London: Adonis & Abbey Publishers Ltd.

————. 2007b. "Religious Conflicts in Nigeria: Paradoxes in the Market Place." Paper presented at the Post Graduate Colloquium, Department of Religious Studies I, University of Bayreuth, Bayreuth, Germany, June 14.

Ostien, Philip, Jamila M. Nasir, and Franz Kogelmann. 2005. *Comparative Perspective on Shari'ah in Nigeria*. Ibadan: Spectrum Books Limited.

Paden, John N. 2006. *Muslim Civil Cultures and Conflict Resolution: The Challenge of Democratic Federalism in Nigeria*. Washington, DC: Brooking Institute Press.

Pippin, Tina. 2002. "Of God and Demons: Blood Sacrifice and Eternal Life in Dracula and the Apocalypse of John." In *Screening Scripture: Intertextual Connections between Scripture and Film*, edited by George Aichele and Richard Walsh, 24–41. Harrisburg, PA: Trinity Press International.

Shuck, Mark. 2005. *Marks of the Beast: The Left Behind Novels and the Struggle for Evangelical Identity*. New York: New York University Press.

Spittler, Russell P. 1994. "Are Pentecostals and Charismatics Fundamentalists? A Review of American Uses of These Categories." In *Charismatic Christianity as a Global Culture*, edited by Karla Poewe. Columbia: University of South Carolina Press.

Stark, Rodney. 2001. *One True God: Historical Consequences of Monotheism*. Princeton: Princeton University Press.

————. 2003. *For the Glory of God: How Monotheism Led to Reformations, Science, Witch-Hunts, and the End of Slavery*. Princeton: Princeton University Press.

Ukah, Asonzeh F.-K. 2003a. "Advertising God: Nigerian Christian Video-Films and the Power of Consumer Culture." *Journal of Religion in Africa* 30(2):203–31.

———. 2003b. "The Redeemed Christian Church of God, Nigeria. Local Identities and Global Processes in African Pentecostalism." Ph.D. dissertation, University of Bayreuth, Bayreuth, Germany, http://opus.ub.uni-bayreuth.de/volltexte/2004/73pdf/Ukah.pdf.

———. 2004a. "Pentecostalism, Religious Expansion and the City: Lesson from the Nigerian Bible Belt." In *Resistance and Expansion: Explorations of Local Vitality in Africa,* edited by Peter Probst and Gerd Spittler, 415–41. Lit Münster.

———. 2004b. "Religious Propaganda in Afrika." In *Plakate in Afrika,* edited by Dieter Kramer and Wendelin Schmidt, 83–88. Frankfurt am Main: Museum der Weltkulturen.

———. 2005. "'Those Who Trade with God Never Lose': The Economics of Pentecostal Activism in Nigeria." In *Christianity and Social Change in Africa: Essays in Honor of John Peel,* edited by Toyin Falola, 251–74. Durham, NC: Carolina Academic Press.

Ukpabio, Helen. 1999. *The Seat of Satan Exposed.* 3rd ed. Calabar: Liberty Foundation Gospel Ministries.

Urban, Hugh B. 2006. "America, Left Behind." *Journal of Religion & Society* 8:1–15.

Varga, Ivan. 1999. "Globalization and Religion. The Case of Pentecostalism." In *Afrika und die Globalisierung,* edited by Hans Peter Hahn and Gerhad Spittler, 337–47. Hamburg: Lit Verlag.

Wellman, James K., and Kyoko Tokuno. 2004. "Is Religious Violence Inevitable?" *Journal for the Scientific Study of Religion* 43(3):291–96.

Zeidan, David. 2003. *The Resurgence of Religion: A Comparative Study of Selected Themes in Christian and Islamic Fundamentalist Discourses.* Leiden: Brill.

CHAPTER 8

"The Domestic Relations Bill" and Inter-Religious Conflict in Uganda

A Muslim Reading of Personal Law and Religious Pluralism in a Postcolonial Society

Abasi Kiyimba

Be fair, for Allah loves those who are fair (and just).
The believers are but a single brotherhood: so make peace and
reconciliation between your two (contending) brothers, and fear Allah,
that you may receive mercy.

—Qur'an, 49: 9–10

Modern Uganda is a British colonial creation, and the educational, legal, and economic systems betray a strong kinship to the systems of the former colonial master. The majority of Ugandan citizens are Christians, divided among Catholics, Anglicans, Orthodox, Adventists, and new Christian sects. But alongside these Christian groups, there exists a sizable Muslim community, whose origin in Uganda predates the earliest Christians by at least thirty years. Despite their minority status, Muslims are quite visible in public affairs, largely because the Christian groups tend to conceive themselves as distinct denominations with longstanding internal social and political power struggles.[1] A sizable number of Ugandans subscribe to traditional religions, but nearly all Ugandans nominally identify themselves with Islam or Christianity.

One of the most conspicuous areas of difference between Muslims and Christians in Uganda has to do with laws regulating marriage, divorce, and inheritance. The laws inherited from Britain had been created in accordance to the colonial principle of "indirect governance," which reified custom and tended to entrench cultural and religious differences and separatism. Statutes governing Muslim marriages and divorce were contained in the Marriage and Divorce of Mohammedans Act, and there were corresponding acts catering to other religious groups. Significantly, the Marriage and Divorce of Mohammedans Act allowed polygamy and divorce, which the Christian groups invariably consider wrong. Ever since the country gained independence in 1962, successive Christian-led governments have attempted to reform the law, and make it consistent with what they describe as "justice and morality appropriate to the position of Uganda as an independent nation."[2]

Owing to the different theological conceptions of morality and marriage, and because the Christian groups have tended to be more secularist than the Muslims, sharp disagreements have followed attempts to reform these laws. The Domestic Relations Bill (DRB), which is currently under debate, represents the latest attempt at reform. Muslims look at the provisions of the proposed law as an attempt to impose upon them Christian conceptions of morality. They also accuse the proponents of the law of being agents of promiscuity because they want to legalize Western social notions such as cohabitation, which the Muslims regard as glorified prostitution.

The disagreement has been sharp and acrimonious, covering a variety of issues in the proposed law but mainly concentrating on the question of polygamy. Christian women have been particularly vocal in the debate, arguing that polygyny, or the marriage of one man to multiple wives, undermines the dignity of women. For their part, Muslims have argued that Christians are interfering in a social arrangement that they do not understand. They have also accused Christians of being hypocritical, since many men who profess Christianity have "official" and "unofficial" wives. They also point to the traditionally Christian societies in Europe and America, where the law prescribes monogamy but allows prostitution to thrive. Some women's groups have added more confusion to this debate by suggesting that if polygamy is accepted for men, women should also be allowed to practice polyandry, the marriage of one woman to multiple men. In response to this, Muslims have said they will not fight this provision if it is tabled for inclusion in the law, since they know Muslim women are not likely to claim the "right" to have more than one man. They insist, however, that they will not be party to any law that includes provisions that are offensive to Islam, and have consistently requested that if the government wants to push ahead with this law in its present form, they should be exempted from it. Finally on this point, Muslims do not accept the accusation that Islamic laws are oppressive to women since Islam presents doctrine that its followers have the option to accept and be Muslims, or reject and follow other faiths. On the specific issue of Muslim marriage laws being unfair to women, Muslim men argue that they only "marry those who have agreed."[3] They argue that the claims of "oppressive Muslim laws" are championed by enemies of Islam, and are swallowed wholesale by those whose Western education has left them ignorant and biased when it comes to the letter and spirit of the teachings of Islam.

Many Ugandan Christians feel that constructing the law so as to accommodate groups who accept polygamy is offensive to Christian sensibilities, inconsistent with principles of gender equality and equity (as they understand it), contrary to common sense, and inconsistent with the correct conceptions of justice, morality, and civilized practice in the twenty-first century. For their part, the Muslims strongly feel that Christians are infringing on their rights by seeking to adopt a legal culture that follows a distinctly Western model, which has historically been conditioned by the Christian domination of Europe, and seems to be devoid of the moral values that Muslims greatly cherish. In particular, they accuse the Christians of being more vocal in their opposition to polygamy than they are to immoral acts like prostitution and homosexuality. Disputes over the legal definition of marriage generate a lot of social and political friction, which in turn threatens the ideal of national unity, as the different religious groups strive to have their norms enshrined in national law.

The conflict over the DRB also provides a variety of extralegal insights into the dynamics of inter-religious tensions, which can eventually lead to violent conflict if they are not appropriately addressed in time. Many Muslims suspect that the DRB is part of a theologically driven majoritarian project to Christianize the Ugandan state. The Muslims therefore regard the bill as a comprehensive threat to Muslim identity in Uganda, and there is a real possibility that the tension it creates could trigger widespread identity-based violence rooted in the deep-seated and longstanding fears of the minority Muslim population. Up to this point, however, protest against the bill has remained nonviolent. It has taken the form of public statements and peaceful demonstrations, but many of these public statements and protests have signaled the potential to rally the community in violent defense against what they regard as Christian aggression. That the conflict has remained nonviolent thus far is a positive sign, and offers the authorities an opportunity to use negotiation and compromise to address disagreements rather than violence or majoritarian repression of minorities, with the aim of building a tolerant and pluralistic civil society in Uganda. The debate over the DRB thus represents far more than abstract legalistic deliberations, as it reveals a nation precariously balanced between conflict and peace. It also raises the question of whether the "majority takes it" approach is the correct way of tackling questions of personal rights and freedoms.

This essay is a contribution to the growing literature and continuing discussion of the role of religion—including religious actors and institutions—in the modern public sphere. It also extends the debate on the question of how pluralistic societies will accommodate all their varying religious components. The essay starts by providing the relevant historical background information, including the origins of the Muslim community in Uganda and a brief overview of the development of marriage law from the colonial period to the present. It then outlines the provisions of the proposed DRB before considering Muslim objections to particular aspects of it. This essay mainly focuses on Muslims' opposition to the DRB and the strength with which they express their grievances, but Christian support for the bill is also examined, highlighting aspects of the debate that make the bill a sensitive nerve for a nation striving to build and maintain peace.[4]

The Muslim Community in Uganda: A Historical Background

Islam was first introduced in the Kingdom of Buganda (the central part of present-day Uganda) by Arab and Swahili Muslims from the East African coast in 1844, during the reign of Kabaka (King) Sunna II. However, while Kabaka Sunna allowed Arab preachers to teach Islam in his court, he did not convert to Islam and did not permit the spread of the religion outside the king's court. His son and successor, Mutesa I, took more interest in the religion, and eventually became Muslim. Mutesa ordered observance of some Muslim customs such as the five daily prayers, fasting in the month of Ramadan, abstinence from alcohol, Muslim burial ceremonies, and prescribed methods of slaughtering animals. He constructed mosques throughout the kingdom and provided several incentives to persuade his subjects to become Muslim, sometimes compelling people to accept his new faith.[5] The other route that Islam used to enter Uganda in the mid- to late nineteenth century was through northern Uganda, where it was preached and practiced by Egyptian ivory traders and Nubian and Sudanese soldiers. By the mid-1870s, the land now known as Uganda was on the road to full Islamization, with Islamic culture enjoying popularity and political power in both the central and the northwest parts of the country. However, the fortunes of Islam began to decline with the coming of Christian missionaries in 1877.

Christian missionaries not only challenged the monopoly of Islam, but also came with a new approach to evangelization. They sought converts through direct preaching to ordinary people, and also built schools and hospitals and introduced other institutions that prepared their converts to manage an emerging colonial society. A combination of these methods of evangelism began to slowly alter the religious demographics of the Kingdom of Buganda, culminating in a power struggle within the kingdom. As this struggle intensified, Christian converts were supported militarily by their religious sponsors, which shifted the power balance away from Muslim domination. But military defeat had the ironic effect of spreading Islam to other parts of the country, as fleeing Muslims took their religion with them to both the western and eastern regions of Uganda. In some places, such as Bugweri County in Busoga (eastern Uganda), Muslim refugees converted traditional leaders, which precipitated the subsequent conversion of these leaders' subjects. The effects of these conversions have rippled through history: thus, today, Bugweri County is the most Islamized rural part of Uganda, with more than 70 percent of the population professing Islam.

THE RIGHTS OF UGANDAN MUSLIMS: A HISTORY OF CONFLICT

When Mutesa I died in November 1884, he was succeeded by his youthful son Mwanga II. The kingdom that Mwanga inherited was deeply divided along religious lines. When Mwanga rejected both Islam and Christianity and allied with the traditionalists, Muslims and Christians joined forces in what has come to be known in Ugandan history as the "unholy alliance," and together they overthrew Mwanga in the August Revolution of 1888. This inter-religious alliance proved successful in revolution but not in governance. Following a power struggle between the former allies, which resulted in Muslims gaining control of the government, Christians were exiled from the kingdom. With their Christian rivals away, the Muslims set about the task of fully Islamizing the country, starting with the installation of a king of their own. The Muslim king, Kalema, was installed on October 12, 1888, and immediately initiated a series of foreign and domestic policies aimed at firmly entrenching Islam. In December 1888, he wrote a forceful letter to the sultan of Zanzibar, which read in part: "I am now the King of Buganda and a Muslim. I believe in Allah and his prophet Muhammad; and I always thank God for that. Please send me your flag, Islamic books, and arms and ammunition to convert the infidels."[6]

Muslim ascendancy did not last long, however. At about the time when the religious wars were starting in Buganda, British colonial policy on the territory was taking a clearer shape. The Imperial British East African (IBEA) Company, the agent of British colonialism operating in the region, had already signed an agreement with the king making Buganda a "British sphere of influence." With material and military support from their European allies, the Christians soon defeated Kalema's forces and turned the tables, driving the Muslims out of the country, to a place in Bunyoro famously known in Uganda conflict history as "Kijungute." The Muslim flight to Bunyoro, in the northwest of Buganda, marked a major downward turn in the fortunes of Islam in Uganda. Islam, which had reached the status of a state religion, was relegated from the center of political authority to the periphery. It was now in danger of becoming extinct in Buganda, as its followers were hunted down and either intimidated into converting to Christianity or forced to seek asylum in neighboring territories.

After a period of protracted negotiations, interrupted frequently by continued fighting, relative peace was achieved with the Mwera Settlement of May 1892.[7] The settlement addressed the burning issues at the time (the late nineteenth century), but these issues remain strikingly relevant to contemporary times. The Mwera Settlement, the first formal agreement in Ugandan history, laid the foundation for the contemporary Muslim claim to differential treatment on matters of personal law. Among other things, the peace agreement provided for the following: Muslims were free to openly greet one another using Islamic salutations of "Asalaam Alaikum"; pork would not be sold in public places, and Muslims were to have a monopoly over the slaughter of animals, as a guarantee against eating "unclean" meat; Muslims could wear their headgear (turbans for men and veils for women), and they would not be forced to remove it, even in courts of law; and most significant for the present discussion, Muslims were left free to govern their family affairs, including matters of marriage, divorce, and inheritance, according to the teachings of Islam. The provision allowing Muslims to govern their family affairs according to the teachings of Islam was particularly dear to them, and it was eventually encoded into law as the Marriage and Divorce of Mohammedans ordinance (and later Act), which the promoters of the DRB now seek to repeal. While the Mwera Settlement did not satisfy everyone, especially hardliners on both sides, it was successful in reducing conflict and creating a platform for a religiously plural Uganda in which Christians and Muslims could harmoniously coexist. Intermittent military confrontation, however, continued until the signing of the Buganda Agreement in 1900.

Muslims and the Law in Postcolonial Uganda

The actual number of Muslims in Uganda is not precisely known. Some speculations put the figure as high as 45 percent and others as low as 10 percent; a more realistic figure seems to be about 25 percent.[8] The U.S. Department of State lists the Ugandan population as 66 percent Christian, 16 percent Muslim, and 18 percent "traditional and other."[9] Regardless of the precise number, it is clear that Muslims are a substantial minority. This minority status is tempered somewhat by the fact that the Christian population is divided among several denominations, including Catholic, Protestant, Orthodox, and Adventist. Despite their internal divisions, Christians hold the reins of political and social power in Uganda, but Muslims have historically wielded substantial economic power, and they continue to exercise reasonable influence in political circles.

The Muslim community in Uganda is for the most part conservative. Most Ugandan Muslims strictly observe Islamic teachings regarding alcohol, food, and marriage. Endogamy is highly encouraged, and intermarriage with Christians is strongly discouraged and can lead to social ostracism, unless the Christian spouse agrees to convert to Islam before the marriage is consummated. Cases of Muslim women who marry non-Muslim men are particularly objectionable, and they attract serious condemnation from the overwhelming majority of Muslims. The combination of the Muslim community's conservatism, their minority status, and a history of marginalization has led to something of an enclave mentality, which makes them sensitive to the slightest forms of attack. They thus assume a defensive posture, to the extent of being willing to use physical confrontation in response to infringements on Islamic teachings. Against the above background, legislation such as the DRB is seen as particularly provocative and threatening to the Muslim community.

Uganda's legal culture and structure is a colonial creation, and closely resembles that of its former British colonial masters, notwithstanding the few legal reforms implemented since independence. This has engendered a complex legal situation. As an African country, the philosophically and experientially remote Western legal system that it operates is only fully accessible to a small minority of its citizens who are Western-educated. When it comes to family law, the legal situation is even more complicated.

When the British introduced colonial rule in Uganda in the late nineteenth century, they recognized the multicultural and multireligious nature of the country and allowed various ethnic and religious groups, including Muslims, to conduct their affairs according to the unique laws that already governed their communities. This was consistent with their policy of "indirect rule," which was used in Uganda by the British colonial administrator Lord Lugard. Whereas customary law varied from one ethnic group to another, Muslims from a variety of ethnic groups generally subscribed to the teachings of the Sharia, or Islamic law. They used this law alongside selected aspects of customary law that were considered not to be in conflict with Islamic teachings. General law, on the other hand, was transplanted in whole from Britain and formally established in Uganda in 1902. Inevitably, much of the general law was directly or indirectly linked to the Christian tradition dominant in Britain. The result of this mixture of customary, religious, and general law was a complex legal system characterized by a high degree of internal contradictions. As a result of this history, domestic matters in Uganda are governed by two types of laws—the customary and religious laws that apply to members of specific communities, and the general or civil law that applies to everyone regardless of their ethnic or religious identity.

By the time Uganda gained independence from Britain in 1962, there were strong feelings in various quarters that legal reforms were necessary. Some laws were considered discriminatory to women, while others disadvantaged the Muslims because they projected Uganda as a de facto Christian state.[10] Legal reform was seen by nearly all stakeholders as absolutely necessary in order to create a society where no citizen would be regarded as inferior to another on account of his or her gender, ethnicity, or religion. The Muslims were particularly hopeful that such reforms would create more legal space for them in the country of their nativity. This would, hopefully, usher in a new era of fairness, especially given the background of political, economic, and educational marginalization during the colonial era.[11] To the Muslims' consternation, the Christian Ugandans who inherited power from their colonial mentors, and who professed recognition of the need for legal reform, did not show any interest in giving more space to the Muslims in the country's legal system.[12] Instead, they made moves to take away even the few concessions that the Muslims had gained during colonial times, especially in the area of personal law.

Although customary, religious, and general laws have worked together in Uganda for some time, customary law is largely unwritten and has been relegated to a lower status than general law. This has created a dichotomy between "written" and "unwritten" law, with the latter being forced into a subordinate position to the former.[13] Because "written" and "unwritten" law exist side by side in the same environment, the implementation of the general law often encounters several problems, since Ugandans continue to govern their lives with a mixture of customary and general laws. For instance, even the Christian Ugandans whose religion clearly forbids polygamy often justify it in their personal lives by referencing their African background. This situation greatly complicates the work of administrators and members of the judiciary, who are supposed to oversee the implementation of the law. There is, therefore, a general acceptance that law reform is necessary, even though there are sharp differences on the direction and extent of the needed reforms. The central issues in the conflict are religion and gender, and these are traditionally sensitive areas in public discussion. On the whole, therefore, the entire subject of "family law reform" has become extremely sensitive and controversial, with the key question being whether Muslims will continue to govern their personal lives according to the teachings of Islam, or whether the law will change to ensure that the entire nation is governed by a singular and unified general law dominated by Christian ideas.[14]

THE KALEMA COMMISSION AND LEGAL REFORM

The most significant attempt to reform Uganda's family laws started in 1962, with the appointment of what came to be known as the Kalema Commission. The commission, appointed by the first president of Uganda, Sir Edward Mutesa, was headed by William W. Kalema, an MP. It had six members: five men and one woman, all

Christian.[15] Its mandate was to "consider the laws and customs regulating marriage, divorce and the status of women in Uganda bearing in mind the need to ensure that those laws and customs while preserving existing traditions and practices as far as possible, should be consistent with justice and morality appropriate to the position of Uganda as an independent nation and make recommendations."[16] The report of the Kalema Commission is to date the most significant reference point in discussions of family law reform in Uganda. It made recommendations for the reform of the laws of marriage, divorce, children, and inheritance, with the professed purpose of creating a just society that did not discriminate against women.

A number of the Kalema Commission's recommendations on the reform of inheritance law were incorporated in the Succession (Amendment) Decree of 1972, which provided for women to inherit from their husbands and fathers, and all children, whether male or female, legitimate or not, to inherit from parents in equal shares.[17] The decree also tried to codify some of the customary practices common to indigenous Ugandans regarding inheritance. For example, it designated a share of 1 percent for customary heirs and 9 percent for other dependent relatives of the extended family. It also provided for the widow to remain in the principal matrimonial holding of the deceased (in trust for the heir) until she remarried or died. Significantly, the Succession Decree compelled all Ugandans, including Muslims, to subscribe to its provisions.

In addition to the various unwritten customary laws,[18] the law relating to marriage in Uganda was governed by four different statutes: the Marriage Ordinance, the Marriage of Africans Ordinance, the Marriage and Divorce of Mohammedans Ordinance, and the Hindu Marriage and Divorce Ordinance.[19] The Kalema Commission recommended that the laws be consolidated into one law, considering it anachronistic to maintain divisions based on religion at a time when the country should be channeling its energy "towards the attainment of unity." The report also claimed that all sections of the community agreed that a uniform law was required to govern marriages in Uganda.[20]

The commission recommended that monogamy should be enshrined in law and polygamy banned, "even though the practice of polygyny and polyandry was still prominent in some communities."[21] The commission acknowledged that it was "aware of the great number of Moslem citizens whose religion allows more than one wife." It noted, however, that "the government was not a religious organization," and that it had information that "the injunction from the Prophet regarding more than one wife is limited to the ability of the man to love equally the two or four wives he has." Observing that it was "very difficult to establish what equal treatment amounts to as well as what equal love demands," the commission therefore recommended monogamy for all.[22] The commission also recommended that a man and a woman should be presumed married if they had lived together for a period of a year or more. The legalizing of cohabitation was particularly objectionable to Muslims, who view such relations as tantamount to prostitution or adultery and consider polygamy a more legitimate and dignified option. In its attempt to impose "unity," the commission essentially disregarded the beliefs of a significant component of the nation's population, and stoked up the debate over the relative worth of Christian versus Muslim values.

By making the above recommendations, the Kalema Commission proposed to add to the long list of laws that impose non-Islamic legal provisions on the Muslims of Uganda, thus further reducing the legal space of Ugandan Muslims.

The Origins of the Domestic Relations Bill

The Uganda Law Reform Commission was established in 1990 by the Uganda Law Reform Commission Act, cap 25; and with the promulgation of the 1995 constitution, the commission became a constitutional commission by virtue of article 248 of the constitution. The commission consists of a chairman and six other commissioners, all of whom are appointed by the president on the advice of the attorney general. The main function of the commission, according to section 10 of the Uganda Law Reform Commission Act, cap 25, is to study and keep under constant review the acts and other laws of Uganda with the view of making recommendations for their systematic improvement, development, modernization, and reform.[23] When the first members of the commission were named, there was no Muslim member, as was the case with the Kalema Commission. Yet this commission was charged with the task of reviewing laws in which Muslims had serious interests.

Among the early tasks that the commission embarked on was that of reforming personal law, which has been controversial in Uganda for a long time. The commission embarked on the task by carrying out a number of studies and consultations. It then wrote a report on the basis of which the DRB was drafted. The studies mainly took the form of random household surveys of about one hundred people per district in ten districts on issues of family law. It also carried out a survey on customary law in four districts and a Sharia study in three districts. In addition, it reviewed reports by nongovernmental organizations (NGOs), and also made consultations with "Islamic countries" before finally producing a report in 1997. In the end, the findings and recommendations of the Law Reform Commission report were not very different from those of the Kalema Commission. Like the Kalema Commission, the Law Reform Commission emphasized "national unity" over diversity in making its recommendations for legal reform. The inherent assumption was that such unity could be achieved by mechanically forcing people to follow the same law.

The Sharia study was carried out by two Muslim university lecturers, Hadija Miiro and Abdu Katende, who were not expertly trained in Sharia but nevertheless did their work fairly well. They found that although Muslims did not fully implement Islamic teachings, there was a widespread feeling among the respondents that any law reforms should be made in the direction of strengthening rather than diluting the application of Islamic guidelines in Muslims' personal lives. Their findings also showed that Muslim women in polygamous marriages felt that Muslim men did not treat their wives equally, but these same women did not think that abolishing polygamy was the solution.[24] These findings do not seem to have been considered when the commission was making its recommendations.

The recommendations of the Law Reform Commission became a source of conflict because they were, in a number of instances, explicitly antagonistic to the Islamic faith. At one point, for example, the commission's report went against the teachings of Islam on inheritance, and stressed in italics that "this provision should be specifically applied to adherents of the Sharia."[25] Cases of this nature in which Islam was directly addressed, and in negative terms, are common in the commission's report, and many were later transplanted into the bill itself. In other instances, the antagonism was only implicit but not less significant. Indeed, Muslims felt unfairly targeted and marginalized by the commission's recommendations; it seemed to them that by drafting a law regulating "all types of marriages in Uganda," the commission had deliberately set out to "fight" Islamic law.

Muslims reacted by rejecting the very process that generated the Law Reform Commission's report. First, they argued that on matters of Islamic law, the consultation process should have included Muslim leaders and those knowledgeable about the Sharia, which it did not. They also argued that Islamic laws were revealed and not generated by consultation with those who did not have knowledge of Islamic teachings. Second, they dismissed the consultations with Muslim countries as irrelevant, since on matters of law, it is the holy books that matter, and not the so-called Muslim states.[26] Third, they questioned the reliability of the consultations with NGOs that were cited in the Law Reform Commission report, since some of the NGOs mentioned (such as the International Federation of Women Lawyers [FIDA]) were perceived to be antagonistic and contemptuous of Islam as a religion.[27] Most damning in Muslim eyes was the fact that the findings of the so-called Sharia study, which the Law Reform Commission itself had commissioned, were not given any weight in the formulation of its recommendations.

Despite Muslim protests, the Law Reform Commission report was transformed into the DRB (first drafted in 1998 and revised several times thereafter), and was forwarded to Parliament for consideration as the Domestic Relations Bill 2003. Its general aim was to consolidate the six different statutes that relate to marriage and divorce in Uganda into one law. It sought to revise divorce law, to give legal status to people living together in cohabitation, and to define the property rights of married people during and at the breakdown of marriage by laying down precise criteria for the redistribution of marital property on divorce in all types of marriages.

Muslims could not halt the preparation of the DRB, but because of their protests, the early drafts underwent a number of modifications. The Law Reform Commission's report had proposed that all polygamous unions be limited to a maximum of two wives, with stringent conditions that included requiring the man to prove in court that he had the ability to sexually satisfy both his wives. In January 1998, the Muslim community made a very widely publicized protest against the proposed law. They arranged for lectures and street protests in at least three Ugandan towns, and crowned the protests with a lecture in Sheraton Hotel, one of Kampala's most prestigious hotels, by the national chairman of the Uganda Muslim Youth Assembly (UMYA).[28] In reaction, drafters of the DRB raised the total number of wives a man could marry to four, as provided for in the Sharia. However, the stringent conditions were retained, with the exception of the one that would have required the man to prove sexual virility in court. Legislators learned that in the attempts to reform personal law, it was not going to be easy to ignore Muslim sensibilities with impunity. This apparent concession notwithstanding, the Muslim community continued to view the attempt to set a common standard in matters of personal law for a multicultural population as both ill-intentioned and misguided, and as representing a danger to peaceful coexistence between Muslims and Christians in Uganda.

Specific Muslim Objections to the Domestic Relations Bill

The DRB has been undergoing changes since Muslims first raised objections to it in 1998. These "improvements" have resulted in the DRB drafts of 1998, 1999, 2000, 2001, and 2003, but to the Muslims, these changes have been merely cosmetic. They still find its spirit negative toward Islam as a social system, and they do not understand why anyone would want to do away with the prevailing atmosphere of religious pluralism and tolerance in the Ugandan legal culture, and impose upon the Muslims an alien system of personal law. While in the past Ugandan Muslims have been known to disagree on matters political and theological, on this issue they have spoken with one voice, which has enabled them to mount formidable opposition to the law and hold it at bay for years. Muslims have raised a number of specific objections to the DRB on issues such as freedom of worship, polygamy, the jurisdiction of qadhis' courts, marriage gifts and the definition of acceptable forms of marriage, divorce, cohabitation, and property rights.

Muslims feel that the DRB negates the constitutional principle of freedom of worship by suggesting that a Muslim marriage can be converted into a Christian one, but not vice versa (sections 51 and 52).[29] In a statement addressed to the Speaker of Parliament, the director of Sharia at the Uganda Muslim Supreme Council said:

As Muslims, we are concerned about the fate of a Christian couple that converts to Islam, and wishes to convert their marriage into an Islamic one. The provisions (on conversion of marriages) either prevent Christians from converting to Islam or they create the ridiculous scenario of an Islamic marriage that is not potentially polygamous. Both are completely unacceptable to the Muslims of Uganda. The provisions are much more than just an obsession with monogamy. They are part of a wider anti-Islamic agenda.[30]

Muslims also reject what they see as cumbersome guidelines for the solemnization of marriage laid down by the DRB, which are designed to supersede the teachings of Islam (sections 9 (1), 29, 30 (2), 33, and 35). According to these guidelines, Muslims would be required, among other things, to give notice to the district registrar of marriages, and have this notice displayed for twenty-one days before the permission is processed. This has prompted the director of Sharia to observe that the "proposed preliminaries are haphazard and place unnecessary obstacles in the way of marriage."[31] Another Muslim organization, the Bridge Foundation, bluntly described the requirement of giving notice before marriage as "a clear reflection of the procedure in church/civil marriages," and pointedly reminded policymakers that "the laws of Allah are supreme."[32]

Another primary Muslim concern was that the drafters of the DRB completely misunderstood and abused Islamic provisions on polygamy by presenting it as a morally unacceptable arrangement. As a result, they have attempted to impose conditions that were tantamount to banning it (section 31). For example, the bill requires the man who wishes to marry a subsequent wife to prove in court that he has the capability to treat his wives equally. This leaves the matter to the discretion of the district registrar of marriages, something to which the Muslims strongly object. In particular, the commission's attempts to limit polygamy while providing for cohabitation has particularly irked the Muslim community. Muslims argue that it is self-defeating to attempt to ban polygamy in a society where prostitution is on the rise, and that a ban on polygamy would further encourage cohabitation and prostitution. The Muslims also point out that polygamy has the additional advantage of taking care of widows. Fatuma Kamulali, chairwoman of the Kampala-based Uganda Muslim Women's Association for Da'wa and Development, observed, "Very many women are looking for husbands. There are many widows. If the law prohibits men from marrying more than one woman, who will marry the widows?"[33] Madina Serunjogi summarized the general Muslim sentiment on this matter when she said that "these people don't understand us and should just leave us alone."[34]

The 1995 constitution of Uganda provides for the establishment of qadhis' courts (art. 129(1)d) to preside over Islamic matters. But the DRB effectively pre-empts the qadhis' courts law by making Islamic law subject to the DRB, nebulous "principles of equity," and any other laws that Parliament may make. Despite constitutional provisions protecting the jurisdiction of Islamic courts, the DRB relegates Islamic law and jurisprudence to second-rate status. In response to this, the director of Sharia has clearly asserted that "Islamic law has its own rules and procedures, and cannot be subject to any other law."[35]

According to Imam Shafi'i,[36] four conditions are necessary for an Islamic marriage to be valid: (1) consent of the parties; (2) consent of the guardian (*wali*); (3) a marriage gift; and (4) two witnesses. In contrast, section 15, subsection 2 of the DRB says: "The consent of a parent relative, clan elder or any other person other than the respective parties to the marriage, shall not be a requirement for the validity of any marriage solemnized, celebrated or contracted under this Act." Likewise, section 20 rules on the marriage gift in a manner that

Muslims find unacceptable, stipulating that "marriage gifts shall not be an essential requirement for any marriage under this Act." Section 15 (2) seeks to take away the traditional right of Muslim parents to consent to the marriages of their daughters, while section 20 denies the Muslim women the right to ask for *mahr* (the mandatory marriage gift that is given to the woman by the man) when they are getting married. Muslims find it offensive that the DRB fails to distinguish between traditional African bride price and Islamic *mahr,* essentially conflating what they see as two distinctly separate practices. By eliminating key provisions of what Sharia requires for a proper Islamic marriage, Muslims argue, the DRB in effect abolishes Muslim marriage.

The DRB's provisions on divorce are equally objectionable to Ugandan Muslims. Section 79 states that "a spouse shall not petition for divorce before the expiry of two years from the date of the marriage which is sought to be dissolved." Islam regards the marriage relationship as a very serious commitment, and divorce is considered only after it has become obvious that the fundamental objectives of matrimony can no longer be realized. If this should be the situation in any relationship, waiting for two years would only create hardships and injustices to the spouses. For example, a spouse could desert another within one month of marriage. Under the provisions of the DRB, the deserted spouse has to wait for two years before petitioning for divorce. Such a situation is seen by Muslims as conducive for one to commit adultery, which is not acceptable to Islam.

The DRB's section on cohabitation begins by stating that it (cohabitation) shall not be considered a marriage, but ends by presuming cohabiting partners to be married if they stay together for ten years (section 13). Muslims see this as the state granting its blessing to adulterous relationships, which is contrary to traditional Islamic values. On the matter of cohabitation, the Sharia study sponsored by the Law Reform Commission concluded that "all [Muslim] respondents were agreeable that they (the cohabiting partners) act contrary to the Sharia and accordingly i.e. if one of them is married, he/she is committing adultery, and should be stoned to death; and if they are both unmarried, they are fornicating and they should be caned 100 strokes."[37] The Muslims are aware that any attempt to have this recommendation incorporated into national law would be greatly resisted by the others, and they do not insist on it. Their greater grievance, however, is that the DRB goes to the other extreme of proposing a legal status for cohabiting partners. This has provoked strong reactions from the Muslim community. Addressing the thousands of Muslims who camped outside the Ugandan Parliament on March 29, 2005, to protest against the DRB, Imaam Kasozi, a prominent Muslim leader in Uganda, declared that "cohabitation is zina (adultery/fornication) in Islam. This law is for shameless people, and they should not attempt to include us in it."[38] It is provisions like these that make Muslims insist that the present arrangement that allows Ugandans to be governed by different marriage laws should be strengthened, instead of being replaced by a "uniform" law that will only cause disharmony without contributing to the betterment of the marriage institution in Uganda.

Another area of Muslim concern is the DRB provision on property rights. Section 66 (2) of the DRB provides that a married person acquires a 20 percent interest in the property of the other if he or she stays with him or her for five years, 30 percent after ten years, and 50 percent after fifteen years. The national chairman of the UMYA dismissed this clause as an irresponsible one because it turns the entire marriage enterprise into a reckless hunt for property and would, if passed into law, have the effect of dispossessing the children and might also deter people with property from marrying legally. This particular clause, the UMYA chairman insists, must have been included by "a woman thief."[39] The director of Sharia at the Uganda Muslim Supreme Council, Sheikh Hussein Rajab Kakooza, described the clause as "an attempt to rob children, whether Muslim or otherwise, of their property."[40]

Muslims also object to section 59 of the DRB, which provides for marriage to a dying partner. They argue that the bill makes it very easy for a dying person to dispossess legitimate heirs by marrying just before he or she dies. Such a marriage is forbidden in Islam because a dying person lacks the capacity to contract a valid marriage that is free of undue influence. Second, this marriage also falls in the general category of marriages that are unlawful and void in Islam because they cannot be consummated. Parties to a valid Islamic marriage should be able to live together to fulfill the objectives of the institution of marriage, which the UMYA national chairman has outlined as "companionship, procreation, social order, social security, and morality."[41] Dying partners, the UMYA chairman argues, cannot fulfill any of the above objectives.

In the first comment by a government official on the DRB saga, Prime Minister Kintu Musoke told the press that the government of Uganda had "no policy of turning all citizens into Christians (and) . . . even if people were to be turned into Christians, there are those who do not subscribe to monogamy." He then shocked his fellow Christians by adding that "yes even myself, I accept I'm a Christian, but I am not a bird which has only one wife."[42] But these conciliatory comments did not cool Muslim tempers. The Eminent Sheikh Abdu Obeid Kamulegeya, former mufti of Uganda, in an angry letter to the chairman of the Law Reform Commission, which was copied to the president of Uganda and to several leaders of Muslim countries, likened the bill to Salman Rushdie's *Satanic Verses*.[43] He described it as divisive and uncalled for, and warned that it would "inevitably pit Muslims against their Christian compatriots (and would cause) a major confrontation between Muslims and the state."[44] And when Justice Sir Harold G. Platt, the chairman of the Uganda Law Reform Commission, invited UMYA chairman Abasi Kiyimba to attend a symposium to discuss the bill, he declined, saying that he had "no interest in presenting his views on a law that seeks to re-write God's divine laws."[45]

COMPETING MODELS OF WOMEN'S RIGHTS

Members of the exclusively Christian pro-DRB women's lobby have attempted to reach out to Muslim women, to "educate" them that if the bill passes into law, it will actually serve their interests. But these efforts have been ignored, and sometimes openly rebuffed. Their greatest frustration has been the opposition they have faced from educated Muslim women. A number of prominent women, including female members of Parliament such as Sauda Mugerwa of Masaka, Lukia Nakadama of Mayuge, and Anifa Kawooya of Sembabule, have taken strong anti-DRB positions. They have expressed resentment at what they consider to be a patronizing approach by non-Muslim women who say they are working on their behalf.[46]

In response to the anti-polygamy sentiments in the DRB, many Muslim women have rallied in defense of the institution of polygamy as an essential part of traditional Islamic marriage practice.[47] Faridah Kakaire, secretary general of the Uganda Muslim Women's Association for Da'wa and Development, admits that it is human to feel jealousy and pain when the husband marries another wife. But she argues that as Muslim women who understand Islamic law, they look at the broader picture. "The same law that hurts you when your husband marries comes to your rescue when your husband dies and you have to marry again but can not get an unmarried man." She further asserts that changing the law "to deny our men from marrying (more than one woman) would be going too far. . . . A man marries to please Allah and not to please people."[48] Hadijah Kibira, the chairperson of the Uganda Muslim Women's Vision, is irritated that Christian women activists have taken it upon themselves to speak for Muslim women: "Do these people think we admire their way of life? Do they think that we do not know about the hypocritical lives they lead?"[49] Together with other members of her organization, Hadijah Kibira has moved around the country educating Muslim women about the DRB and its dangers for the Muslim community. They also consistently urge Muslim men to treat their wives justly. This will please Allah, they urge, and also prevent the detractors of Islam from taking advantage of Muslim abuses of Islamic law, real or perceived, to further their ends. As is implied in the above comment by Hadija Kibira, a number of Muslim women, while supporting the general Muslim objection to the bill, have also privately expressed disapproval of the way the men sometimes handle the institution of polygamy. They have, however, described these as internal matters to be sorted out after defeating "the external enemy."[50]

Under the provisions of the proposed law, if a Muslim man should decide to marry a second wife without fulfilling the DRB's rigorous conditions, the new wife will not be recognized as "legal." On the other hand, Muslim women argue that when they marry according to Islamic law, they are full wives regardless of whether they marry as first or fourth wives. They are therefore alarmed that the DRB intends to turn them into *concubines* overnight. Addressing a seminar organized by the UMYA during the month of Ramadan in 2003 to discuss the DRB, Sarah Nakabuye told a mixed male and female audience that "the Muslim women in this gathering know that when a woman decides to marry a man, she marries him because she loves him. So does it matter whether the man is already married or not, for as long as he has not exceeded the ceiling of four?"[51]

Promoters of the DRB argue that they are endorsing the interests of all women, including (or especially) Muslim women. Where advocates of the bill see it as promoting equality among the sexes, however, Muslims argue that it undermines Islamic provisions on the responsibilities of men and women in marriage. They point specifically to section 63, which vaguely declares that "both spouses shall have the duty to maintain their family." This has been widely understood to mean that the woman will have an equal responsibility to support the family financially, whereas in Islam, it is the duty of the man to provide financial support for the family. Women are not prohibited from contributing to the financial sustenance of the family, but Muslim women are concerned that this provision of the DRB will give legal protection to men who are reluctant to fulfill their obligations, since it places an equal burden on wives. Speaking on the Muslim-owned Voice of Africa Radio, Hajat Mastura Nakanwagi asked: "Who are they to attempt to take away what God has given us [the right to be maintained by men]? How can such a law claim to serve the interests of the Muslim woman?"[52] Furthermore, the secretary of the Bridge Foundation, Mariam Kasule, has also told the speaker of Parliament in a strongly worded communication that Muslim women look at section 63 of the DRB as "an attempt to rob them of their right to maintenance, and irresponsible men will want to use this provision as a justification for pushing the burden of maintaining the family on the woman."[53] This provision, perhaps more than any other, reveals the starkly contrasting definitions of women's rights and equality held by the different communities within Uganda. Both sides claim to be protecting the best interests of women, but approach the issue from entirely different if not conflicting perspectives, and with very different results.

THE DOMESTIC RELATIONS BILL AND THE THREAT
OF VIOLENCE

Thus far we have traced Muslim objections to the various provisions of the DRB in a largely abstract manner. However, a cross section of Ugandan Muslims have gone beyond simply expressing dissent with the bill's contents to expressly warning of possible inter-religious conflict if the bill passes into law, thereby infringing on their right to practice marriage according to Islamic tradition. The issue takes on greater resonance as Muslims assert that it is not just about marriage practice, but about what they see as a concerted effort by Uganda's Christian majority to Christianize the state. Debates over the DRB thus indicate that it is a potential trigger for the broadening and deepening tension between the country's Christian and Muslim populations. Journalist Lara Santoro has observed that the bill "pitted Muslims against Christians, traditionalists against progressives."[54] The threat of violence hangs over the public discussion of the bill, even though up to this point no violence has been reported.

Various Muslim groups that traditionally have their internal disagreements have all univocally rejected the bill. The mufti of Uganda, Sheikh Shaban Ramadhan Mubajje, has insisted, "The Qur'an caters for every aspect of marriage, children and relationships. There is no need for making another law for Muslims. A man can marry depending on his ability to maintain and sustain the marriages."[55] After discussing the bill at length with the management team at the Uganda Muslim Supreme Council, he said in a statement addressed to the Speaker of Parliament, "It is neither possible nor necessary to improve the DRB to the satisfaction of Muslims. Therefore, we pray that we be excluded from the application of this law."[56]

Many Christians see Muslim opposition to the bill as sectarian and backward. In response to the position taken by Muslim leaders, the outspoken born-again Christian MP Miria Matembe retorted, "There is no need to listen to religious leaders who are against the DRB because they have for long failed to address the plight of women in their prayer sessions. Those religious leaders are not honest, they should shut up."[57] Miria Matembe, Dora Byamukama, Sheila Kawamara, Winnie Byangima, and other prominent women activists have also attempted to suggest that Muslims are overreacting because they have either not understood the DRB or have not read the Qur'an "correctly," for the Qur'an does not allow them to oppress women.[58] This kind of belligerent rhetoric is partly responsible for the worsening "DRB crisis," as it has come to be known in Uganda.

On March 29, 2005, Muslims took to the streets to demonstrate against the bill. It was probably the largest demonstration that Kampala has seen, with more than twenty thousand Muslim men and women dressed in white robes and chanting, "Allah Akbar! Allah Akbar!" Protesters carried banners with messages such as "The DRB is contradicting Islam," "Muslims not party to the DRB," "The Quran is the constitution of Allah," and "Muslims should enjoy freedom of worship."[59] One demonstrator, Haruna Bukulu, plainly stated the position of many Muslims on the matter: "Islamic law has been there since it was passed on from Allah to the Prophet Muhammad, it cannot be re-written now. . . . It is not compulsory to have more (wives), but if the need is there, I can. Men and women are equal in many ways, but equality is not uniformity."[60]

One banner displayed at the nonviolent demonstration on March 29, 2005, carried the ominous message: "Don't force us into terrorism." As far back as 1998, when the debate became public, it was obvious that the proposed law was potentially divisive and could lead to a serious breakdown in Christian-Muslim relations in the country, and even a breach of peace and security. The banner that said "Don't force us into terrorism" was a significant pointer in this direction. Many Ugandans found it alarming, but the banner revealed the feeling of anger that many Muslims felt in the face of what they saw as unwarranted interference in their religious lives.

Even moderate clerics such as the district khadi of Kampala, Sheikh Sirman Kasule Ndirangwa, have been quite uncompromising. He declared: "Other cultures want to overcome Islam, but we will not allow it. People are willing to die so that no one will trample over them. God gave us guidelines on how to handle marriage. Telling us how many women we should marry makes the Bill ridiculous and infringes on our freedom of worship."[61] Another prominent Muslim leader, Sheikh Haruna Jemba, has said that "we should not listen to these people. For them, they have the option of having sex outside

marriage whereas for us, our only option is to marry. So if they try
to get in our way, we should just fight them."[62] And Sheikh Nuhu
Muzata has told Muslims in the country to prepare for a time when
fighting in defense of the Qur'an will not be just an option but an obligation: "This time will come on the day they pass this Bill."[63] Muslims look at the DRB as an attempt to impose on them "Christian
values,"[64] and will not countenance having those who do not believe
as they do interpreting Islam for them. They have openly declared
that they will never obey the proposed law if it should be passed by
Parliament, and they look at the determination by some Ugandans to
push ahead with it as an attempt to turn them into outlaws.

Significantly, the Muslim demonstration of March 29, 2005, had
a very large female component; some observers even suggested that
women outnumbered men at the event. This should have served to
dispel the thinking that the opposition to the DRB in the Muslim
community was "a male thing." But Sylvia Tamale, a professor of law
at Makerere University and an outspoken human rights activist, dismissed the female participation in the demonstration as an instance
of "the slave using the master's language."[65] In other words, the Muslim women do not understand what is good for them, they are simply
doing what their men would like them to do, in the same way the
slave would act in obedience to the master. "It is us (the Christian
women) who know the right thing, and they should let us speak for
them," Sylvia Tamale seems to be saying. Comments similar to this
have been made by other prominent Christian women activists, such
as Dora Byamukama, Solome Kimbugwe, and Sheila Kawamara.
They are perceived by Muslims as arrogant and belligerent, even im-
perialistic, and they actually strengthen the Muslim resolve to fight
the bill to the bitter end. In a country with a history of bloody religious conflicts, this approach to questions of inter-religious coexistence is simply a recipe for disaster, and borders on the irresponsible.

Because they feel beleaguered, Muslims have been reported in the
press as vowing to resort to *jihad* (holy war) over the DRB. In an eye-
catching headline entitled "Muslims Threaten Holy War over DRB,"
the national chairman of the UMYA was quoted as saying, "The Muslim community has been provoked for long. I may not be the one to
fight but there are Muslims ready to go for Jihad. We shall fight this

battle to the end in any form."[66] He is also reported, in the same article, to have told journalists that "Jamil Mukulu has actually released a recorded tape calling upon Muslims to join him [in a guerrilla war against the government] and fight against the Bill." Jamil Mukulu is a Muslim cleric and formerly a prominent preacher in Kampala who is now leader of the Allied Democratic Forces (ADF). His rebel group, based in the DR Congo, is reportedly Muslim-dominated, and has been fighting the government of President Yoweri Museveni for years, accusing it of mismanaging the country. In this same tape, Jamil Mukulu is said to have urged Muslims to compile the list of the big-headed Bakafiri (infidels) who are causing all this trouble, so that they can deal with them when the time is right.[67] Whether it is true or not that Jamil Mukulu is already using the DRB to mobilize Muslims for violent conflict, the fact is that the sentiments of many Muslims on this issue tend to flow in a more militant direction.

Two months after the Muslim demonstration, President Museveni declared that the DRB was not urgently needed, and could be shelved temporarily to allow for consultations with all stakeholders. He said the delay would calm Muslims and other men who feel the DRB is infringing on their rights.[68] Christian women reacted by calling a demonstration to press for the DRB to be passed.[69] Unlike the Muslim demonstration, which had attracted tens of thousands however, this one attracted about two hundred people, mainly women. As they walked through the streets of Kampala, they chanted "No DRB, No Kisanja"—meaning they would deny President Museveni their votes in the 2006 elections. Even though the Christian demonstration had fewer people than the Muslim one, it revealed the continuing power of the DRB debate to polarize Ugandan society. Speaking after the demonstration, the outspoken born-again Christian parliamentarian Miria Matembe declared that "Muslims, who constitute a smaller percentage of the country's population, should not force their views on the majority."[70] In response to the Christian demonstration, Muslims restated their determination to fight the bill to the bitter end.[71] There is a sizable number of Christians who are puzzled by the proposed law, and they watch the raging DRB debate with bemusement. They do not understand why anyone would want to prevent Muslims from marrying the women allowed to them by their religion. Some of them have loudly wondered why government is disturbing the Muslims. "If the Muslims want to marry four women, let them. After all, they are their women. Why should it bother me?"[72] This apparent aloofness on the part of some Christians notwithstanding, Muslims have continued to mobilize angry, defensive, and potentially militant sentiments within the Muslim community. This situation could easily degenerate into violent conflict if the issue is not handled with sensitivity.

RELIGIOUS PLURALISM AND DEMOCRACY

The debate over the DRB goes beyond the simple proposal that the state should regulate marriage, which most Ugandan Muslims do not in itself reject per se. It poses stark questions about the nature of pluralistic society and democratic government. Can a majority pass legislation if the values inherent in the law contradict those held by minorities? At what point does government by the people become tyranny of the majority? How does a state mediate the competing truth claims of its diverse religious and ethnic communities, especially in cases where their values, and particularly the application of them, are seemingly incompatible? Many nations in the West have reconciled these contradictions by creating avowedly secular societies in which all religions, including those of the majority or minority, are presumably separated from political power. The secular solution, which itself is fraught with contradictions and perils, is rejected by many Ugandans of various religious persuasions, who deeply feel that religion should have a strong personal and public presence.

Ugandan Muslims feel that the DRB crosses the line of acceptable government by the majority. They believe that the bill is actually a cloak for a larger project of Christianization, pointing not only to the bill's various provisions discussed earlier but also to what they see as the imperial attitude of the Christians who have supported the bill. Indeed, all the people associated with drafting and publicly defending the bill are Christian, and some of them have publicly testified of their "born-again" status.[73] Muslims also complain about the all-Christian composition of the Law Reform Commission, stressing that institutions of the state are supposed to be representative and inclusive of members of different faiths. The Law Reform Commission did attempt to negotiate with the Ugandan Muslim community on a number of occasions, and twice met with the top Muslim leadership at the Uganda Muslim Supreme Council. Many Muslims saw these meetings simply as token gestures, since the commission made contact with Muslim leaders after the bill had already been drafted. And even when these meetings took place, the entire nine-person Law Reform Commission team (including members of the commission and technocrats) was Christian. So it was more of powerfully placed Christians negotiating with adamant Muslims than a neutral government organ making consultations with stakeholders. Muslim fears of Christian influence behind the process were further exacerbated in December 2004, when a delegation from the Uganda Muslim Supreme Council presented a memorandum opposing the DRB to the Parliamentary Committee on Legal Affairs. Two MPs, Tom Kayongo and Idah Mehangye, had to be reminded that they were in the committee session in their capacity as MPs and national leaders, not as representatives of the Christian community. This was after they had repeatedly defended the provisions of the DRB against Muslim criticism by citing verses from the Bible.[74]

Muslims are concerned that apart from Prime Minister Kintu Musoke's famous remark about not being "a bird which has only one wife" (cited earlier), no prominent Christians have gone on record as conceding that Muslims have a point. All this tends to reinforce Muslim fears that the DRB is part of a broad strategy by Christians to impose their beliefs and values on them using the state apparatus. In a communication to the then-editor of *The Monitor,* Onyango Oboo, the national chairman of the UMYA (Abasi Kiyimba), asked: "Do you realize that from the way the debate on this Bill has gone, [the Muslims] are on one side and Christians (including yourself) are on the other? Where are those broad-minded objective non-Ugandans that are willing to concede that the Muslims have a point when they insist on governing their lives using their religious teachings, not those invented by mortals like them? Instead, what we continue to read in *The Monitor* is the same anti-Muslim rhetoric that women activists have been voicing from the beginning. Parliament may pass this law and thus give it legality, but it will never gain legitimacy, not in the Muslim community."[75] Prior to this letter, the same UMYA chairman had angrily declared in a January 1998 statement that it was "shameful that thirty-five years into independence, some Christian fundamentalists hiding behind the law would now like to interfere with the fundamental aspects of the Islamic religion by imposing Christian marriage laws on Muslims."[76]

So far, the worst has not happened. Despite tensions and even threats, violence has not broken out. Ugandan Muslims have argued that in the spirit of avoiding further conflict, the DRB reforms should be abandoned and the current legal code that is more sensitive to religious pluralism be maintained and strengthened. Compromise is not an option with what they see as a deeply flawed bill. Some Muslims are even willing to accommodate women activists like Linda Nabusayi Wamboka, who believe that the right to have multiple spouses should be extended to women, if it is granted to men.[77] The defining rhetoric of the Muslim community throughout the DRB debate has been that it is necessary in a plural state to genuinely respect cultural and religious diversity, and they believe that the DRB violates both the spirit and fact of the nation's diverse religious heritage. They acknowledge the fact that Christians believe polygamy is wrong, but they refuse to accept that such a belief should be enshrined in national marriage law to be applied to everybody. The solution is to work out a legal arrangement that accommodates every community. This is not an easy task, and some of the attempts at it have met with resistance. But the cost of failure may be too dear for the Ugandan posterity.[78]

CONCLUSION

In a country with a fair number of pressing problems, one of which is unity, it should surprise many that the opportunity to build unity in diversity should be passed up. The arrangement of the family is of course very important, and it is right that public debate should focus on it. But it is unfortunate that this should become a point of possible violent conflict. However, while the discussion seems to be about family and marriage on the surface of it, almost every Ugandan knows that it takes the form of a binaristic religious debate between Muslims and Christians that is more than one-and-a-half centuries old. At various moments in the country's history, this debate has degenerated into violent conflict, a situation that few right-thinking Ugandans would like to replay. Ugandans belong to different ethnic groups that have elaborate cultures, but their views and practices in the area of marriage are strongly informed by their religious beliefs, which are mainly Christian and Muslim. It is therefore not surprising that in the DRB debate Ugandans of various ethnic backgrounds have taken positions that are strongly aligned with one of the two religions.

The undercurrents of gender and sex in the debate are strong, with leading women activists attempting to suggest that their positions are informed by a general pro-woman perception of gender relations rather than religiously partisan assessments of the matter. But the problem that has continuously dodged them is that the *DRB coalition*[79] is exclusively Christian, and some of its members are publicly known to be *born-again* Christians.[80]

A number of Ugandan Christian men practice polygamy, and they justify it as being part of their heritage as Baganda, Banyankole, Basoga, Lugbara, and so on. But when it comes to looking at themselves in comparison with their Muslim countrymen, they tend to regard themselves as infinitely superior, because they nominally subscribe to a culture that is endorsed by the seemingly more "universal" Western culture. Indeed, the general flow of the DRB debate tends to suggest that the Christians perceive the Muslim belief in the legitimacy of polygamy as backward, and they even accuse them of using religion as a pretext to oppress women. One Christian writer has even suggested that the Muslims live in a different century, and that the DRB will "drag them kicking and screaming into the twenty-first century."[81] This imagined leverage in the social hierarchy often leads Christians to imagine that they have the right to dictate terms to the seemingly "inferior" Muslims, including an attempt to impose upon them a compulsory culture of monogamy.[82]

The debate on marriage law is just one example of instances when Muslims are made to feel that they are being treated as aliens in their own country, sometimes by people from the same ethnic community or even the same clan. This feeling often drives the Muslims into desperate states of mind, and makes them speak and act in ways that make it even harder for the others to understand them. Utterances like "Don't drive us to terrorism" directly result from the feeling that the others are determined to push them harder against the wall. These outbursts also tend to confirm general suspicions that there may be some among the Muslims who are ready to use extremist approaches to confront the situation.

The reality is that Uganda is a multireligious country, and it would be wrong to front the argument that the majority must have their way. Similarly, it would be a betrayal to future generations for this "majority" to use the law to perpetuate conflict by enacting laws that the Muslims will never accept. After all, the Muslims argue, the present numerical superiority of the Christians in Uganda is the product of a violent and unjust history in which the colonial masters favored the Christians against the Muslims. Because the Ugandan society is a pluralistic society with deeply divided religious communities, the whole DRB undertaking seems to be an impossible task. Its attempts to legislate a monolithic interpretation of marriage and divorce are likely to continue to meet with stiff opposition, especially from the Muslims. The sooner it is abandoned, the better for Uganda as a country.[83]

While the talk about violent resistance to the bill is widespread among the Muslims, the voices of common sense within the Muslim community have consistently stated that they recognize that they are destined to share the same country with the others, and they are committed to peace-building as part of the search for a meaningful existence. However, even these voices of common sense are not willing to be culturally subsumed by Christianity, as the bill seems to propose. They insist that Uganda's religious diversity should continue to inform both its culture and its laws.

It is the duty of the more rational voices among the Muslims to prevail on the other members of the Muslim community whose sentiments tend more toward violence to realize that it is in their interests to continue with a peaceful engagement with their countrymen and countrywomen, rather than wielding the threat of violence to get their way. But it must also be recognized that we live in an era where the responses of individuals and groups to social and political pressures are becoming increasingly difficult to predict. The state must therefore not permit groups or individuals, however socially powerful, to use its structures to push for the enactment of laws that could be detrimental to community harmony.

In the interest of peace-building, both Muslims and Christians must be prepared to look beyond the binaristic *us-them* thinking. They must be prepared to accept that it is possible for all of them to be fully Ugandan, even when their marriage and other domestic arrangements are different. The precedent for such parallel laws for different communities has a long history within and outside Uganda. It has, in the past, helped the country to show respect for minority rights, and to build a national culture of tolerance and peaceful coexistence. In the present circumstances, it would necessarily entail a degree of legal autonomy for Muslims, at least in this one area of family law. Fortunately, qadhis' courts are already provided for in the Ugandan constitution, and what is required is to enact a law or a set of laws that would operationalize them and properly incorporate them into the general body of Ugandan laws. This should be done with the full involvement of the Muslim community, and without any intimidation or manipulation, as has been the case in the past.[84] Once this is done, Uganda will have the opportunity to demonstrate to its neighbors and others that living under separate domestic laws is not as great a calamity as some groups would want to make it appear.

NOTES

1. Catholics and Protestants (Anglicans) are on record as fighting bitter battles described as the Wa-Faransa/Waingereza wars, which resulted in inter-religious animosity that led one Anglican to assert that "I would rather be ruled by a dog than by a Catholic" (Abasi Kiyimba, "The Muslim Community in Uganda Through One Hundred and Forty Years," *Journal of African Religion and Philosophy* 1, no. 2 [1990]: 99). They also constantly fight over schools, and even maintain separate educational and social institutions.

2. These were part of the terms of reference for the Kalema Commission, which was the first serious attempt to reform Uganda's family laws. See *Report of the Commission on Marriage, Divorce and the Status of Women*

(Entebbe Government Printers, 1965), 1 (under the Chairmanship of the Hon. W. W. Kalema, MP).

3. UMYA chairman Abasi Kiyimba told a seminar this in Sheraton Hotel in January 1998.

4. The term *Christians* is used here in a very general sense, since the debate has been greatly polarized, with all the proponents of the bill being Christians and all the opponents being Muslim. It would be deceptive, however, to suggest that all Ugandan Christians support the bill. Christian men are particularly silent in the debate, and have left the debate to the women. The Christian women who participate in the debate attempt to present themselves as general advocates of a fair law, but they present very thinly veiled Christian positions. The other point to note is that whereas the bill is officially a government bill, the Muslim ministers in President Museveni's government have maintained a loud silence. It is logical to assume that they do not support the bill, and probably fear to go against the tide in their own community, but they are bound by the principles of collective responsibility and cannot oppose it publicly.

5. For one example of coercion, see Badru Kakungulu and Abdu Kasozi, *Abasiimba Obuyisiraamu Mu Uganda* (The Planters of Islam in Uganda) (Kampala: Equator Books, 1977), 11.

6. *Uganda Journal* 14, no. 1 (1950): 28. Kalema's letter was written on December 12, 1888.

7. The Lugard-Mbogo talks at Mwera have been recorded in varying detail by different historians, and to get a comprehensive picture of what was agreed at Mwera one has to rely on several sources. What we provide here is a summary of the key issues, as they have been recorded by several historians. These historians include Sheikh Abdallah Sekimwanyi, *Ebafaayo by'Obusiraamu* (A History of Islam), MS, 1900; Sheikh Abdu Karim Nyanzi, *Ebyafaayo by'Entalo z'Eddiini mu Buganda* (The History of Religious Wars in Buganda); F. D. Lugard, *British East Africa* (1894), Apolo Kagwa, *Bassekabaka ba Buganda* (The Kings of Buganda) (1902); Robert A. Ashe, *Chronicles of Uganda* (1894); Albert Lugolobi, *Ekitabo Mbulire* (Forewarned) 1933; James Miti, *History of Buganda* (1938); Hamu Mukasa, *Simuda Nyuma* (Go Forward), vol. 3: Entalo Zeddiini (The Religious Wars), MS, 1939; P. L. McDermott, *British East Africa or IBEA* (1893); H. H. Austin, *With Macdonald in Uganda* (1903), *Macdonald, Soldiering & Surveying in British East Africa 1891–94;* Henry Colville, *The Land of Nile Springs* (1895); G. Portal, *The British Mission to Uganda* (1893); Sir Harry Johnston, *The Uganda Protectorate* (1902); and Asuman Wamala's "Eye Witness Account" in Professor N. Q. King's *Christian and Muslims in Africa* (1971).

8. Ali Kettani, *Journal of the Institute of Muslim Minority Affairs* 4 (1984); Radio Uganda report of Anglican Archbishop's speech, April 13, 1985; Abasi Kiyimba, "The Problem of Muslim Education in Uganda," *Journal of the Institute of Muslim Minority Affairs* 7, no. 1 (1986): 252.

9. While it is usual for statistics in Western scholarship about Uganda to refer to traditional religions and assign them a percentage, the reality is that nearly all Ugandan identify themselves as Christian or Muslim.

10. Laws and practices like the Marriage Act and the Oath Act are framed in a manner that makes non-Christians feel like they are the guests of the Christian community in Uganda.

11. For example, the total education budget for the year 1944 was 134,000 pounds sterling, but Muslim education was allocated 213 pounds sterling. The rest went to Christian schools. See Kiyimba, "The Problem of Muslim Education in Uganda."

12. There are many laws and conventional practices in Uganda that Muslims cite as biased in favor of the Christians. Muslim women have, for example, consistently cited the practice of forcing them to remove their headscarves when they are being photographed for passports or for voters' registration exercises while Catholic nuns do not have to, but the details relating to this are outside the scope of this essay.

13. The term *unwritten law* is uncritically used in the draft Domestic Relations Law to imply Islamic law as well as other laws, despite the fact that Sharia has existed in written form for more than 1400 years, more than 12 centuries before the colonial introduction of general law into Uganda.

14. Muslims seem to have conceded that it would be difficult if not impossible to win concessions on the application of the other laws of Islam, such as those that relate to commerce (prohibition of interest), punishment of the crimes of adultery and fornication by stoning to death or whipping, and punishment of the thief by cutting off his hands. So they do raise them for discussion, and have concentrated on personal law.

15. The Kalema Commission was appointed on January, 14, 1964, and it submitted its report on July 30, 1965. The members of the commission were W. W. Kalema, MP (chairman), H. B. Nkojo (member), Ben Otim Etura (member), W. B. Mwangu (member), M. M. Kabuzi (member), and V. C. R. A. C. Crabbe (member and secretary). It should be noted that the first female appointee to the commission was Irene Bisamunyu. When she failed to serve on the commission, the appointing authority made a point of replacing her with another female member (Marian Marjorie Kabuzi). The Muslim complaint is that no Muslim was appointed to the commission, even though the nature of its task demanded it.

16. See *Report of the Commission on Marriage, Divorce and the Status of Women,* 1.

17. By virtue of the Succession (Amendment) Decree, all children of an intestate deceased person get 75 percent of the estate, which is to be divided equally among them.

18. The Kalema Report (9–19) documents the customary marriage laws of fifteen indigenous communities in Uganda.

19. These laws were reprinted and re-designated "Acts" by the Laws (Revised Edition) Act, 1965. Note that the Marriage Act provides for both Christian and civil marriages.

20. The absence of a Muslim member on the commission made it easy for it to say this. Otherwise, the Muslim community could never have been party to such an "agreement." Indeed, a close examination of the list of respondents and of the people from whom memoranda were received shows that the entire activity of the Kalema Commission was really a Christian affair.

21. Kalema Commission Report on Ankole in western Uganda (9–10). The commission, however, does cite instances of polyandry in Uganda.

22. See page 44 of the commission's report. Non-Muslim scholars often make reference, in error, to the Prophet's injunction that allegedly refers to the ability of the man to "love" his wives equally. Muslims know that there is no such injunction, and they find arguments by Christians based on the alleged existence of such an injunction extremely irritating. This is one of the points that make Muslims believe that any attempts by others to understand Islam from a Western mindset can only lead to misunderstanding, frustration, disagreement, and conflict, especially because observations such as those made by the commission usually arise out of arrogance and ignorance of Islamic teachings. That is why Muslims think that the laws on personal matters should be maintained as separate laws.

23. http://www.ulrc.go.ug/about_ULRC/ulrc_brief.php.

24. A copy of the report of the Sharia study is available in the records of the Uganda Muslim Youth Assembly.

25. This was in reference to the Sharia requirement that children born outside wedlock should not inherit from the father. A copy of the first report of the Law Reform Commission is available in the records of the Uganda Muslim Youth Assembly.

26. See communication by the director of Sharia Uganda Muslim Supreme Council to the Speaker of Parliament, February 10, 2004, 2.

27. Ibid.

28. The lecture was published in *The Vicegerent* of January 1998, by the Uganda Muslim Youth Assembly (UMYA). Dr. Abasi Kiyimba, the author of

this essay, is also the UMYA chairman. Within the body of the essay, reference is constantly to "the UMYA Chairman" to avoid repeated reproduction of the names of the author in the body of the essay.

29. These articles do not directly use the terms *Islamic* and *Christian*. Instead, they talk about "potentially polygamous marriages" and "monogamous" marriages, but the Muslims have seen through these thin veils.

30. Statement from the Uganda Muslim Supreme Council signed by Sheikh Hussein Rajab Kakooza, director of Sharia, February 10, 2004, 9.

31. Ibid., 8.

32. The Bridge Foundation communication to the Speaker of Parliament is available in the records of the Uganda Muslim Youth Assembly.

33. See Evelyn Kiapi Matsamura, "Ugandan Muslims Demand Limits in Women's Rights Bill," Inter Press Service (an international news agency with its head office in Vienna), April 7, 2005.

34. Madina Serunjogi is a teacher of Islam and history, and was until 2009 the deputy headmistress of Bweyogere Secondary School. She is also a committee member of the Uganda Muslim Women's Association. She holds an MA in Religious Studies from Makerere University.

35. Statement from the Uganda Muslim Supreme Council signed by Sheikh Hussein Rajab Kakooza, director of Sharia, February 10, 2004, 14.

36. Shafi'i is one of the four most prominent imams who excelled in scholarship that laid down the law used in the day to day implementation of Islam by Muslims.

37. Hadija Nassanga Miiro and Haji Abdu Katende, Report of the Domestic Relations Project (Sharia study), April 1997, 14.

38. *New Vision,* March 30, 2005 (article entitled "Muslims Insist on Polygamy").

39. Abasi Kiyimba, national chairman of the Uganda Muslim Youth Assembly (UMYA), in an interview with *New Vision,* December 2004.

40. Statement from the Uganda Muslim Supreme Council signed by Sheikh Hussein Rajab Kakooza, director of Sharia, February 10, 2004, 13.

41. Abasi Kiyimba, national chairman of UMYA, in a statement published in *The Vicegerent,* no. 1 (1998): 3.

42. *The Monitor,* January 10, 1998.

43. Sir Ahmed Salman Rushdie, the British-Indian novelist and essayist, achieved literary prominence with his second novel *Midnight's Children* (1981), which won the Booker Prize of 1981. He has several other works to his name. He caused a major international controversy with his fourth novel *The Satanic Verses* (1988), which offended Muslims worldwide and was the cause of violent protests in several countries that have sizable Muslim populations. On February 14, 1989, the Supreme Leader of Iran, Ayatollah Ruhollah

Khomeini, issued a *fatwa* (religious ruling) condemning him to death, and offering a substantial prize for whoever would execute that sentence (http://en.wikipedia.org/wiki/Salman_Rushdie).

44. January 22, 1998.

45. *The Monitor,* January 20, 1998.

46. For example, after MP Idah Mehangye said that Islamic laws only serve the interests of men and are not fair to Muslim women. Lukia Naka-dama, a Muslim MP and now a minister in President Museveni's government, retorted, "Why are you complaining on our behalf?" This was during a session the Legal and Parliamentary Affairs Committee convened on Tuesday, December 7, 2004, attended by the present writer. See report in *New Vision,* December 8, 2004, 5.

47. See Matsamura, "Ugandan Muslims Demand Limits in Women's Rights Bill."

48. Fridah Kakaire in a personal interview on March 21, 2005. Also see Matsamura, "Ugandan Muslims Demand Limits in Women's Rights Bill."

49. Hadijah Kibira holds an MA in geography from Makerere University, and is the deputy head teacher of Wakiso School for the Deaf. She is also the chairperson of the Uganda Muslim Women's Vision. She made the remark while addressing a Muslim women's seminar at Entebbe Kitooro mosque in October 2004.

50. In seminars and other discussions organized internally within the community, Muslim women regularly criticize Muslim men for not strictly observing the Islamic standards of justice in dealing with their wives. Sarah Nakabuye, quoted later in the essay, has been quite vocal on this matter. But she insists that this is an internal matter within the community, and non-Muslims should not be allowed to interfere because they also have their own problems.

51. See *New Vision,* May 7, 2005, article by Mariam Nalunkuuma. Sarah Nakabuye is the treasurer of the Uganda Muslim Women Vision.

52. Mstura Nakanwagi is a prominent woman preacher affiliated with the Uganda Muslim Women Vision. She made this comment in October 2004.

53. Mariam Kasule is a lawyer in Kampala. A copy of her communication, March 9, 2004, is available in the records of the Uganda Muslim Youth Assembly.

54. Lara Santoro, "First Wives Club Unites in Africa," *Christian Science Monitor,* January 23, 1998.

55. See Matsamura, "Ugandan Muslims Demand Limits in Women's Rights Bill."

56. Statement by the mufti, March 29, 2005, addressed to the Speaker of Parliament.

57. Hon. Miria Matembe, MP, Mbarara District, has repeatedly expressed this view in public debates. "Religious leaders opposed to the DRB" was a thinly veiled reference to Muslim leaders, since no other religion has objected to the DRB. Even the provision of cohabitation has not attracted any memorable objections from Christian leaders, whereas of course Christianity does not approve of cohabitation.

58. Miria Matembe was speaking on WBS television in April 2005.

59. *New Vision*, March 30, 2005 (article entitled "Muslims Insist on Polygamy").

60. "Uganda Muslims Demonstrate in Defense of Polygamy," on the http://atheism.about.com/b/a/158062.htm, visited on October 12, 2005.

61. *New Vision*, March 30, 2005 (article entitled "Muslims Insist on Polygamy").

62. Sheikh Haruna Jemba is a lecturer at Makerere University and chairman of the Kampala District Muslim Council. He was speaking on Voice of Africa Radio on March 30, 2005.

63. Sheikh Nuhu Muzata, a graduate of Madina University (Saudi Arabia) and a prominent Muslim preacher, was speaking at a seminar organized by the Makerere University Muslim Students' Association in April 2005.

64. Santoro, "First Wives Club Unites in Africa."

65. Sylvia Tamale was until 2008 the dean of Makerere University's Faculty of Law. She made this remark while speaking on Radio Capital's *Capital Gang* program on April 6, 2005.

66. "Uganda Muslims Demonstrate in Defense of Polygamy" on the website http://atheism.about.com/b/a/158062.htm, visited on October 12, 2005.

67. Santon who quotes Kiyimba in "First Wives Club Unites in Africa."

68. *The Monitor*, May 5, 2005.

69. http://www.docstoc.com/docs/17936389/No-DRB-No-Kisanja---Women; also see *The Monitor*, May 5, 2005. I am sure the Christian women would object to my continued use of the expression "Christian women" in this sense. They would like to portray themselves as an objective non-denominational group fighting for a general women's cause. But the reality is that Muslim women have disowned them, and their side is entirely Christian. And remarks such as those by Miria Matembe quoted earlier (dismissing Muslims as a minority) actually serve to smoke them out of their inadequate "hiding place."

70. *The Monitor*, May 5, 2005.

71. The district kadhi of Kampala, Sheikh Sirman Kasule Ndirangwa, went on Radio Simba on that same day to denounce the Christian women's demonstration as misguided.

72. Joseph Mukwaya, a resident of Nakulabye city suburb, interviewed on March 29, 2005, by *The Vicegerent* after the Muslims had demonstrated in protest against the bill.

73. These include Miria Matembe, Winnie Byanyima, Solome Kimbugwe, Margaret Oguli Oumo, Percy Tuhairwe, Sheila Kawamara, Dora Byamukama, and Jacqueline Asiimwe.

74. The present writer attended and addressed this session of the Legal and Parliamentary Affairs Committee, in his capacity as National Chairman of the Uganda Muslim Youth Assembly (UMYA).

75. The full five-page letter, dated February 3, 1999, is available in the records of the Uganda Muslim Youth Assembly.

76. *The Vicegerent*, January 1998.

77. See "Do Not Tilt Bill against Women," *The Observer*, December 16, 2004. Muslims are sure that few Ugandan women will ever wish to be granted such a concession, but they have declared that they will not fight that request if a clearly identified group requests for it—provided, of course, it is not made to apply across the board.

78. Since the year 2003, when the current version of the bill was drafted, the public debate has been characterized by argument and counterargument on the "correct" form that the proposed law should take. As a result, the atmosphere surrounding the "DRB debate" has continued to be tense. In 2007, the government decided to break up the law into two versions: one for the Muslims and one for the others. The Muslims were requested to propose a draft of "their law," which they did. Since the submission of the Muslim draft bill in the latter part of 2007, a team of Muslim representatives has been in dialogue with the Law Reform Commission to see how these proposals could be consolidated into law. Following these negotiations, the Law Reform Commission announced that DRB would be split into two, to give birth to separate laws for Muslims and Christians. (See *New Vision*, April 21, 2008, "Domestic Relations Bill Split into Two"). And in May 2008, the Speaker of Parliament, Edward Sekandi, told a visiting delegation from the Club of Madrid, an international and nonpartisan organization made up of former world leaders to promote democracy, that the 8th Parliament—which expired in May 2011—would pass the DRB (http://www.ugpulse.com/articles/daily/news.asp?about=8th+parliament+to+pass+DRB+-+Ssekandi+&ID=5789). *New Vision*, September 23, 2009, also reported that "the Deputy Attorney General Freddie Ruhindi while addressing Parliament revealed that the Government will soon bring a bill to establish Islamic Khadi courts. The bill that seeks to operationalize Article 129 of the constitution, will give guidelines on how Khadi courts can administer justice to the Moslem community, and that in these courts Moslems will be free to apply Sharia Law in accordance to

their religion." As we write (April 22, 2011) neither of the two versions of the DRB has been passed into law, nor has the qadhis' courts bill been passed.

Some Christian groups have strongly objected to any arrangement that would enshrine polygamy in the national law, regardless of whether it is intended to apply to the Muslims alone or other groups. Others have argued that they (the Christians) should not be lumped together with the Hindus, Bahais, and others while Muslims are given their distinct law. The most recent development is that Pastor Umar Mulinde of the Gospel Life Church International, who describes himself as national chairman of the Ex-Moslems Task Force, has petitioned the Speaker of Parliament not to pass the Muslim version of the DRB into law, and to amend the constitution to delete article 129(1)(d) which provides for qadhis' courts, arguing that "*Qadhi* Courts should operate privately among Muslims who adhere to the Islamic faith and accept its authority, but such courts should never have the judicial power of the state" (*New Vision,* April 19, 2011). For their part, Muslims continue to insist that they will not settle for anything less than total exclusion from the general law. Given the above circumstances, the bill is still very much part of the volatile public debate, with different groups sticking to known positions.

79. The women who support the enactment of the DRB in its present form have formed an organization called the DRB coalition. Its membership is entirely Christian.

80. Miria Matembe is only one example of the pro-DRB debaters who make no secret of being born-again Christians. The problem that she and others in her category pose for the DRB debate is that they are seen as selling a very Christian agenda. They have failed to satisfy Muslims that whereas they are strongly Christian in their general social identity, they discuss the DRB as general nonreligious partisan leaders.

81. Joseph Bbosa, "Marriage Property under the Domestic Relations Bill," *The Monitor,* May 17, 2005.

82. It should be stressed that throughout the entire course of the DRB debate, Muslims have consistently pointed out that while Islam permits polygamy, it does not decree it for all its followers. It is an option for those who can manage the stiff conditions it imposes.

83. As political scientist Leonard Binder argues, it is not possible for outsiders to make totalizing interpretations of "non-historical" phenomena such as Islam because its cultural "essence" cannot be "accessible to those who are not indigenous to that culture." The regulation of marriage and divorce in pluralistic Uganda is not a unitary matter that can be given a single interpretation. Only Muslims can fully access the essence of marriage and divorce in Islam. The DRB fails at the "totalizing" task in large part because it fails to recognize the Islamic essence of marriage and defaults to what the

drafters know best, namely the traditional Western and Christian model of marriage.

84. Successive Ugandan governments have attempted to influence the decisions that Muslims make, even in the running of their internal affairs. This is particularly the case when it comes to the choosing of leaders. See Kiyimba, "The Muslim Community in Uganda Through One Hundred and Forty Years."

Contributors

Rosalind I. J. Hackett (Ph.D. 1986, University of Aberdeen) is professor and head of religious studies, adjunct in anthropology, and faculty associate at the Howard H. Baker, Jr. Center for Public Policy, at the University of Tennessee, Knoxville. She was a Rockefeller Research Fellow at the Kroc Institute of International Peace Studies at the University of Notre Dame from 2003 to 2004. She has published widely on religion in Africa, notably on new religious movements (for example, *New Religious Movements in Nigeria*, ed. 1987), as well as on art, media, gender, conflict, and religious freedom in the African context. Her latest book is *Proselytization Revisited: Right Talk, Free Markets, and Culture Wars* (ed.) (Equinox, 2008). Forthcoming publications include: *New Media and Religious Transformations in Africa* (co-edited with Ben Soares) and *The Anthropology of Global Evangelicalism and Pentecostalism* (co-edited with Simon Coleman) (NYU Press). In 2010, she was re-elected president of the International Association for the History of Religions and will serve until 2015.

Abasi Kiyimba is an associate professor in the Department of Literature, and deputy dean of the Faculty of Arts at Makerere University in Uganda. He holds a BA in literature and language from Makerere University, an M.Litt. in literary linguistics from the University of Strathclyde, Glasgow, and a Ph.D. in literature from the University of Dar es Salaam in Tanzania. He has taught and published on a number of literary subjects, including African oral literature, children's literature, gender in literature, literary linguistics, and twentieth-century African literature. He is also the national chairman of the Uganda Muslim Youth Assembly (UMYA), and has done research and published on a number of Islamic subjects. His articles have ranged over the following topics: "The Problem of Muslim Education in Uganda," "Islam in

Uganda through One Hundred and Forty Years," "Modern Science: A Muslim Perspective," "Islam on the Education of Muslim Women," "Images of Islam in the Ugandan Press," and "Hajj—the Fifth Pillar of Islam."

Isabel Mukonyora holds a doctorate in Theology from the University of Oxford, and a Master of Letters Degree in the History of Religions from the University of Aberdeen in Scotland. She is an Associate Professor in the Department of Philosophy and Religion, Western Kentucky University. She teaches a variety of classes on Early, Modern and Post-colonial Christianity, as well as Women, Religion, and Ecology. Her publications respond to many topical questions about religion and women, social justice, and, more recently, ecology in African Religions. Isabel is the author of *Wandering a Gendered Wilderness: Suffering & Healing in an African Initiated Church* (New York: Peter Lang Publishing, 2007).

Charles Schaefer is associate professor of history at Valparaiso University and chair of the International Service Program. He taught at Addis Ababa University from 1992 through 1994 as a Fulbright Lecturer. He was also Country Specialist for Ethiopia for Amnesty International, USA, from 2006 through early 2009. Much of his research has been on historical methods of peace and reconciliation in Ethiopia, but he has also written on elections and human rights issues. His latest work is *The Ethiopian Red Terror Trials: Transitional Justice Challenged* (co-editor, James Currey, 2009).

James Howard Smith received his Ph.D. in social-cultural anthropology from the University of Chicago in 2002, and is currently associate professor of anthropology at the University of California, Davis. He was a Rockefeller Research Fellow at the Kroc Institute of International Peace Studies at the University of Notre Dame from 2003 to 2004. His research interests include the cultural politics of time; the social life of globalized substances; changing local understandings of "development"; religious utopias and neo-traditionalist movements; resource struggles and politics in Africa; conflict, violence, and concepts of peace; witchcraft and sorcery in Africa; contemporary state transformation; the cultural and political consequences of "neoliberalism"; Africa (especially East and Central). Smith is the author of *Bewitching Development: Witchcraft and the Reinvention of Development in Neoliberal Kenya* (University of Chicago Press, Series in the Practices of Meaning, 2008), and has written scholarly articles for *Comparative Studies in Society and History*, the *Journal of Religion in Africa*, the *American Ethnologist*, and *Ethnography*. He is currently conducting collaborative research on the social life and political economy of coltan mining in the Democratic Republic of Congo.

ASONZEH F.-K. UKAH is a lecturer and research fellow in the Department for the History of Religions at the University of Bayreuth in Germany. He holds a Ph.D. in history of religions from the University of Bayreuth, Germany. Ukah's research interest focuses on African Pentecostalism, religious advertising, religion and media, as well as religious popular culture in Africa. He has published numerous academic papers in English, Spanish, and German. He is the author of *A New Paradigm of Pentecostal Power: A Study of the Redeemed Christian Church of God in Nigeria* (Africa World Press, 2008). He is a member of a research team at the University of Bayreuth working on a project titled "Tradition and Innovation: Old and New Churches in the Religious Market of South Africa."

KOEN VLASSENROOT is lecturer at the Faculty of Political and Social Science of the University of Ghent and coordinator of the Conflict Research Group. He is also the director of the Central Africa Programme of Egmont, the Royal Institute of International Relations. He has published numerous book chapters and articles in international academic journals on conflict dynamics, militia formation, governance and state formation, land issues, and food security in eastern DR Congo and the Great Lakes Region. He is the editor (with Tim Allen) of *The Lord's Resistance Army: Myth and Reality* (London: Zed Press, 2010). He obtained his Ph.D. in political science from the University of Ghent in 2002.

GRACE NYATUGAH WAMUE-NGARE is senior lecturer at Kenyatta University. From 1990 to 2007, she taught in the Department of

Philosophy and Religious Studies. Her Ph.D. is in the area of gender, African religion, and culture. In January 2008, she moved to the newly created department of Gender and Development in the same university, where she continues research, together with the development of teaching manuals, in this area. Among her many publications on gender and religion in Africa is the book she co-edited with Mary Getui, *Violence against Women: Reflections by Kenyan Women Theologians.* (Acton Publishers, 1996.). Wamue's interests in religion and politics began with her master's research on Agikuyu and the Mau Mau, and this has continued with her ongoing investigations and publications on the Mungiki people. She is currently writing a book on this neo-traditional movement.

Index